This book was scribed on Pallanganmiddang Country.

It's breathtakingly beautiful, and fertile beyond imagination. It's our home.

On this patch we've realised our lifelong dream of planting and nurturing a heritage orchard and berry farm. Our practices are regenerative, and we mimic Mother Nature in every way we can. We've made our mark on this land; as the years plod on and generations pass, we hope that these well-intentioned actions bear fruit.

But that's just our story.

What I can't tell you is the story of this land before white settlement. I don't know how the hills rolled, where the creek flowed, how the sun fell, which plants and animals flourished, or what kinds of patterns and pathways were made by the people who walked this country for tens of thousands of years.

This land is stolen. Our forefathers rewrote the rules to separate people from place – people who are inseparable from place. For all of the work that our family has done, it's little more than a hiccup within the timeless stewardship of First Nations peoples.

Today, I acknowledge that this place I call 'home' was never ceded. Whatever the piece of paper says, we cannot own this land demarcated by palings and wire any more than we can own the sun, air or birdsong.

As current custodians, we pledge to learn as much as we can about its Indigenous past, especially the stories and wisdom of those who came before us. We stand in awe and recognition of the rich culture that propagated and maintained a complex food-production system on this brittle continent for countless generations; it is a way of landscape-scale farming that we may never fully comprehend. We cannot heal the damage, but we will spend our lifetime trying.

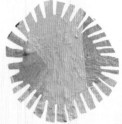

FUTURE-STEADING

PRACTICAL SKILLS, RECIPES +
RITUALS FOR A SIMPLER LIFE

FUTURE-STEADING

LIVE LIKE TOMORROW MATTERS

JADE MILES
Black Barn Farm

murdoch books
Sydney | London

CONTENTS

PART TWO: THE HOW, SEASON BY SEASON

Preface

On fire ... time for change

**LET ME TAKE YOU BACK TO
THE BEGINNING OF 2020 ...**

3 January

*As the mushrooming clouds of bushfire smoke
threatened villages in our valley and the evacuation
notices went out, it suddenly got real.*

*Charlie's day out fighting fires yesterday was
long and hard, and something in his voice was
adamant when he asked me not to be here with
the kids tomorrow while he is not here but in the
bush. I resisted, of course, but actually he is right.
So I'm prepping, packing the car, moving the horses
out and kissing the geese, chickens and sheep on
the heads, wishing them luck and heading off.*

*Our cars are full of petrol, our phones are charged,
our fire box with woollen blankets and coats plus
emergency rations is by the door, and I have a
battery-operated radio. I've got the emergency
app on my phone, and I'm alert with a plan of
action in the back of my mind. Am I being
overcautious? Having someone in our household
who works in fire management not only heightens
our sense of responsibility but also means that we
must be prepared at home so he can be sure his
family is safe while he is away at another fire.*

DO YOU HAVE A FIRE PLAN?

6 January

Each day is the same ... but not the same! At daybreak, he dons the smoky clothes that he dumped by the door at the end of his 12-, 14-, 16-hour shift the night before, and leaves for more of the same. 'Where is he today?' I don't know. 'What time will he be back?' Late? I don't know. 'How long will these fires burn?' I don't know. 'Is he safe?' I don't know that either. He assures me they are well trained and always put safety first, but fires are unpredictable and things happen ... They did, and now his heart races until it wakes him in the night.

He is part of a crew I have never met, relying on comradeship I cannot fathom. His head swims with maps and briefings, incidents and strategies. He speaks a different language and has a fortitude that I can only imagine. He is building memories that I cannot share.

It's like groundhog day on a bed of quicksand. I don't know what to expect, because no one does. As the wife at home, I do know that the days pass, the oppressive smoke gives the antsy kids sore throats and headaches, the farm is mine to keep ticking along, the niggle of worry is just below the surface, the need to keep life 'normal' is critical, and any fire plan that I have to enact for my own safety and that of the farm will need to be undertaken on my own.

Yet I'm grateful. Despite my now embedded dread of summer and the inevitable fires that come with it, I have my house, my garden, my kids, the most incredible support from relentless daily messages, a husband who comes home more often than not, a village that has not faced fires this season, and a country that has a rising desire to see genuine change.

We must change, we will change. We have been bad house guests for too long, and Mother Nature is done. As the landlady, she holds the ultimate power – and unless WE CHANGE, we will be done, too.

I was so grateful for those on the front line of this ... but they can't do it on our behalf forever. It's time for all of us to consider what our role in this is. What will you do? How will you CHANGE?

8 January

The pantry is bare, and so is my resilience. Fortunately, the food co-op reopens today, so I'll refill my jars with wholefoods and locally grown food. I'll share a cup of tea with whichever volunteer is staffing the shop, and see other members who've become like family. It's time to come out of the cocoon I've been in while Charlie has been fighting the fires and the smoke has blanketed the farm, which I've not been courageous enough to leave. It's been a foggy, heady, grit-your-teeth kind of week.

But for all of its heartache, I chiefly feel buoyed by the sense that our country is galvanising, becoming resolved and clearly seeing what it needs to do!

11 January

I waved him off for night shift and waited for the change to come. My restless head and listless body found calm in the mundane … I planted more corn, watered the patch and stood in the chicken coop while the angry wind blew hard in every direction, trying to make up her mind. And while she did … I made up my mind, too.

I'm a list writer. So I sit here now, with the wind buffeting the windows and doors, the sky getting heavier and texts from worried friends shooting in like gunfire. I'm writing my list of everything I can do to make a difference, as just one person wondering what can be done.

WHAT DOES YOUR LIST INCLUDE?

13 January

He is on night shift this week. He spends 14 hours each night walking through the bush with a drip torch in hand, back-burning, raking, rescuing dazed wildlife and putting out spot fires.

I imagine there's an eerie, time-stands-still kind of loneliness that stretches into the inky night, but he tells me there's jovial banter, two-way radio instructions and plenty to do in the glow of the burning bush, so time actually ticks by quickly.

He is not contactable once he drives out our gates, so I distract myself with anything on offer and a reassuring internal monologue that loops.

Despite the long nights, he returns each morning to resume his role as father and farmer, doing his best to be present for the kids' stories and to help me edge along my to-do list. Today, we strung wire in the hoop house so that I could get the tomatoes onto strings. I couldn't do it on my own. While the bed was beckoning, he stood upright for just a little longer to be the second pair of hands I needed and to feel like we're standing side by side – in this together.

The smoke-filled air, emergency app and fire roster are the sun we're orbiting at the moment. A usual summer family rhythm doesn't exist, but

somehow he knows that even just one cup of tea, one quick round of cards and one small need-your-help-on-this job makes all the difference to us, at home waiting for this to all come to an end.

He is tucked up asleep now, and the house is quiet so we don't wake him. My breathing is slow, the kids aren't bickering, and the house feels complete … until tonight, when he drives out the gates again.

14 January

The smoke cleared, the garden winked green, the marigolds bobbed, and we were lured towards this feeling of simple bygone summers. It's not, of course, and perhaps it can't be again, but I'm confronted to find that my deep desire for this memory to be the reality is as strong as my determination not to forget the fires.

As much as I yearn for it to be my favourite season again, I am clutching to the earnest commitment that I made to myself, my kids, my fire-fighting husband and the hundreds and hundreds of individuals who have been made homeless, lost business income, been stranded, felt fearful, been inconvenienced – and, most of all, become galvanised in their commitment to create a different world.

I will not be dissuaded from my commitment to making individual change.

I hope I'm not alone!

These words from my diary still lock my throat and make my heart race. It was the summer that galvanised my desire to write this book.

As our climate warms and our country cooks, we Australians are now accustomed to bracing ourselves for hot summers. But in 2019–20, country and city cousins were united when our collective eyes were opened to the burden that we now face nationwide – actually worldwide.

The grief of our nation shook us hard to the core, shouting WAKE UP like never before!

We can no longer be apathetic or ignorant about the impact of climate change. We need to adapt and build hardened, in-this-together resilience as awake individuals who live in connected communities where each and every one of us – regardless of race, age, sex or income – has a right to live vitally. But we can't expect this to be the responsibility of everyone else. We each need to look hard at ourselves and consider:

◆ how reliant we are on extractive industries
◆ how much waste we generate
◆ how committed we are to our localised food systems
◆ how much we contribute to the wellbeing of our communities
◆ how much we consume
◆ what happiness or success really is
◆ how much knowledge we have of the natural world
◆ whether we respect the seasons
◆ how we show respect for one another.

Most importantly, we have to assess our genuine desire for change.

I know that we are each capable of starting right now in our own households and our own communities in our own ways. This will look different for everyone, and that's to be celebrated. For me, the first step was to start a podcast and write this book. It's been one hell of a learning curve, and the climb is still steep. The words I've written will never be complete or indeed right for everyone, but they will spur thoughts and start conversations between people – all of us!

We cannot let all of the heartbreak, hard work, fear and fire in our bellies go to waste. Now is the time for individual and then collective change.

Are you with me?

PART ONE

THE WHY

Introduction

Hello! How lovely to be held in the palm of your hand

As you turn the pages of this book, I invite you to open your head, heart and soul to the idea of living like tomorrow matters. To love every minute of today while cultivating a rich and fertile future. In theory, it's paradoxical. In practice, it's a deeply rewarding, deliciously challenging and rather muddy pursuit.

We're a family of five – two adults and three chilluns – living at Black Barn Farm, an 8 hectare (20 acre) orchard complete with feathered and furry menagerie in north-eastern Victoria, Australia. Depending on the day (and species), we're stubborn, idealistic, practical, whimsical, determined, exhausted and peckish.

If you popped in for a spontaneous cup of tea, you'd probably find me (Jade) weeding the vegie patch while fielding a call from the local food co-op. Charlie might be in the orchard or waist-deep in a research paper detailing the most effective organic pest-control methods. And the kids would be roaming on their bikes, testing recipes in the kitchen or – in a flurry of responsibility and initiative – feeding the chickens or fishing for dinner.

For the better part of a lifetime, we've pursued a considerate, regenerative, hands-in-the-dirt existence – we've coined the term 'futuresteading' for this way of life. We haven't always got it right, but we have amassed a personal inventory of experiments, failures and revelations. These are hard-won lessons about identity, community and what makes a good life.

On these pages, I'll share the most practical and evocative parts of our story. Whether you're seeking a fail-safe pickling recipe or inspiration to start living like tomorrow matters, there's something to tickle your fancy, I'm sure.

And before you ask, a life in the countryside complete with enamel milk jugs isn't a prerequisite for making use of this book. While you may notice some pretty imagery (thanks to a talented photographer and golden afternoon light), the principles and philosophy can be applied anywhere, whether you're in a high-rise urban rental or a backyard caravan.

In fact, I'm not inviting you to move to the countryside and become self-sufficient. I'm challenging the current paradigm – the story of endless growth and chronic consumption that is making a meal of our future. I believe that we can all do our bit, concrete or literal jungle dwellers alike.

To plant a tree is to believe in tomorrow. To plant an orchard of fruiting trees is the ultimate act of optimism.

THE FUTURE IS IN OUR HANDS

None of us can escape it, this future. We'll be present in our children and our children's children, or as ghosts, compost or atoms – depending on your beliefs. We have a duty of care to this land and every human and non-human thing that springs from it, and we are cared for in turn. The time to start exercising our custodial responsibility is now.

It's time to share stories, challenge norms, tap out of consumerism, celebrate local, cultivate connections and actively seek slow. It's time to lead lives with more ritual and less rubbish, more culture and less consumption, more seed-sowing and less scrolling. We have to build tribes, put down roots, shadow the seasons and draw insight from our disillusionment. It's time to eat with intention. What we put into our mouths (or grow and prepare ourselves) is a thrice-daily statement of purpose. Make it local. Make it count. It's time to accept that we are part of, not in control of, the natural world. It's time to dive into futuresteading.

If you're feeling overwhelmed by the magnitude of this task, then keep reading. You'll soon discover that something as small as a pot of mint on your balcony can amount to activism, or simply observing the seasons can forge a relationship with Mother Nature that is so strong you'll defend her no matter what.

Most of all, this book aims to fill us with hope. Not an addictive and false sense of 'hopium', but a practical and evocative stimulant for change. The sharing of deeply considered ideas and a compassionate way of life will provoke thought, challenge norms, encourage simplicity and provide tools to create rituals that will connect folk to themselves, to others, to the natural world and to the powerful pull of a seasonally evolving year.

Wherever you live and whatever stage you're at, you can write a new story with your choices. You can do things that feel good and are meaningful and achievable, on any scale. And you can find comfort in the ever-expanding tapestry of like-minded people who are strengthening their commitment and pulling together for a better tomorrow, today.

I'm so glad that our stories can overlap.

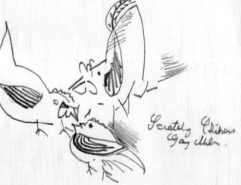

What is futuresteading?

Simply put, futuresteading is *living like tomorrow matters*.

The term riffs on 'homesteading' and has roots in permaculture. Actions are localised, simplified, slow and food-oriented – but, most of all, cultural. How can we supplant our current, hurtling-towards-destruction culture with a new one that values tomorrow?

Futuresteading starts with gently guiding our thoughts and actions towards a sense of permanence. We need to reimagine our routines and rituals so that they give back to – not take from – the planet. Our decisions should contribute to a steady, vibrant, vital and joyful tomorrow. Futuresteading asks: what tiny but significant thing can we do to make a positive change right now? Then it celebrates the act of having a go.

Futuresteading honours contradiction. It acknowledges that living with integrity involves accepting the straight-up hypocrisy of everyday life; that thinking deeply about tomorrow means being okay to live in today; and that pursuing an earnest and noble existence works best with a big old belly laugh and by encouraging a small group of individuals to bring a magnitude of change.

Futuresteading is a mindset powered by real people and local places, not faceless corporations or government. It defines success as a healthy family, great relationships, an elegantly frugal household, a tight-knit community, acts of kindness, creative fulfilment, integrity, ritual, connection to the natural world and simply being human. In celebrating everything that money can't buy, success is suddenly within everyone's reach.

Futuresteading is not a prescription but an invitation to honour the future in ways that work for you. Far from insignificant, your actions and intentions add to and energise the change that's happening right now within our communities and beneath our feet. Can you feel it?

We can all do it, starting right now.

'There are millions who know the world's problems but very few who are willing to change their actions to reflect this. Now is the time to be excited about beginning a radical transformation.'

Rob Greenfield, environmental activist dedicated to sustainability

What does a futuresteader look like?

You! You've been brave enough to pick up a book with a nonsensical name, so my guess is that you also have a whimsical and curious disposition. You're not afraid to ponder the powerful question 'what if?', and you'll sit comfortably with the answer or action spurred by that question.

What if ...

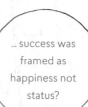

... we all acknowledged when we had enough and shared the abundance with others?

... we prioritised mental health and soil health over wealth?

... we all valued the food on our plate and treated it like it was the foundation of our life?

... education was about experience rather than excellence?

... success was framed as happiness not status?

... helping others made you feel as good as earning money?

... we each contributed equally to building our communities so they could be the most incredible places?

... we decided to repair rather than replace?

... we worked on love projects as often as we worked on industrial projects?

... growing food was as celebrated as growing dollars?

... we could spend time each week learning skills from our elders and teaching skills to our children?

... we were stronger as the sum of the parts?

... we honoured our individual gifts by using them rather than sidelining them as mere hobbies?

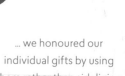

Ponderings do not require complexity to embrace the power of curiosity. Experiments with everyday life evoke childhood fascination and a chance to marvel at the world's magic.

What if ...

... I took my showers in the dark?

... I got to know my backyard magpie family?

... I could only take three foods to the island where I'd see out my days? (It would be potato, cheese and avocado for me.)

... I ate nothing but my body weight in beans for more than 40 days? (My brother actually did this.)

... my life depended on learning how to play a musical instrument?

... I invited a perfect stranger to tea because they had a friendly face?

... I had the courage to publicly honour the gifts that I give to the world?

... I began a collection (that would never be complete) of heritage apple trees? (Hello, Black Barn Farm!)

... I replaced a new 'thing' with a new 'skill'?

... I let go of the riverbank and just floated down the stream, away from stability and financial return but towards an unknown place that followed my heart?

... I committed to only eating food that I foraged?

... I never bought another present but made them all instead?

... I committed to only buying second-hand goods?

... I mapped the miles on everything I purchased?

... I had to carry my waste on my back for the rest of my life?

... I considered the lives of the generations that were still to come?

... I went screen-free for 48 hours every week?

Why is futuresteading so important?

Grim pictures aren't my favourite thing to paint, but illustrating the reality of our current situation places futuresteading in context. After all, futuresteading is a response to a culture that isn't working. Before we make a mad dash towards a better one, it helps to understand the issues and connect the dots to our whole-system issues.

Could it be that, as a people, we have become accustomed to an abundance of readily available, inexpensive, single-use consumables and choice? The reality of anything ever becoming scarce is so far removed from our expectations that we have not only forgotten historical memories of poverty and starvation, but also imagined ourselves into a false reality of endless abundance, enough to lure us into thinking that we will never need survival skills again.

Think again ...

Dwindling biodiversity

Biodiversity = resilience, but only 10 per cent of food varieties from 100 years ago still exist today. In addition, one-third of all insects are now endangered. Species extinction is happening more rapidly than ever before.

Global hunger

Some 805 million people around the world are undernourished.

Fewer forests

Around 19 million hectares (47 million acres) of forest are cleared every year for development and food production.

Disconnected eaters

Around 60 per cent of the global population are urban dwellers who do not have the ability to easily grow the majority of their own food, or to connect to the person who does.

Gross inequality

There is an ever-widening wealth gap. The six wealthiest individuals on Earth own as much as the poorest 60 per cent of the rest of the world. Poverty = decreased access to fair and equitable income, education, health care and employment.

Rampant food waste

Due to long supply chains, 50 per cent of the world's food is wasted. Some produce is never picked on farms; anything sold cheaply by wholesalers is seen as disposable. Restaurants choose only prime cuts of meat, getting rid of the rest.

Corporate domination

Just 12 multinational companies own 90 per cent of all the brands on supermarket shelves. Their focus is on their bottom line, not on the farmer, the consumer or regional community health.

Declining food literacy

When people eat less homegrown food and spend more time dining out or eating pre-prepared food, their knowledge of where food comes from, how to cook it, when produce is in season and the nutritional value of food decreases significantly.

Disease and pandemics

There are exploding rates of cancer, obesity and infertility. Global pandemic is a reality.

Topsoil loss

Around 24 billion tonnes are lost annually. This equates to 3.4 tonnes lost every year for every person on the planet. Soils store more than 4 trillion tonnes of carbon.

Gig economy

Around 44 million people worldwide now work in the gig economy. The downsides to this economy include financial instability, decreased loyalty, short-termism and decreased legacy thinking.

Climate emergency

We are now experiencing unstable weather patterns, including extreme droughts and floods. This has led to rising seas, erosion, health emergencies, food shortages, species extinctions, adaptation costs and negative economic impacts.

E-waste

Around 50 million tonnes of e-waste – such as computers and smartphones – are thrown away annually. This equates to 70 per cent of the world's overall toxic waste.

Global political discontent

There is growing disillusionment with and loss of trust in the governments of the world.

Fossil-fuel depletion

The extraction of fossil fuels is occurring at unsustainable rates. Fossil fuels are expected to be depleted by 2060.

'Going plastic free is like an on-ramp to a multilane freeway of learning why we need to change.'

Erin Rhoads, author and plastic-free activist

Antibiotic overuse

Up to half of antibiotic use in humans is unnecessary or inappropriate. Overuse leads to antibiotic resistance in disease-causing organisms.

Plastic proliferation

Some 300 million tonnes of plastic are wasted annually. This equates to 53 kilograms (117 pounds) of plastic per person. Around 40 per cent of all plastics are single-use items.

Financial debt

By 2017, global debt had reached US$184 trillion – or US$86,000 per person. This is more than two and a half times the average income. The world's economies rely on an endless growth model to avoid collapse.

A sobering reality ...

So where do we begin?

What's your annual carbon footprint? How much waste do you generate? Asking these questions and then following up with an audit of your own habits is a great place to start.

MEET YOUR EATS

The one thing we all do – eating – is a powerful place to begin.

Participating in and promoting food systems that are local, secure, sustainable and socially inclusive is powerful, because it's a movement of many values: human health concerns, animal welfare, agricultural sustainability, ecological sustainability, food justice and political empowerment. It is occurring internationally and carries political and social clout.

Additionally, it's taking shape at a grassroots level, ensuring that its heart beats strongly with deeply committed ideals. This means that, regardless of government support, it will continue to thrive.

Long supply chains that leave our poor growers backed into a financial corner result in decaying rural and farming communities, and threaten our nation's food security. In the last 100 years, we have seen the degradation hit from all angles:

+ lower seed and soil biodiversity
+ higher suicide rates among farmers
+ longer paths to market
+ lower profits for growers
+ obesity and other health issues
+ higher levels of food waste
+ higher levels of food scarcity
+ greater levels of environmental degradation due to food production
+ an overall sense of disconnection from one another.

We are all eaters, regardless of our age, sex, house size or political alignment. Our need to eat crosses generations and country borders; this provides us with a good opportunity to connect to one another through food. What we choose to buy makes a difference to someone else:

+ to our local growers, who are struggling to inspire the interest of the next generation
+ to our children, who are increasingly becoming disconnected from their food sources
+ to our friends and family, who may be unaware of their food's provenance (who grew it, how they grew it, where they grew it)
+ to our community members, who are more disconnected from one another than ever before.

Farmers need more than just other farmers by their sides. Yes, they understand each other's journey intimately, but a rich and vibrant food system can only be brought to life when conscientious futuresteaders come together as celebrators, connectors, advocates, creatives and eaters. We all form a complex tapestry that celebrates food and the people who grow it.

Thankfully, this new-old-new-again way of thinking allows us to lead a connected life, consider our heritage, rebuild our traditions and deeply honour the food we eat. And the process begins with a local food system that focuses on home-based food production.

GET THE KIDS ON IT

Connecting our kids with their food is an opportunity to change our path and the story we tell as humans. Sowing the seed of knowledge about food growing, pollinating, ripening, picking and cooking is endlessly rewarding. It helps to upskill our future generations in a fundamental way that is pure, practical and primal.

When I deliver school programs, I ask the kids where their food comes from. Around 90 per cent of the time they say 'the supermarket'. Sometimes they say 'the farm'. Very occasionally they say 'we grow it'. Never do they say 'we forage it'. I outline the difference between long and short supply chains, price takers versus price makers, and I talk about Australia's 'just in time' approach: we only have three days' worth of food on the shelves. I ask them what would happen if we were to experience a calamity.

It's a powerful conversation that actually challenges their belief that we will always have food available. Before COVID-19, it was an entirely esoteric conversation, as never in their lifetimes had they not been able to eat what and when they wanted. Since COVID-19, I can now reference a real event where short supply chains were far more robust than long supply chains. I ask them to ponder what they would do if our food supply was genuinely threatened beyond toilet paper and flour shortages – most kids are still adamant that this could never happen.

Although it's hard to truly imagine what it would be like to suddenly have no access to food, tickle your memory bank a little and dust off what it felt like during the first weeks of COVID-19 lockdown. We all watched as shelves were stripped bare and our usual social etiquette was overcome by self-protection. Without access to food security, our society displays very different behaviours. Sadly, I can now share with my schoolkids real examples of the fragile long supply chain in our food system.

In contrast, during that first week of lockdown, I placed an order for flour with a farmer friend who grows and mills their own, I offered food from our garden to neighbours, I gave away jars of homemade relish and I foraged basketfuls of roadside apples for our winter stores.

Sadly, our connection to food has been eroded by a system that relies on long supply chains. We are no longer equipped with food literacy skills, we can't connect to the seasons of abundance or famine, and we don't know how to feed ourselves without 'ducking to the shops'. We don't hold our small-scale family-owned farms on deserving pedestals, because we have traded the value of their noble work for more prestigious, money-making industries.

But when our highly financed, globalised existence shows cracks, I'm grateful that I know where my food comes from.

A vision for a new tomorrow

What's your vision for tomorrow? What gift will you offer to the collaborative patchwork of regenerative existence? We all have a role to play, and together we can build a very different tomorrow.

When our world ground to a halt in the face of a pandemic, we were offered the gift of time to deeply contemplate the vision of what we wanted our life to look like. It's now up to each of us individually to follow through and start taking steps towards making this vision a reality.

It's okay for us to have slightly different visions, but they will only become reality if we have the gumption to share them. We need to get past our fear of sharing, even if we suspect that the gap between our hope and our reality will be painfully wide. We need to develop a willingness to share for the sake of a better world.

It's time to be practical, nourishing and connected while we create a world of regeneration. Please don't be overwhelmed by the process. Let it add to the foundation of knowledge that will spur us on collectively in our actions to create a better future – because tomorrow matters.

It's time to be practical, nourishing and connected while we create a world of regeneration.

FUTURE-STEADING PILLARS

Let's fill our cup! I welcome you as one of the brave, and thank you for showing up. Not just for reading this book, but also for being someone who is driven by conscientious consideration for our world and the part you play in this deeply complex web.

While the world spins, buffeted by the competing global issues of disease, climate instability, inequality and the faceless, endless push for economic growth, it can become overwhelming to try to work out where we can each make a difference. But we can!

Seven simple principles

While avoiding hard and fast rules, futuresteading does have some basic principles. Interpret these as you like, with actions to suit life as you know it.

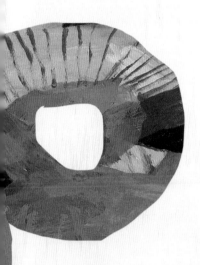

➊ Meet Mother Nature

Bring your awareness back to the infinite potential of a connected existence. See your surroundings as a gift. Notice the subtle patterns, the beauty, the evolution, the fragility and the strength of Mother Nature. Be in awe of her, be respectful and courteous to her, and assume a manner of gratitude.

➋ Celebrate simple

Give yourself space to breathe and to really see, hear and feel abundance. Having less allows you to appreciate and value what sits in your hands and heart. Strip back the white noise to give yourself room to discover the magic in the simplest of wonders.

➌ Make your place

Hold your heritage, stories, memories and hopes in your heart. More than a home or a mark on a map, your place fans your deepest sense of belonging and enables curiosity and commitment to your people, yourself and your culture.

➍ Seek ritual

Create patterns and rhythms, rites of passage and processes. Seek moments alone for deep nourishment, growth and healing. Build time with your people for tomfoolery, conviviality and alternative points of view. Rituals are repetitive and cathartic.

➎ Create your clans

You are as strong as those with whom you build your life; they are an extension of yourself. Choose to be in unison, hand in hand and heart to heart; favour collectivism over individualism. Contribute your piece to the sum of the parts.

➏ Salute the seasons

Notice, respond to, adapt to and embrace the in-the-moment reality of where the outside patterns lead you.

➐ Love local

A powerful spiral begins with the individual and coils outwards, with those closest to you receiving the most energy, love and attention. The community that builds is bound by mutual trust, obligation and reciprocity that empowers all.

① Meet Mother Nature

If you go into the woods today … the kids will run and jump and squeal and explore, their imaginations will leap about, and you will all feel dwarfed, calmed and deeply satiated by an unidentified yearning. Your voices will be muffled, and your busy minds will be stilled by the magnificence of the trees – longstanding, weather-beaten, upright sentinels of wisdom. I recommend going into the woods today.

At Black Barn Farm, our life is mostly outdoors. It extends from the boundaries of our farm to the roadsides where foraged foods are found, the nearby bushland for bushwalks, the pine forests for mushroom hunting, the not-too-far-away mountains to escape the heat or revel in the snow, the abundant rivers for paddling and fishing and picnics, our own dam for daily dips when it's hot, and the woodlots we frequent for the sake of our warmth. We eat by the fire and under stars for seven months of the year, and ride our bikes or walk instead of driving where possible. Rather than changing our habits when the weather shifts, we change our clothes.

Let's get dirty

The dirt under our feet nourishes the foundation of all our needs. It's also the world's single most effective carbon sink. Soils are much better than forests, which actually emit as much carbon as they absorb, and slightly better than oceans, which store only marginally more carbon than they create. The world's soils are superb carbon sinks because they need ongoing additions of carbon to thrive and stay alive. Once we modify our soils, they will transform our food – ultimately renewing our globe.

Fortunately, both soils and human biology heal fast – but only if we halt the assault. So the time to grasp our opportunity to change is now. If you can live regeneratively, existing in a way that closely mimics the natural world, then do it. If you can't, then support those who do.

For a while there, Charlie and I were heavily burdened by the weight of this, but slowly – once we were growing our own food and transforming the soil from which it came – we began to see it as an opportunity to reconnect. We started with food, and you could, too. Buy local, fresh and seasonal food, and share it generously with those you love. This brings us into fellowship, allowing us to exchange with comrades, be human and love unconditionally.

'My obsession with soil and regenerative agriculture is an obsession with feeding the world, and preserving our topsoil so that we can feed the world into future generations.'

Sadie Chrestman, co-owner of Fat Pig Farm

Right: Our orchard is biodiverse and has intentionally curvaceous and contoured rows to maximise water infiltration.

Fortunately, both soils and human biology heal fast – but only if we halt the assault. So the time to grasp our opportunity to change is now.

Mimic Mother Nature

Mother Nature is messy. Yet within the chaos, there is a repetitive and intentional patterning that forms a rich biodiversity. It allows each and every contributor to become the strongest, most robust version of themselves they can.

Our orchard is messy! To the uninitiated – and even some of our closest friends – our orchard looks like an unmanaged wilderness. Not so long ago, while we shared a cider, a good friend quipped casually, 'It'll be great when you have some time to manage your orchard properly, as it must be so hard seeing it so full of weeds and in such a state.' It was a jarring comment, not just because it was a little rude, but because we had assumed that someone so close to us would know that our orchard is growing exactly as we intended.

You see, we intentionally planted an orchard with no straight rows. Also, we intentionally:

- planted out only 3 hectares (7½ acres) of orchard so we could observe it closely
- left big strips of unslashed grass in the middle of our wavy rows for biodiversity
- avoided creating bare earth patches to maintain topsoil
- sourced and grafted more than 100 fruit varieties, again for biodiversity
- grafted onto multiple varieties of rootstock for disease minimisation
- underplanted with diverse species
- used biological solutions for pest management.

We did all of this on purpose, as it mimics Mother Nature's approach to creating a

vibrant, biodiverse, sustainable ecosystem, which is exactly the kind of environment in which we want our food to grow. The trouble is that we've become accustomed to manicured spaces as a representation of success, and see environments that reflect the natural world as 'untamed', 'uncontrolled' and 'unproductive'. I know where I want my food to grow, though – do you?

Are you listening?

The natural world allows each of us to exist; it literally provides the air we breathe, the water we drink and the food we eat, and it regulates the atmosphere on which we depend. Unfortunately, our increasingly urban population has lost sight of this fact. We need to understand that each person sitting in an apartment is still reliant on all of those ecosystems for their existence, even if they can't see, smell, hear or taste any part of nature's vital services.

Although our comprehension of our evolutionary relationship with the natural world is waning, our intuitive response to being in nature is unwavering. It's called biophilia and, put simply, it's our innate desire to seek a deep connection with the natural world.

Our need to rewild, seek fundamental skills and recalibrate our connection to Mother Nature is surging with each global crisis. Fortunately, we have primal knowledge thanks to our hunter-gatherer ancestors, who deeply understood our surroundings, seasonal cycles and foundational needs, but we cannot expect to discover and absorb these skills once more without first acknowledging their value and taking the time to reconnect with them. Our opportunity to then finetune these skills requires us to use them in real environments.

Adapting our lives to accommodate this may be confronting and feel foreign, but in some countries it's quite a deeply entrenched way of life. Norwegians have built their entire culture around what they call *friluftsliv* – pronounced *free-loofts-liv* – which translates to 'free air life'. It refers to their commitment to a life spent exploring and appreciating nature. A tree change is perhaps not just for ideologists or romantics, but also for those with a genuine desire to rebuild their own world and the way they connect to it.

When Mother Nature provides conflict, she also gives us a great opportunity for transformation. But we can only transform if we are listening ... not only with our ears, but also with our eyes, our heart and our primal intuition. As beings of the earth, we have the knowledge but we need to take the time and truly have the desire to make the necessary changes.

Mother Nature has an incredibly powerful and ruthless way of ensuring balance. Our role now is to find a way to transform in order to bring balance to our world before it is too late. My head, heart, senses and intuition are listening. Are yours?

NOT JUST *ON* THE EARTH, BUT *OF* THE EARTH

To regenerate something is to return it to better than its original state. This can be applied to just about anything, but it can only happen if we pare back, aspire for less, seek simplicity and, most importantly, acknowledge that we are each just a tiny speck that comes from the natural world. We are not above it, in control of it or the creator of it – we are 'of it'. The more deeply connected we are to the natural world, the better placed we are to mimic it, learn from it and regenerate it.

'Adopting simple skills is burgeoning because it nourishes the people you love and gives you a sense of hope.'

Sophie Hansen, author and blogger at *Local Is Lovely*

MOTHER NATURE ENCHANTMENT

Tune in to the natural world any way you can.

- Cloud watch ... take a pillow.
- Get to know your watershed – where does your water flow from and to?
- Grow plants from seeds (steer clear of hybrids).
- Make a treehouse (this is for grown-ups, too).
- Whittle a piece of wood.
- Press flowers.
- Let the kids decorate the table each night with natural items chosen to mark the seasons.
- Pick posies of roadside flowers, and put them next to your bed.
- Collect leaves for a bowl.
- Go scrumping for roadside fare.
- Paint stones, and tell many stories with them.
- Go on treasure hunts in nature, and use your finds to make a mandala, crown or mask.

❷ Celebrate simple

If you were to leave your life today and pack only the things you truly need, without a doubt you would have a light load. When you pare back the noise from the stuff you acquire, what's left is what matters; when you focus your energy on what remains, these treasures thrive and become your true wealth.

Take comfort in simple recipes, simple homes, simple schedules, simple pleasures and simple expectations. This everyday stuff forms the bricks of our existence – sniffing fresh herbs, feeling the sun on your back, hearing the warble of a magpie, snapping and eating an asparagus spear, having a chat with a childhood friend. It's not always easy to keep things simple (in fact, simplicity often comes after complexity), but the more we set our sights on simple, the less we need to seek the elusive state of balance. It's not only a kinder and more joyful way to live, but it's also pretty darn liberating.

Life from scratch

Building resilience calls on the skills, desire and ingredients for a life that cherishes a from-scratch approach. It's often referred to as the simple stuff, but I like to call it the fundamental stuff. If I'm honest, it's not really simple at all. Learning to live a life from scratch takes a million moving parts of interconnected things that can all come undone. But once you know how to do it, build a rhythm around it and make it happen, the parts fit together seamlessly and the daily rituals take care of themselves.

A from-scratch childhood preset my adult inclination, and you could argue that my knowledge is innate. But in seeking ways to share these skills, I've had to unpick and understand how to create a from-scratch mindset. When recalibration is required, answer these simple questions:

- How resilient and adaptable would you be if your daily conveniences were interrupted?
- Do you grow any food of your own, or buy it direct from a farmer?
- Do you store bulk foods?
- Do you make your meals from scratch?
- Do you have a mind library of non-shop-bought solutions for your needs?
- Do you have a large store of vegie-garden seeds?
- Do you rely on a daily visit to a supermarket for food?
- Do you have a well-stocked medical kit or well-stocked herbal medicine garden?
- Can you deal with injuries and ailments?
- Can you make your own clothes?
- Have you created a community that will respond to your call for help?

Resilience and adaptability are our individual choice, but having from-scratch skills is enriching, empowering and fundamental to a futuresteading life.

> **'I see us moving closer to a sharing mentality where the definition of success is not so stuff addicted – this is liberating.'**
>
> Brenna Quinlan, permaculture illustrator

Reframing success

You *can* have it all! But to the detriment of what? Our environmental stability, our connection to each other, our commitment to reducing plastic use, our regard for food? It's a wired, hazy, fast-paced, exhausting state of existence where we live but don't thrive.

In today's developed nations, the concept of success lures us with the idea that we can and, in fact, should expect to have it all. But our expectations don't get to the heart of the problem: we're living beyond our means. We exist on a finite planet with finite resources, yet we live in ways that assume there is an infinite ability to continue business as usual and see success as a big house, fancy cars, global access and countless gadgets.

If, on the other hand, success were defined as a healthy family, great relationships, an elegantly frugal household, a tight-knit community, random acts of kindness, creative fulfilment and integrity – all the things that money can't buy – then we'd be happier with less. Reducing our consumption would be no biggie. When we champion the simple, human stuff, not the material stuff, suddenly success is within everyone's reach. And it doesn't cost a cent.

Integrating limits to growth into our Western culture has been nothing short of impossible, as it presents an inconvenient truth that our habits must shift and our priorities must realign with the natural world. Perhaps we should take a leaf from the Iroquois Nation's Law, which considers the needs of the seven generations to follow (this equates to 140 years). When making decisions now, we should have a deep concern and respect for the legacy that is left for those who come afterwards.

Simple is sacred

It can be hard to swim against the flow of the Western world, and I acknowledge that having the headspace to seek something out of the ordinary is only afforded to those who genuinely have enough. I'm fortunate to be in this position. Although many may consider our 'enough' to be less than most, I've had time to ponder the ways to see magic in the tiniest of things and to give space to celebrate them. In this country, abundance and beauty twinkles everywhere if you open your eyes, use the right lens and let delight follow.

Actively seeking these moments and acknowledging the joy they bring to me, our kids and friends is a conscious decision. I'm not just talking about four-leaf clovers, bunches of roses and fresh eggs (although they tickle my fancy, too) – I'm talking about even smaller wonders: a scent in the wind, lichen on a branch or an impromptu cup of tea with a neighbour.

You know that feeling of having something exciting to look forward to – it sits in the back of your mind, bubbles to the top at odd times and makes you grin. What are your simple pleasures?

CHOOSE SIMPLICITY

Seeking the simple life is simple, really.

- Make your presents and be proud to give them.
- Read books aloud to each other.
- Drink fresh, icy-cold, non-homogenised milk with the cream still on top.
- Eat snack plates on weekends.
- Have a bath with a friend ... not a spa, but a bath (I did this at age 22 to relive a childhood memory – what a hoot!). Wear a swimming costume and take wine.
- Laugh. Out loud. Right from your belly.
- Walk out the door with no time frame to return.
- Have a cup of tea at sunrise in your own special spot.
- Start a collection of something that's easy to find: pine cones, sticks, pressed flowers, feathers.
- Have a boiled egg with a sprinkle of salt for dinner.
- Write a letter and post it.
- Take a good friend for a ride on your bike.
- Look for the beauty in all things.
- Dance or sing without inhibition.
- Sit under a tree, and look up into the leaves.
- Race raindrops down windows.

Less was best!

Our house was old and cold. We wanted it to be warm and comfortable. Lucky for us, it took us four years to secure a builder. We were lucky, because the four-year wait gave us a chance to realise that being on the farm full-time rather than working for the man was actually what we wanted. It forced us to genuinely assess what we really needed. What we planned to be grand was eventually scaled down to be sun-filled and cosy – and it didn't break the bank.

Most of the materials used were second-hand, and we painted walls, sanded floors and built the stone steps ourselves. Our view is of the garden, there's a seat in the sun, and the bank account is balanced – so our long days off the farm, where we worked to pay for it all, are now behind us. By being cleverly frugal, we gave ourselves the gift of time – a present we'd rather have than a cathedral ceiling any day. Patience can be a virtue after all!

START WITH WHAT YOU'VE GOT

The best advice we got when starting on our path of intentional simplicity was to start with what you've got. Not only does this reduce the need for unnecessary consumption, but it also lets you set a pace of change that's sustainable for you while you rebuild habits. In addition, it encourages you to be creative and realise that solutions to just about every problem are right under your nose.

❸ Make your place

Our sense of place is our foundation. It influences the decisions we make, how we interact with others and our relationship with self, and it's the first step in realising the part we play in the world. While we can't control everything, we can regulate our own impact and take our role in the world seriously (not earnestly – that's exhausting) by making decisions that consider the generations yet to come and honour those who came before us. Our place is so much more than things. It's a deep remembering that sits in the cool of the rivers, the swaying of the trees and the warmth of the sun. Your place is yours and yours alone!

It begins at home

Our homes form the skeletal structure of our lives, which today are lived more 'out' than 'in'. However, you don't need to own your home to generate a strong connection to place. By simply filling a space with good intention, creativity and energy, you infuse it with life, hope and honour. It might be a rental property, but you can create a place to belong through ritual, appreciation and simple acts.

Our homes are where we rest, have space for thought and are 'held' between moments of busyness. For most, our lives are not home-based. We honour those working away from home with titles and positions, while value has eroded for those committed to home-based pursuits. Economic growth has flourished but to the detriment of those who can grow food, sew clothes, raise children, volunteer for community groups, create a garden, cook from scratch and be happy with less.

This slow, persistent demise has resulted in the home no longer being a place of bustling and intentional industry, connectivity and productivity. Instead, it's a comfortable if sterile port at which we dock between convenient solutions and activities, such as pre-packaged or takeaway food, store-bought presents, kids' activities and our jobs.

Interestingly, during the COVID-19 lockdown, we recalibrated our homes as the centrepiece of our decision-making. They returned to being a place of centring, nurturing, feeding, growing, learning and mess-making. Family rituals and a connection to self, to others and to fundamental skills such as growing, sewing, cooking, fire-lighting and fixing became the core focus of our priorities, rather than titles, careers, business meetings, dollars, endless stuff and endless growth.

Creating 'place' is not just about making a home. It's about really belonging! Being part of and contributing to your community, and knowing that you can honour your strengths because those around you will encourage these gifts to shine. The more comfortable you are with your strengths, the more inclined you are to offer them to others; when everyone is supported while doing this, the entire community benefits. When there is harmony and everyone has found their sense of place, together you can ebb and flow to the rhythms of your world.

Finding my place

Midway through writing this book, I moved 'home' for ten weeks. My nostalgic desire to be back in the rolling green hills of my childhood was a need as great as breathing. I missed the soft, gentle light, the sickly sweet smell of recently baled silage and the unmistakable red mud of Victoria's dairy country.

As expected, while I was at home, the generations on both sides of the family were loud and present. There were Saturday cups of tea and Sunday drives to old haunts, evening walks through paddocks and picnics where a house once stood, as well as new stories from Gran. The kids attended my childhood school and had sleepovers with cousins twice removed. Absorbing it all, I became convinced that this was how I needed to live ... forever. And I breathed more fully than I had ever done in my adult life.

In my childhood patch, I became my fullest, truest and strongest self. I was never alone, but I could hide when needed, fly high when desired and ponder safely when things were uncertain. There's no doubt that when your roots are deep, your sense of belonging is unquestioned. From there, you can face the challenges of hard questions, problematic relationships and difficult circumstances, overcoming these hardships with a resolve that often falters when you are alone.

My childhood home still held me, and as long as my enormous family – with its generations of stories and belonging – still called it home, it would always hold me. But somewhere along my life I had undergone a transforming rite of passage from child to adult; my own clear vision and my sense of place had shifted.

I realised that home now was where I'd raised my children, creating for them what my childhood place had been to me. We were deeply entrenched in our community, with 20 years of experiences and loyal friendships that had ridden the tides of joy and endured the hardships of soul-breaking effort. We'd founded a community-owned food co-operative that entrenched us even further, and our vision of building a small-scale orchard that fed, connected, inspired and educated had been two decades in the crafting.

This story would be different if I'd ventured home earlier, but the irony is that it was my dad who actually unlocked my desire to call another part of the world home.

Charlie and I had been living in a little town for a decade, but we both worked away from home and never got involved in village life. One day when our twins were not yet one, Charlie was away with work, and our car broke down. I called my dad to ask if I might borrow one of his three cars, as we couldn't afford to get ours fixed. His response? 'Do you have any seeds? A good pram? Good walking shoes?'

I was confused by his abstract advice. He went on to explain: 'I suggest you put those little boys in the pram, walk into town and buy what you need to grow some vegies. If you've got no money, then you'd better get growing so you've at least got food, and if you've got no car then you'd best get walking.'

I hung up, hurt and miffed but determined to prove that I could push through. I sat, I thought, I put the kids in the pram and I walked into town. I bought seeds, walked home and planted them.

Over the next six months, I began to make my place. I found a daily rhythm in watering, weeding and planning around the food I grew. I paced the roads with my two little boys and began recognising faces, starting conversations and saying yes to being involved. I slowed my rhythm to reflect the pace of 18-month-olds rather than holding on tightly to our pre-baby life. I became happy in my home-based existence in a way that had eluded me until then. I stopped fighting and became accepting of my reality. I also realised that this had been my dad's intended lesson.

After not speaking to him for months, I finally called him. Just before I hung up, he asked, 'So, you got your car fixed then?'

'No thanks to you,' I retorted.

All he said was: 'It was better this way.'

The connections I found to my home, my kids, myself and my community during that time were the flagstones of the life to which we're now wedded. So wedded that even the prospect of moving to my childhood hills could not lure me back. I have a new place now!

Strength from place

With a strong sense of place, managing the hard stuff is easier and we can take on challenges without backing away. The things that need the most work are usually the most rewarding, and often these are human things. Those wedded to their place have the support and grounding to step up

and work through problems, navigating with tools that are honed as they go.

These skills are some of the hardest to develop, yet some of the most important in our ability to create towns, communities, households and ideas. We all have a unique sense of where we belong, but being conscious of it and considering it as quite possibly the most important foundation in your life will allow you the freedom to make decisions about what matters, not what appeals!

MAKING YOUR PLACE REQUIRES:

- ✦ patience – all good things take time
- ✦ kindness and honesty – especially to yourself but also to others
- ✦ gumption – just give it a go
- ✦ courage – it might not work, but you tried and learned
- ✦ a vision – it'll hold you in tough times
- ✦ a conscious awareness of your surroundings, both inside and out
- ✦ awareness of your senses
- ✦ acceptance that it's not linear or sensible but erratic and emotional
- ✦ recognition that those who came before us left a legacy on which to build
- ✦ understanding that what we do will impact those still to come
- ✦ a foundation of memories.

For me, having my hands in the dirt is the most grounding and place-making act of all. It assures me that I can feed my people and create a space of prettiness to nourish our hearts. Where you live and how you tick will influence how you make your place, but it's your own journey – and with it comes the ability to tell stories, share meals, grow dreams and develop a culture that is worth fighting for.

❹ Seek ritual

Start your day with a freshly brewed pot, walk the block, split the wood, call a friend, write letters, doodle on paper and weed while you talk. The way we spend our minutes is how we spend our days, and in no time at all it amounts to our life.

Humans are by nature inclined to repeat their practices. It keeps us calm, builds our confidence and assures us of who we are. This is ritual.

The way we live our lives is based on our deeply held values, which have evolved through kinship, memory markers and our desire for what's to come. We challenge, question, encourage and participate in the activities that lift us up and fill our cup. This is ritual.

A home of ritual

Home is so much more than a place to store our stuff. It's the place to build our rituals, and a place of nourishment and deep, soothing safety. It's where conversations explore more, lessons are learned and unlearned, and mess and rest mash together. We grow, recover, breathe, unmask and are free in our home.

One of my regular rituals is the intentional 'let it go' feeling at around 6 pm each night, when the push of the day subsides. I take my first deep breath for the day, and gain perspective by observing a summary of the day's events. Even though I've considered myself a morning person all my life, I find the mornings mildly overwhelming. I'm definitely not a night owl; in fact, I revel in the shutdown of the house that symbolically screams, 'No more, I'm done!': the curtains are drawn, the fire is stoked, the chickens are locked away and dinner is cooked. Perhaps I'll start calling myself a 'twilight owl'. It's definitely my favourite time of day.

Rebuilding culture with ritual

Today we live in a world that is paced beyond our ancestors' imaginations, and one that has replaced cultural richness with suffocating consumerism. Our leaders are driven by elections rather than legacy thinking, so short-termism dominates our culture and has removed our desire to stop, take time and ritualise our lives.

We have landed in this scenario after many decades of postwar boom. No generation or ideology has successfully carried the torch in protest against the relentless erosion of our ability to think about others in what has become a narcissistic and impatient way of life. By considering those who came before us and those who are yet to come, we shift our cultural heartbeat from instantaneous satisfaction to one of slow respect. We make wiser decisions and value attributes that differ greatly from productivity, yield and margins.

By acknowledging and celebrating our own daily rhythm, the pace of our broader community and the influence of the seasonal shifts, we awaken to the world around us and to the opportunities to honour ritual. Not only does this connect us more deeply to annual changes, but it also rebuilds our community scaffolding so that it holds us all and keeps us safe – just as it did in pre-industrial times.

Seeking ritual can be slow and personal, or it can be paced and connecting. Powerful rituals are those that repeat in line with events that are bigger than you. It may be as simple as seeking an afternoon breeze or as convivial as an annual winter wassail.

Acknowledge the existence of rituals, nod your encouragement and support those who seek to create more. The gift offered by ritual is a rich tapestry that is capable of weaving us all together.

PICK A RITUAL

To obtain rewards from rituals, just start with:

- a daily mantra – I set mine on my morning walk
- a deep breath – I repeat this during the day to reset my body
- a fresh pot of tea in the morning sun – I pick fresh herbs and add honey
- seasonal bonfires with your closest folk – give them a theme
- an annual trip to the bush – pitch tents, fly-fish, pan for gold and talk late around the camp fire
- a weekly call to those you don't see often
- a daily adventure in your own backyard – whether it's big or small, make it intentional
- gratitude at the dinner table – we each share a good, bad and funny story from the day just gone
- a repeated activity on certain days of the year – birthdays, Easter, Christmas
- drinking in a thunderstorm – stand in the wild wind, breathe in the energy and then run from the rain.

'We have to start finding out what binds us and what we have in common – because it's far more than what divides us.'

Sadie Chrestman, co-owner of Fat Pig Farm

❺ Create your clans

Build your community. Of course, I don't mean the bricks and mortar – I mean the heartbeats and casseroles, the conversation and collaboration. I mean all the good stuff that comes from feeling like you have a deeply entrenched place in the world: people have your back, you feel like you belong, and you've got folk you can call on to celebrate the rock-star moments, or drink tea with and perk you up after the falls.

Creating community sparks a primal desire in each of us. For some, it comes naturally; for others, it's a minefield of human complexity that holds little appeal. Some people (like us) tackle this sport from both sides of the field – we are capable of getting in and playing the game, but equally inclined to sometimes back away.

Like many, I long wrangled with this hot/cold trait, and the feeling of 'belonging' eluded me. In the end, I decided that I just hadn't found my people. Then we started growing food, and the feeling of being an outsider shifted markedly. The jury is still out on what caused this shift: us settling into what we had desired for a long time, or attracting different people into our lives through farming.

Eating food that came from our own patch grounded us, through both the growing process and the sudden ability to swap, share and banter about new tricks with others who were also growing food. It was profound to learn that, through the act of growing food, we were no longer remote from others; we finally found connection, fulfilment and ultimately our sense of community.

Growing food kickstarted our paradigm shift away from being passive about our most critical daily act: eating. And it spurred us to consider the supply chain, production methods and waste outcome of everything else we consumed. The shift was gradual, but it joined the dots in our life completely.

We are only as strong as the community of which we are part. In a genuine quest to be community-sufficient rather than self-sufficient, you need to seek out those who are as wedded to this lifestyle as you are. It's not necessary to share your preferred political party, earning capacity, age or career, as what you are building is bigger than this – and it requires a commitment to the wellbeing and upskilling of the people around you. It will take effort, compromise and unwavering contribution, but it will be worth it.

Find your people through food

Following a four-month 'food systems' research trip to Vermont, Charlie and I joined with a group of like-minded folk in our town to establish our local food co-op. We learned a lot from this journey. Working voluntarily and cooperatively was massive, complicated and messy, but for all of the heartaches, the reward was ultimately in the community that it created.

What we don't grow ourselves at Black Barn Farm we buy from the food co-op. It's community-owned and nearly 100 per cent

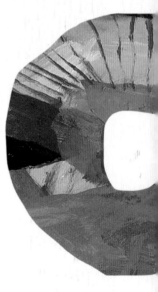

volunteer-run, so as you would expect it's not open 24/7, is sometimes low on stock because cash flow is tight, and it sometimes takes longer to process sales because new people are learning the ropes. Rather than getting frustrated, I just accept that I don't need convenience and speed to make my shopping experience extraordinary. Instead, I value the time that so many people contribute; the chance to buy in-season, locally grown food; and the idea that I belong to something bigger than all of its members. I simply commit to shopping fortnightly, buy what I can, and adjust my meals around my purchases. I ride the co-op's highs and lows, and stick with it because it's only as strong as the community that backs it.

As important as the food it provides is the community it creates. The co-op regularly hosts potluck dinners, morning teas, skills workshops and schools programs, and the building it manages supports other community groups and initiatives. It drives a sense of solidarity and raises a much-deserved toast to every single contributor to our local food system. It's been one hell of a ride, with plenty of potholes and near misses, but it was a community effort – and that's commendable in itself.

Making small changes

It would be unrealistic to think that you can do all of these things all of the time. But as you adapt to a more conscious way of making decisions, a preference for a more organic outcome becomes second nature.

Slowly but surely, we shifted our life away from being constantly busy, earning a decent living so we could buy our solutions but having no time, to one where we were both working part-time and had less cash but enough time to spend it doing slower, simpler, more meaningful things. This ultimately gave us the chance to connect with and contribute to our community.

EMBRACE SIMPLICITY
Seek folk who consider this normal.

- Clothing: commit to only buying second-hand clothing or swapping items with friends. If, unlike me, you can sew, you could also make your own.
- Gifts: transition to predominantly giving homemade/grown/ upcycled gifts.
- Transport: consider first if you could walk, ride or not go at all, rather than using a car.
- Holidays: pitch a tent at home or invite people for picnics, rather than going away for holidays.
- Relaxation: take bushwalks and host yoga classes.
- Gardening: grow from seeds, plants given to you, or cuttings rather than shop-bought plants.
- Food: grow your own herbs, fruits and vegies, and then swap with other people.
- Home: make your home small, warm and cosy rather than big, glossy and expensive, so you owe little and minimise running costs.
- Stuff: you really need stuff? If you do, then visit an op shop. There's nothing you can't find, and the thrill of the hunt becomes addictive. Try to follow the 'one in, one out' rule – for every item bought, donate another.

Left: Hand-watering the kitchen garden is time-consuming but fun when standing side by side with our WWOOFers.

The wonder of WWOOFers

I often forget that not everyone knows what I'm talking about when I mention WWOOFers. Eventually, someone usually plucks up the courage to ask, 'What's a WWOOFer?' In short, WWOOF stands for World Wide Opportunities on Organic Farms, and WWOOFers are people who volunteer to work on these farms. Despite the organisation's name, anyone can engage in this activity, whether they're in the city or country, have a plot of land or not.

The beauty of WWOOF is that you can open your house to folk you've never met but who willingly join you in comradeship and hard work on your path to creating a dream. A grateful intimacy bonds you, grounds you and fills you with a confidence to keep on going as you churn through the list of jobs.

A deep sense of community is established as you navigate everything from shower times and food preferences to self-discovery and new skills. You all adapt and learn from one another as different customs, languages and cultures mesh together. Conversation is real and raw. While you work side by side, a friendship quickly forms that might otherwise have taken years.

A day of repetitive work that may have been mundane when done alone becomes animated and exciting with others by your side. It's like everyone in the mix willingly offers their truest selves, and magic is made thanks to that honesty and vulnerability.

The best part is that even once they leave, what remains is a warming sense that you belong to an incredible network of humans who 'get you', support you and love you, so you've got a world of folk who have your back. In return, they have a bolthole to always call home. After all their hard work, they've earned the right to consider your place a little bit theirs.

'You are only as healthy and
strong as your community –
if the future concerns you,
then become the most useful
node of knowledge in your
community and willingly
share that knowledge.'

**Kirsten Bradley, permaculture educator
at Milkwood**

FINDING SOLIDARITY

Without a doubt, the best way to
settle impatience, reinvigorate a
vision and renew your energy is to
seek out those who've trodden the
path before you and who willingly
share the magic, mistakes, joy and
heartache of their journey. You don't
need to re-create their exact vision,
but if you know that you share
fundamental values then there will
be lessons in their stories. At the very
least, they won't tell you that it's not
worth it, it's too hard or you must be
bloody crazy – they will understand
your language, see your burning desire
and encourage you to have a go. This
is solidarity at its finest. You are not
alone in your desire to make change
a reality sooner rather than later, so
find your soldiers and connect.

CONNECT TO YOUR CLAN
Creating community is not so hard.

- Compliment people –
  acknowledge that we are
  all trying to do our best.
- Gather people – realise
  that humans rely on
  interconnectedness and
  interdependence.
- Hear others – seek to understand
  people's best intentions.
- Drop your walls and be kind –
  smile, wave, write a note or leave
  a flower.
- Share abundance – deliver a
  cooked meal or share your
  newspaper after you're done.
- Offer to help older people – dig
  a hole, weed a garden or hold
  their hand to cross the road.
- Join a group – such as a food
  co-op, Landcare, climate-action
  team or book club.
- Connect and conquer – create
  a brains trust to think through
  your worries.
- Think collaboratively – share
  tools with a friend, car pool or
  split a subscription.
- Create a hub at home – arrange
  a food/plant swap, street library
  or seed saving.

⑥ Salute the seasons

The seasonal pull waits for no one; it is dictated by forces stronger than anyone, and it impacts us all. What we wear, what we eat and how we spend our days used to be influenced by the seasons more than any other factor, but this is happening less and less in our modern world. We flick on the aircon when it's too hot, buy fruit and vegies whenever we want them, and persist with a pace that disregards the natural rhythm of the year. While the convenience of a seasonally disconnected life feels virtuous, it's not how we've been designed to tick. Seasons are Mother Nature's way of prompting us to align our actions with the forces that create our world – if we ignore these, then we are in contempt of our evolution.

Nothing connects us to the seasons like growing food. Once, we all grew and celebrated seasonal food. We understood how precarious it was. When was the last time you ate an apple and considered the name of the farmer who grew it? Sadly, for most people in the Western world, our connection to what we eat, where it came from, how it was grown, who it was grown by and its nutritional value gets lost on the plate that sits next to our computer screen while we work through lunch. Instead, we trust the labels, ignore the boundless packaging and choose convenience and price over provenance and seasonality. The result is that food is no longer something we celebrate; rather, it's a low-cost, low-value commodity that attracts apathy and waste. Our connection to food has changed from rich and sacred to benign and purposeless.

Also lost are cultivation skills, connection to the earth, respect for the farmer and, sadly, regional vibrancy. Long supply chains make our family farmers faceless price takers rather than celebrated champions. While this might enable us to buy cheap food now, these farmers eventually break down and walk away from their farms, leaving multinational companies to fill the gaps with disastrous monoculture, a singular focus on maximising yield and more mechanisation. The impact of this on rural Australia and ultimately our food sovereignty is devastating. Fortunately, our need to eat means that we can all make a difference simply by asking a few more questions, connecting to our food and, ultimately, making an effort to see food as a resource to be celebrated. After all, it's fundamental to our existence!

Celebrate the farmers who feed us

The orcharding life is more raw and real than any path I've journeyed on before. I'm proud to stand tall as a farmer and utterly grateful to others who've also committed their life to the production of food, especially our regenerative comrades who honour and nurture the soil. They are noble growers of food, and their desire to know the people who are eating what they grow allows them to celebrate food and stay true to their beliefs.

As eaters and growers, we can instil far-reaching change. Together, we are powerful and can rise to salute our farmers, increasing our respect for food as a sacred joy to be cherished. Today, as you read this, I challenge you to find out where your food comes from, how it is grown and who grows it.

Hooray for homesteading

A guaranteed way of getting cosy with seasonal life is to grow your own food. A pot of tomatoes and basil in summer and a winter crop of brassicas on the balcony will stroke your seasonal senses. The best place and time to start growing your own food is here and now. Start small, with what you've got, and remind yourself that all good things take time. The skills you learn by doing are powerful and yours to keep, add to and get carried away with. Once you start, you might find it hard to stop.

If the joy of fresh food and seasonal life tickles your primal desires, then you may end up like us: homesteading. This can be a full-time job and requires skills that are slowly being forgotten as more and more of us become city-based office workers. But for those who seek something else in their life, homesteading is a diverse, rewarding and exciting way to live.

It's anything but the 'simple life', but it does connect you deeply to the natural world, demand that you observe the seasons, and reward you with homegrown food in abundance. Actually, feeding a family requires a pretty serious commitment and quite a lot of work, but this doesn't mean that you shouldn't still grow whatever you have space and time for. Picking corn and beans fresh from the garden will still feel virtuous, even if you have had to buy everything else on the plate.

Regardless of your scale, be mindful that seasonality is central to your food-growing rhythm. We eat like kings at Black Barn Farm, straight from the garden, from February until May (late summer to late autumn). Once the weather chills and our harvest slows, we get stuck into the pantry stores, with a little top-up from a sleepy winter garden of kale and cabbage from June. Then we limp through the spring hunger gap from September to November before the new-season produce starts to appear. We eat fresh food again, but it's not until February that peak abundance rolls around once more.

You really can begin immediately and build your toolkit at the same time as your skills and network. You don't need to buy anything new; sharing tools with friends is a good idea at the start.

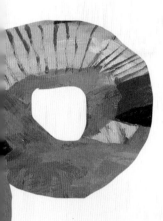

Ultimately you will need:

- jars – these can be Fowlers jars, or any jars with tight-fitting lids that have been saved over time or bought in op shops
- appropriate and adequate storage space – this needs to be cool and dry with no sunlight, and located close to your kitchen
- a large pot – with a capacity of 10 litres (340 fl oz)
- an outdoor sink, tap or laundry to clean vegies
- carrier baskets that drain
- good secateurs
- adequate freezer space
- a benchtop prep area, inside or out
- a dehydrator – a store-bought machine or homemade rack (potentially both)
- a potting area – within a courtyard, balcony, backyard or garage
- a storage solution for your seeds (see page 246 for details)
- a garden diary
- garden tools – a hand trowel, hand fork, rake, shovel, spade, gloves and stakes
- a good watering system and watering-can (ensure that it has a soft spray)
- space to grow food – a paddock, backyard, nature strip, pots or raised beds alongside the driveway
- a compost heap – even a small heap using lawn clippings, food scraps and roadside leaves will return a worthy amount of compost
- a worm farm – these can be any size, starting as small as a bucket
- a chicken coop (or quail coop if space is tight)
- most importantly – gumption, creativity and persistence.

❼ Love local

Committing to going local doesn't mean just looking inwards. Actually, it's important that you think global but act local. And the power of localising is profound. It starts in the home, where you value the stable, nourishing space in which you spend more time than any other; where you grow and cook food, observe the seasons, connect to the land, gather your people, understand your watershed, express creativity, and learn and share all you can.

Then you prioritise your community of family, friends, school, work and volunteer committees, as they form the core of your world. Support where you can, with time, kindness, ideas and financial contribution.

Why? Because if you build the best backyard you can, and everyone else does the same, then energy, opportunities, money, connection and community spirit will emerge from where the heart beats strongest. You may need to seek ideas, knowledge and opportunities from afar, but your priority stays closer to home.

A tree grows strongest when its roots are deep. In fact, Helena Norberg-Hodge, founder and director of Local Futures, says, 'Throughout human history, our cultural traditions, societies, personalities and even our bodies have evolved in relationship with community and local ecosystems.' We are designed to live where we evolve.

Seek a short supply chain

For all of its assets, going local is harder than you might think, because our Western world is geared towards growth and global markets in the name of progress. This means that imported technology, food, skills and labour are often cheaper. But we've lost a lot. In the name of reconnecting with each other, our environment and our human nature, going local can rebuild our self-reliance, quality of life and hope for a vibrant future that relies on thriving human-scale, short-supply economies.

Nothing is more local than food from a short supply chain, where growers sell within their nearby markets. Along with enhanced relationships, a reduction in both travel and packaging requirements and the payment of fair prices to the farmer, the other bonuses include transparency of growing practices, the sharing of food literacy, and healthier humans eating food that is suited to their gut biomes. The broader power of locally grown food is that it keeps money in the community, which in turn maintains that community's vibrancy, connection and opportunities for the ongoing viability of small-scale, family-owned farms. Supporting local farmers is a powerful act.

Futuresteading is about empowering individuals and communities to take back ownership of food, health, energy and local environment, little by little. By growing vegies, practising herbal medicine, harnessing natural energy, composting, harvesting water, building and repairing, bartering with neighbours, and finding joy in simplicity, you seize power from the big guns and pull it back down to Earth … where the people are. Where changing the world is something you do every day, bit by bit, in your own backyard.

GO LOCAL
Make local your mantra.

- Buy your gifts from local makers.
- Buy your food from local growers.
- Send your kids to local schools.
- Commit to local causes.
- Contribute to local committees.
- Attend local events.
- Buy your energy from a local grid.
- Employ local people.
- Keep your money in community banks.
- Dine at local cafes and restaurants.

Do you futurestead to honour the generation that came before you? Or are you upskilling so you can then share that knowledge with the generation coming after you?

A life surrounded by elders is a fortunate one. The seeds they sow in our minds make us who we are. You adopt their knowledge by osmosis, observation, emulation, storytelling and standing side by side. My pop showed me that it's possible to work three jobs and still find time to help your children evolve their dreams. Gran taught multitasking by milking a cow, hand-washing clothes and baking while simultaneously wrangling grandkids and great-grandkids. The need to 'just keep doing' regardless of life's vagaries was Mum's dominant lesson, and Dad instilled a great respect for creativity.

While children take for granted this regular contact with kin, the sensibility of adulthood sheds light on the sheer delight of it. I now realise how bloody lucky I was to share mornings with my great-grandmother as she knitted coat-hanger covers from shredded plastic bread bags, and afternoons with Gran as she harvested rhubarb and apples to make pies from scratch. I cherish the times spent helping my mum to bottle home brew and preserved fruits, and my earliest memory of being lulled to sleep by the rocking motion while I was on Dad's back as he dug fence-post holes.

My childhood was relatively bare of material possessions, although I still have many of the wooden toys made by my dad. However, it is the gift of generational knowledge that has made me a grateful adult who actively passes on these shards of the past to my kids. Not only because the knowledge is invaluable, but also because my kids have been able to connect with and find belonging and value in their heritage.

Each one of us has deeply rooted, multigenerational knowledge. Some of us tap into it more than others.

Sometimes the insights are so ingrained that they feel more like intuition than skills that have been learned, but we can unravel where our lessons came from and honour our family teachers.

'Social success is about giving more to the world than we take. Deeply held success really comes when it's more than just about looking after yourself and is a commitment to something bigger than ourselves.'

Alexx Stuart, author of *Low Tox Life*

FOLLOW YOUR INTUITION

Futuresteading with families is intuitive and instinctive, and it thrives on the sentiment of 'hand-me-downs' – be they possessions or pieces of knowledge. It's also lubricated by a healthy dose of sentimentality. These are the things that nourish family life.

Our kids are at the core of what drives many of us. What will their lives look like in this world that sustains us? Becoming puritanical and earnest about your lifestyle choices won't engage and lure the next generation, so in the second half of this book I have included plenty of ideas on how to encourage kids to become involved. But before you roll up your sleeves, here are a few ideas to chew on:

- Keep it light and fun.
- Set a realistic pace for change.
- Don't trip over the small stuff.
- Keep the conversation gentle – it isn't life or death.
- Fan the embers of curiosity until their individual fires of interest ignite.
- Build rapture for the outside world so it's not a foreign place.
- Let kids wander/discover/learn on their own – in a way that works for them.
- Find like-minded families who are at a similar stage in their change journey.
- Make it a game, and instil a sense of magic.
- Set small, achievable tasks so kids are spurred on by little wins.
- Create an activities box with natural materials.
- Let kids grow their own food.
- Shake the hand of the farmer who grows the food you can't.
- Dress for outside days, and go out whenever you can.
- Celebrate the seasons.
- Build family rituals that occur daily, monthly and yearly.
- Know your family rhythm – what's your pace, style, preference and taste?
- Make it YOUR path – adapt what others are doing to suit what works for you.
- Stop comparing yourself to others – let your changes and challenges be yours to navigate.
- Lead by example – it's powerful.

Real skills for kids

When we give our kids real skills, we take seriously the vital importance of raising a generation that is adaptable and capable of facing an uncertain future. School is not the place to learn these skills; our teachers are already working hard to ensure that kids can read, write and master maths. As parents, mentors and friends, we need to take on this upskilling task – and if we combine our efforts, it doesn't have to be difficult.

Do you have an uncle who fishes? A friend who makes bread? A cousin who rides horses? An acquaintance who can weave? A community member who goes bushwalking? Can a coach inspire? A big brother build? A neighbour make herbal medicine? A local group share a vegie garden? There are so many ways to engage our kids in learning skills that are critical right now, and doing it with others can make it more memorable. Kids are more likely to connect with diverse knowledge if they experience the world with more people than just their immediate family.

FROM LITTLE THINGS BIG THINGS GROW

Getting kids to grow herbs, fruits and vegies is a powerful way to connect them to their food, to their family and to the seasons. It gets you all outside together, creating something with purpose, and it shows them in real time – reinforcing patience – how incredible it is that from a tiny seed we can produce something delicious. They learn how to identify pests and weeds, nurture plants during hot and cold weather, understand when something is ready to be picked and savour it when it's on their plate.

Left: Whet the kids' appetite by getting them involved.

Right: Our winter wassail is one way we build community through annual traditions.

Rewrite the storybook

We're responsible for guiding our children to build a story that differs from our own. Instead of inspiring them to contribute to growth, let's create a storyline that:

- builds resilience in an uncertain world
- celebrates simple
- is happy with less
- seeks delight in the outside world
- uses our imagination
- understands seasonal cycles
- grows our own food and can use it all
- deals with boredom creatively
- makes time to discover our gifts
- owns our mistakes
- converses about the big issues
- accepts and celebrates differences
- formulates our own opinions
- is confident to challenge norms
- breeds individualism
- celebrates empathy and kindness.

Of course, we've got to make it relevant to our kids, but imagine if the next generation was offered support to participate in this story. They would be exceptional humans indeed.

MILESTONES AND FAMILY RITUALS

Our families are the place of greatest belonging. It's also the place best suited to guiding us gently through significant, memorable and valued rites of passage. Creating rituals and actively celebrating milestones are easy to do and reinforce potent bonds. So join forces with your clan and create memorable experiences such as:

- coming-of-age milestones
- symbolic artworks
- nature mandalas
- annual men's/women's hiking/ camping trips
- musical creations
- men's/women's ceremonies
- shared multigenerational meals
- entrance-to-adulthood gatherings
- facilitated camp-fire conversations
- solitude challenges.

KEEPING IT REAL – OUR FAMILY STORY

As a family of five, our transition to this way of life has been slow and in response to lots of things: health, time, new knowledge, support from others, growing seasons, money … the list goes on. We've made mistakes every step of the way, often with things that we thought would be easy (such as raising meat birds), and discovered how simple it can be to adapt to some things (such as making herbal tea).

We haven't got everything right. Just like you, we're human, we're trying and we're transitioning. There are still plenty of changes to make, but focusing on the things that we're not doing correctly – or at all – takes away from the things we have got right and can perform well. It's all any of us can do.

Void of romance, rich in ritual

The way we choose to live our days is the way we spend our lives. Regardless of where and how you dare to live your life, the decisions you make are best directed by values that transcend your every day.

Our choices and decisions led us exactly to where we are. This is the reality for most of us. Charlie and I are farmers! Just to be clear, though, you don't have to farm to futurestead – this is just our life. We left professional careers, where the income was regular and our title was easily explained, because we knew that we needed more, for us and for our kids. Not more money or status, but more family time and gritty, experience-laden wealth. Now, our days flow without formality, facades or bureaucracy. We make our own decisions, change our mind if we wish to, and go slower if we need to. Our kids are entrenched in this life, too, so we face our celebrations and challenges together. While the reality of farming is anything but romantic, it's disappointing

that it's rarely encouraged or saluted. It's such a shame! For while it is indeed void of glory, it certainly isn't void of gloriousness.

The hours we work are long. We work in the rain, we work when no customers come, we work until we get blisters – and every day is a work day. The financial reward for our efforts is low, but our days are ours, and we adapt according to our needs. No day is ever the same, and the simple production of food is more deeply satisfying than we ever imagined. Regular money no longer lands in the bank, so our creative approach to paring our needs back is a never-ending challenge, but it sifts the needs from the wants and gives us time to assess what matters.

Our lungs work hard with the physical exertion, but the air we breathe is clean, and we stop to eat lunch outside every day. Life is now ours to make mistakes (doing too much too quickly), overcome challenges (birds in the orchard) and be deeply connected to our community – so really, we wouldn't change a thing!

A futuresteading family life is messy, noisy and argumentative. We debate our ideology and nag to get jobs done. Our vision has been a long, clear one and it's definitely taking shape, but not without massive sacrifices: spontaneity, restfulness and sometimes joy and frivolity. I'm incredibly grateful for the way our kids view their world, and hope that they can see past the things they don't have and realise what they do have: bare feet, paddock picnics, dam swims, bush biking – and quality family time.

An image of hope

For us, our hope looks something like my own childhood:

◆ The only rule was to stay within view of home, to have something on your head and be back before dark.
◆ Your bike was your freedom, and you laboured in the dirt making dugout forts.
◆ You rode your neighbour's horse bareback in a swimming costume (it's as uncomfortable as it sounds) to the creek, then jumped off a log into the swimming hole, and dried out in the sun next to the pile of freshwater mussels you'd just gathered.
◆ Shoes were unnecessary, and you could roam anywhere at full speed without the slightest foot falter.
◆ Your days were unplanned and unruled.
◆ You dashed nude to the creek from the hayshed cubby that made you all scratchy, before raiding the vegie garden or orchard for a feast.
◆ You filled buckets to brimming with freshly picked mushrooms.
◆ You painted yourself from top to toe in cow poo and dried in the sun until it cracked, then climbed into the cow trough to rinse clean.

I was especially lucky as a child, because my neighbours were my best friends, and my multitude of cousins lived close by. Their parents were as preoccupied as mine doing grown-up things, so we were left to enjoy adult-free adventures that were as crazy as our imaginations allowed. Our activities brimmed with magic that built creativity, independence and immunity beyond our wildest dreams.

My desire to give my children this same experience nagged at me until we made it real. What I didn't realise was that behind the scenes of my idyllic childhood, my parents were juggling the complexities of life. These are now ours to manoeuvre. While the issues feel all-encompassing at times, I think that my kids are as oblivious to them as I was back then – and if they're not, then perhaps this reality is an important lesson.

More than anything, my wish for the next generation is that their childhood builds a foundation which encourages them to be 'awake' to the natural world, considered in their actions and aware of the impact their decisions will have. I want their 'woken' life to be rich with deep friendships, ritual, purpose and an appreciation of their role in contributing to the greater good.

I hope that they are guided by collectivism rather than individualism, but that they have the courage to be individuals who don't fit inside anyone's pigeonholed expectations. I long for their childlike curiosity to take them into adulthood, and for them to find awe in simplicity. I hope that they are nimble, adaptable and entrepreneurial in spirit. But most of all, I simply want them to know love, to laugh often and to be true to themselves. This is resilience!

Part of the dream

At age twelve, between settling into high school and adjusting to life with WWOOFers, our twin boys launched their own little business, making and selling fresh apple-cider doughnuts alongside our pick-your-own-apples business. It definitely wasn't without its challenges, but they committed to the three-month season with gusto (mostly) and wrangled the fine art of rostering their friends, wages, start-up repayments, painfully quiet days, bad weather, awkward customer-service moments, new systems and more.

What I'm most proud of is their commitment to turning up, day in and day out, rain, hail or shine. They scrubbed their equipment, filled the quiet days with card games and soccer, and created systems to help on the busy days. They learned that creating something from scratch can bring immense frustration, challenge you beyond belief and even make you cry (thanks to a few nasty customers), but it also offers enormous rewards, opportunities to learn, and satisfaction when you nut out the problems. There were definitely difficult days, but at the end of it they walked just a little bit taller because they knew that they could do it.

It doesn't matter whether or not the business continues. What matters is that they stepped up with an idea to be part of our dream. They took a chance, engaged in something that was bigger than themselves, and proved without a doubt that they were 'awake' and had the gumption to give something a go!

HONOUR OUR PAST

When I was young, I never saw my parents and grandparents as old. As the daughter of a hospital matron, I spent a lot of time in the local nursing home, helping the 'pink ladies' freshen the flowers and chatting to the patients. By their side I learned to knit, sang songs and drew endless pictures to brighten their rooms; I was probably irritating, but I considered them my friends.

My regard for older generations solidified early, and I was rewarded for my eagerness to hear their stories and seek their knowledge bank of wisdom. They lived in a time of less, but their skills, work ethic, statesmanship, stewardship and stoicism filled the gaps. They had dreams and lived good lives, but they were made of different stuff.

Now my grandmother is old. Luckily, I've had 43 years of her knowledge and her glass-half-full attitude. I know that her skills were born of a life that was hard, and her version of 'simple' was not a choice but reality. The food that she fed to her family (rabbit, venison, fresh milk, roadside fruits and homegrown vegies) was 'organic' by default, not bought from a shop or romantically called scrumping. Her 'local life' meant that she rarely left her district, and she has never travelled overseas, although family and multigenerational friends have surrounded her for her entire life. A need to feed her family turned her thumb a shade of green and blended beautifully with Grandad's love of hunting, so no one ever went hungry. As a side benefit, it intertwined them with the seasons and the outside world, although the idea of 'grounding' or rewilding makes her eyes grow wide.

She shakes her head at all of this and can't imagine how her way of life has influenced mine or why we seek to replicate any part of it. She will have none of the romantics and is quick to keep it real, but without realising it she has laid the foundation stones for a generational reawakening – and for that I'm truly thankful.

The gratitude I owe her is more visceral than words allow. Instead, I'm blowing out the cobwebs, keeping romance at bay and finding ways to incorporate granny skills – now! Here's to asking questions and sharing stories with all of those grans out there who deserve not just to be respected but also to be revered.

Sometimes the answer to the challenges of the future lies in the solutions of the past.

So now you've got the lowdown on futuresteading. But what do you do with it, and where do you begin? Importantly, how do you make it relevant to you and the life you lead? This obviously differs for each of us, depending on where and how we live. Regardless of your path, the second half of this book will tickle your senses, stimulate your head, soothe your heart and lay idea cornerstones on which you can build your own ritual-rich, seasonal life where you're awake to your surroundings and deeply (yet joyfully) committed to observation, simplification and the celebration of less.

The anecdotes, rhythms and rituals highlighted in the upcoming pages are the stories and experiences of my own life, some from childhood but more from Black Barn Farm in recent years. Yes, we're on land in the southern temperate state of Victoria, where we homestead our days away, and I know this isn't everyone's reality. But by sharing my experience through storytelling, I hope to pass on knowledge in a way that is easy to understand.

While the anecdotes might appear to have little relevance to your life, please hold on to your hat and put judgement aside. I urge you to read them anyway and consider the kernels of universal truth that lurk there.

Your seasons may differ, your access to land may be thwarted, and your friends might be ritual averse, but I promise you that with the simplest of tweaks to your lens, you could apply something from nearly every story to your own life.

This is where the philosophy of futuresteading gets real.

It's where we get dirt under our fingernails, chicken poo on our boots, homegrown food in our belly and love in our heart thanks to all the people we'll gather around us. We'll make our way through six (yes six!) seasons in the following chapters:

Awakening	**Harvest**
Alive	**The turning**
High heat	**Deep chill**

I know that we're accustomed to a four-season year, but there are many cultures – Australian Indigenous cultures included – that identify more than four seasons, usually through a deep connection to the production or availability of food. The evolving year is a palette of goodness that can be defined by seasonal offerings on endless rotation. The six chapters ahead will encourage the gentle act of 'noticing and participating' in this cycle.

Within these seasonal chapters is a swathe of ideas for connecting to the moment and building a rhythm all of your own that is deeply wedded to your local offerings. Some suggestions are as simple as stargazing, while others require more planning and deeper knowledge. These chapters will come to life through five essential actions:

1. grow
2. ritual
3. feast
4. nourish
5. create

Chosen with intention, these descriptions of our actions serve to create a well-rounded life that relishes simplicity without the disappointment of scarcity. They allow frugality to shine with joy! So what does each action mean when looking through a futuresteading lens?

Grow

To grow is to nurture from the smallest of seeds. It all starts and ends in the dirt! Growing food, animals, humans and stuff. It all relies on the soil under our feet. If this is healthy, then we all thrive.

In the garden

Growing food is the single most hopeful, fulfilling, regrouping, empowering act that I undertake. It forces me to have patience – things grow as seasons pass and can't be hurried. It soothes a busy mind – the tasks are all-consuming, so my head, heart and soul are always in the moment. It teaches lessons through incredible failures and accidental successes.

There are no judgements and no rules. The time frames are dictated by forces much bigger than me, so I am humbled by perspective, relinquish my ability to influence and simply do what I can: press my hands into the soil, feel the seeds slide through my fingers, read the seasons, revel in my observations and share my wins.

It's a solo pursuit but a deeply connecting one, too. The rewards are plentiful, even if there is not always an abundance of food produced – the lessons learned are worth the shortfall.

Food growing is my foundation and has been my keel for as long as I can remember. I've been able to grow things wherever I am, and you can, too: in a pot, in a box, on a windowsill or in a hanging basket.

Planting a seed seems like a simple act, but it's actually a powerful one that rekindles a primal flame within each of us. It connects us to past knowledge and reminds us that we are a vital part of the natural world, not separate from it.

Grow diversity

Diversity is the giver of life. This can manifest in many ways: soil diversity, seed diversity, political belief diversity, thought diversity as well as social diversity.

Diversity is a complex, interwoven fabric that provides the strength we need in order to work together. It balances tension, ebbing and flowing to create a harmony that does not exist in a monocultural environment. Mother Nature knows this and has created a web rich in diverse layers that all help each other. However, we humans have sought to streamline and simplify our thinking away from diversity and towards a monocultural mentality.

As a kid, I was encouraged emphatically to 'bloody think' and to 'create your own bloody box … and make sure it's not square'. I want the world my kids inherit to be vibrant, rich in opportunities, tuned in to the natural world, and both respectful and encouraging of contrasting thoughts and ideas – because diversity is the giver of life!

Go on – give it a 'grow'!

Ritual

A ritual is a sacred, customary way of celebrating a culture while building the traditions of a community. Perhaps one of the most intuitive and continuously practised rituals of humankind is that of storytelling. As a powerful communication medium – whether written, drawn or oral – stories have played a important role in sharing knowledge, connecting us to each other and to place, and allowing us to be enriched, educated and enhanced since the beginning of time.

Telling a yarn might seem innocuous, but those with a talent for it have found their place in the history books and in positions of leadership. We are drawn to the whimsy, potential and camaraderie within stories, knowing that, having read, heard or seen the words, we will be richer for them. Let each of us become a raconteur in our own right, and let the stories we tell create change.

Connecting to ancient wisdom

There's a reason why we at Black Barn Farm often reference names and terms that seem like they belong to another time. We feel that myth, ritual and ancient wisdom offer a richness that eludes our frenetic lives in the current day. Our desire is not to return to the Dark Ages – far from it – but we believe that the whispers of truth sitting in the knowledge from our past are like a remembering, a stirring of a bone-deep knowing. It is this knowledge that we want to absorb, so we can connect to each other, to the natural world and to our place.

DECORATIVE OR STRUCTURAL?

In the past, what may have appeared merely decorative still had structural purpose within its cultural depth. Christmas and Easter are wonderful examples of this – they were once culturally important celebrations of new life and family togetherness. However, consumerism has largely drowned their purpose, as David Fleming alludes to in *Surviving the Future*. He quotes T. S. Eliot's lament in *Ash Wednesday* about how what were once 'wings to fly' eventually become 'merely vans to beat the air', rendering these events only decorative.

Feast

A feast is a celebratory meal where we eat and drink sumptuously. But shouldn't this be the definition of every meal? I'm not suggesting that gluttony be normalised – I'm asking whether our enjoyment of food should be so palpable that even the simplest of morsels is valued and cherished. After all, food is the lifeblood of existence.

The celebration of food begins with knowledge of nature's vagaries and an understanding of how vicarious food growing can be. We need to be reminded that overpackaged foods on overstuffed shelves in overlit shops is not the truth of where food comes from or how we were designed to exist – devoid of comprehension about how the food on our plate came to be.

Once we truly understand our reliance on food and the processes that create it, we can appreciate how a finely sliced homegrown apple topped with a little fresh goat curd and a just-cracked, new-season walnut is not merely a snack but a worthy feast.

I recently quipped that a shopping list is fraught with problems, as it assumes abundance and disregards reality. What a shopping list ought to say is something like 'Food for seven days for five people'. With this sort of list in hand, you can fulfil the brief with whatever food you can find.

RECIPE CONFESSION

I've included plenty of recipes in the six seasonal chapters. But I have a confession to make: I'm allergic to recipes. It's the whole exactness thing that makes me uneasy. You see, our life is entirely dictated by the season we're in; the abundance we've grown, foraged or swapped; and the stores on my pantry shelves. I adapt recipe ideas to suit what I have, make hay while the sun shines and make do when there's not much.

Over time, we've amassed a range of seasonal feasts that we create and eat. While they differ a little each time, they follow an annual pattern that offers stability and familiarity but doesn't lose sleep over the details. The jars we use come under much the same mindset: while we have a few sets of proper Fowlers jars that we've collected over the years from paddock-clearing sales, the majority of them are recycled from our co-op and come in all shapes and sizes.

I've done my level best to ignore my recipe allergy so that I can present a collated range of feasts, which you can use as a base to whip up creations that work for you, your garden, your time, your budget and your taste. Try new things, swap one thing for another, spice things up, remove the meat, add some kick – start with the base recipes within these pages, and see where creativity takes you. And if your finished product weighs a little less or serves a few more, that's okay.

'Living in reciprocity is what drives me – I want to give back so that the transaction becomes a cycle rather than a one-direction consumer relationship. That way I can nourish it, and it can nourish me.'

Taj Scicluna (The Perma Pixie), **permaculture educator**

 Nourish

 Create

When we nourish both ourselves and others by offering food or other acts of kindness, we replenish the reserves, and we gain the strength to sing our best song.

Sometimes, you need to stand alone and do your own thing for a while … not forever, but just long enough to be sure that what you stand for is true to who you are. Then, without a doubt, you will feel the need to find others to stand with, and together you will all grow in rewarding and worthwhile ways.

While feeling nourished looks different for each person, one of the simplest ways for humans to feel safe, nurtured and complete is to 'belong'. There's no more effective way to feel like you belong than by acknowledging and sharing your personal gifts with the community that surrounds you.

Take your time, change your mind, be led by that voice inside … but be sure to listen closely and respond in a way that's always kind.

This is the noble act of bringing something into existence. Imagine if you could create without rules, boundaries or judgement. Imagine that you had the gift of time to daydream and then to bring into being all manner of brilliance that might serve no specific purpose. Without the pressure for your creation to 'be' or 'do' something, you might produce the most wondrous thing ever known. Or perhaps it would simply be a cathartic and creative rest.

The art of creating is what makes us human. While mastery only comes naturally to some, the process of trying and exploring alternative ways to bring something to life where there was nothing before is as valuable as the outcome itself.

We once hosted a quiet lady at a weaving workshop, who seemed frustrated for most of the day. The next day, I received an effusive email from her. She said that her day had been one of the most rewarding, nourishing and liberating experiences that she could recall since childhood. Creating something from nothing had brought joy in abundance. She signed off with the words 'I can breathe again'.

PART TWO

THE HOW, SEASON BY SEASON

AWAKENING

It's like Mother Nature knows that the weight of the curtains – usually pulled closed to lock in the heat – are now too cumbersome, that our days of fireside cups of tea are starting to feel suffocating and that we are drawn outside by the sun's whispered promise of fresh air and warmth on our skin. Having spent months under the nurturing blanket of winter's quiet time of reflection and solitude, we seek reconnection to our people, we are inspired to see new life, and we impatiently quicken our step towards outside days. As we awaken from the winter slumber, we are rested and ready for the coming months of vibrant action.

And just in the nick of time, as the winter food stores are low, creating the annual spring hunger gap. The chickens respond to the call, delivering daily eggs, while asparagus crowns tentatively push through the frosty ground and reach for the sky. They are the perfect duo for creating hearty breakfasts and cheesy quiche dinners.

Dried herbal teas are replaced with fresh new leaves of mint, rosemary, verbena and chamomile, or perhaps a quick squeeze from the last lemons. Mulched garden beds that are looking bare will soon have a beard of new growth as perennials and bulbs push through. It's time to chop wood ahead of the summer drying days, and to open your seed collection to kickstart the vegie garden.

If you hang the sheets outside in the sun, they'll dry quickly in the breeze for the first time in months. Pack a picnic with mates not seen since autumn. Daffodil and tulip blooms nod in the breeze, while jasmine and roses dance together at twilight, blending their heady scents. Breathe deeply, and experience the sensorial overload of the season.

Fill the house with overstuffed vases of wattle blossoms, and fling open every door and window to flush the dust from the mantle.

This is the season to lose layers, go cloud watching, prepare for summer and WAKE UP!

This is the season of Ostara – the spring equinox – when renewed energy and sharpened minds are ready for the 'awakening' that marches us towards something exciting. Appreciate this time through a commitment to observation and, more importantly, by being outside, getting your hands busy and your feet dirty, and tickling your senses in all the right ways.

Ritual

CLOTHES SWAP

Pop the cork, spread the tablecloth and rummage in your wardrobe. It's time for a purposeful sojourn with mates and ultimately a new look for the warming months. When you do this is up to you, but I love popping out from the deepest of winter days to be greeted by a brisk outdoor brunch or afternoon tea with friends who fling no longer worn wardrobe items towards each other. We swap garments to our heart's content, until everyone has new outfits to see them through spring. You get a whole new look with not a cent spent; good clothes are redistributed, and you rekindle relationships with your crew.

WONDERFUL WWOOFERS

Inviting strangers into your home requires a leap of faith and a magnitude of trust. It's not for everyone, but regularly hosting folk on our farm has become an annual ritual each spring and autumn.

For us, it works best when they come for a minimum of three weeks and stay for up to three months. The first ten days are spent working each other out and finding our way around a new rhythm where we 'host' and 'teach' extensively. We bide our time with every new WWOOFer, knowing that – almost by magic – everyone will arise halfway through week two with an innate understanding of what needs to be done, and they just get on with it.

Our days are quite fluid, with a few consistent key routines. Breakfast is on the table by 7.30 am, and we brief everyone about the day over eggs or porridge. We host a planning meeting on Sundays over beers and fireside dinners. There are fixed jobs allocated every day: meal preparation, chicken feeding, hoop-house work, brooder-box checking, wood carting and mushroom foraging. Rules are few, but our expectations are clear from the beginning when we send an introductory letter to all inquiries. Everyone cooks, everyone cleans, the cook never washes up, there are no screens at the table, and you can never ask the same question too many times.

Mostly, WWOOFers work about six hours a day in return for food and board. 'Work' is a broad term and varies depending on the season and weather, but to be honest, when there are so many hands on deck, the days fly past amid shenanigans and interesting banter. Our converted packing shed becomes their home, so they have their own space where they can get online, take an afternoon nap, do yoga, brew a pot of tea or quietly read from our library, having selected just the titles to suit their learning journey.

For months at a time (we host WWOOFers from September to December, and again from February to May), we operate as a tight-knit crew that is working towards a common goal. Everyone takes on jobs of all descriptions: trench digging, apple picking, irrigating, fencing, washing dishes, cooking, vegie gardening, mulching, sheep wrangling, child wrangling … the list goes on and on. So when our WWOOFing season ends, our house and farm feel extremely quiet. But the real emptiness comes from no longer having rich conversations, a mashup of cultures, different types of food, deep belly laughs and our own little home-based community.

Having strangers around took some getting used to, but there's no doubt that WWOOFers fill our life with goodness. I'd urge you to consider how you can form a community in your own backyard – the rewards are immeasurable.

BIRDS, BUZZING AND BEASTS

Birdsong at dawn is a poet's muse. It's the momentary tickling of your senses at daybreak before the sun has even tipped her honey-like light through the sleepy bedroom window.

Each spring, we wait with anticipation to hear the sharp and spritely call from the little striated pardalote that signals the awakening of the year. Having been north during the cold months, he returns to our windowsill to dance his jittery, bouncing jig and sing his pure notes until at last, sometimes weeks later, he is no longer solo – his little lady has joined him.

We feel privileged to watch their antics for a week or two, knowing that their routine is finetuned. It will soon take them from view and tuck them into our verandah, where they share the sitting for 19 patient days. The greatest reward is the fleeting presentation of their new family on the windowsill for admiration before they are gone, out into the world, until next year.

Gorgeous goslings

As gloriously cute as the babies are, the mating season for geese is noisy and aggressive, and it takes unsuspecting prisoners by surprise if they get caught between a randy gent and his ladylove. An overt show of male dominance entertains us daily for weeks, until our mamas finally nestle atop their eggs for their 35-day slog. The success rate can be very low, especially with Toulouse geese; it's not uncommon for the mamas to sit on 40 eggs between them and hatch only six goslings.

Just before the eggs hatch, the gaggle abandons their daily farm ramblings and comes together near the nesting mamas, milling around like listless soldiers waiting for something to happen. They won't let us anywhere near them as hatching day nears, so we monitor our calendar meticulously and sneak peeks from strange places until finally we catch a glimpse of new life. Then it's important to separate the geese from the ganders and to keep the mamas locked in with their babies for a few days so the little balls of fluff don't get marched all over the farm.

Within a week of hatching, the gaggle settles and they come together again.

Right: Toulouse geese are large, majestic and placid – except during breeding season, when they get noisy and assertive.

Each adult takes turns standing guard and watching for overhead threats, which are very real – one year we lost more than half of our goslings to eagles!

Hive health

The striated pardalote brings our attention to the marching of another year, as does a haze of cloudy smoke through which appears the vision of a man in a suit that covers him from top to toe. It's time to check the health of the hives and to hang our hopes on starting a new colony or two by catching a passing spring swarm.

Deafened by the whirring hum coming from the great amorphous cloud wrapped around a tree trunk, the beekeeper does his best to capture this natural wonder in a home that he hopes will convince the bees to stay. With plenty of failures under our belt, these antics are more in the spirit of connecting a little more closely with these incredible creatures, with the added

bonus of some sweet honey to fill our cupboards and cups of tea. Come harvest season, we all suit up and get among the golden goodness.

Roosters and clucky hens

Suddenly, after weeks of lifting the lid, there it is in the straw: the first soft pink egg! The first is always the most joyful; it is usually small and alone, but with longer days, more sunshine and plenty of time scratching in the garden beds, the chickens soon fill the nesting boxes to overflowing with eggs in pale blue, white, chocolate brown and various shades of pink and orange. Our event and workshop visitors inevitably feast on egg dishes in spring, as it's what we have in abundance.

Once egg production has started, so has our breeding season. We wait until dark and then don head torches to venture into pens and reorder according to breed. We pluck chickens from perches, flipping them

Far left: This happy hive sits beneath deciduous trees, so it's warm in winter and cool in summer.

Left: There's nothing like holding fluffy gosling goodness in your hand.

Right: Geese (top) and chickens (bottom) will be busy with breeding this season.

upside down and holding them under our armpits, and then we scurry in and out of each pen and place the sleepy, wobbly hens back on a new perches. Soon we have all five pens looking uniform according to breed.

Now we really take stock of our birds. We don't like to leave roosters with any less than three hens each, but more often than not we've lost a few key players (including the rooster) to foxes during the winter months. These bastard predators are out and about all year but are especially active in early spring when feeding their newborn cubs, so they have more gumption and go. They scatter the hens into hiding, but often the rooster will puff out his chest and take them on. Sadly, we are yet to have a rooster who has won the fight.

When we lose a rooster, we lose our ability to create more of that breed, so numerous texts, emails and conversations at the post office turn to finding a suitable replacement that needs rehoming. It leads

to night-time dashes to neighbours near and far to collect randy roosters looking for a harem of their own.

It's ideal to let the hens naturally get clucky, stuff their nest full of eggs and then sit. Eggs have a much higher hatch rate under a hen than in an incubator, and it removes the need to have a brooder box with a heat lamp in our shed for six weeks. This doesn't always play out, however, so inevitably we dust off the incubator, fill it with 48 eggs and wait for 21 days.

While this involves more intervention from us, it has the bonus of giving the kids (big and small) the chance to get cosy with the fluffy, wiggly, unpredictable chicks. Every season the kids decide on their favourite, name it and develop a bond through lots of handling and adventures in jacket pockets and under jumpers. Then it comes time for all the chicks to move into their new pens, ready to begin life as chickens rather than toys.

'Living in a culture that relies on mechanisation has trapped us into thinking we are machines, too, but actually our bodies and minds much prefer life at an ecological pace.'

Meg Ulman, blogger at *Artist as Family*

  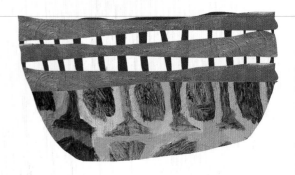

POTLUCK WITH YOUR PEOPLE

At this time of year, it's especially cup-filling to reconnect over a meal. It's a gentle way to break the drought after months of hibernation. It tickles you pink to the tips of your toes as you bask in reconnecting with those who make your community. These are the trusted, real, human, get-in-boots-and-all friends who much prefer vulnerability and honesty to three courses and fine linen.

What could possibly beat a gathering of your people, each with a pot of food (usually whatever was in their fridge), half a loaf of bread, the last of their homemade chutney or last night's half-drunk bottle of wine? This must surely be the simplest way to dine without expectations, where everyone mucks in to make it a quick and easy night of laughter and conviviality rather than one of slaving in the kitchen and cleaning the house.

Potlucks are first and foremost about people and togetherness, then comes the meal, which is inevitably incredible, as the array on offer is astounding. Lastly, it's about the setting. While being warm and dry matters, it can honestly be little more than a shed that has had the floor swept just five minutes before everyone arrives. We usually host our potluck dinners in work boots and jackets.

The beauty of the potluck meal is that it can be arranged last minute if the opportunity – and, in some cases, the need – arises. We have one set of farming friends who are excellent at sending a late-afternoon text suggesting that a potluck is 'needed' to get us, them or both off the farm. It's a gift, as it comes from a place of caring that only they understand, and even if we are frantically trying to finish a paddock project, they fill the gaps, muck in for the last half-hour of work and help us make a meal using their fridge leftovers and ours.

Create

WEAVE SOME MAGIC

Weaving has been a cherished skill for as long as we've had a desire to be dry, to cart food, to carry babies and to clothe ourselves. More often than not, women honed this skill and passed it from one generation to the next. The need to learn came from necessity, but the process of creating brought women together and connected them through sharing, talking and just being.

We seemingly have no pressing need for this skill anymore, as we have ready-made plastics, clothes, prams and rugs. But not only do these things generate a pile of single-use synthetics beyond our imagination, they also strip us of the chance to create with natural materials, to come together, to share and to build important rituals and traditions.

In today's busy world, we sometimes gift ourselves the chance to learn weaving as a form of mindfulness. But imagine if we could see it as the much-cherished skill it once was. We would consider the time it took to make sturdy, useful things of beauty a necessary part of life, because it reunited us with each other, ourselves and the natural world that offers us the materials in abundance throughout the seasons.

At Black Barn Farm, we host a full weekend each year just as the awakening begins at the end of winter, while the natural materials are still malleable. We gather and share while we wrangle applewood, hazelwood, grapevine, birch, poplar, willow and flax (mostly foraged from our pruning piles) into birds' nests, spheres, domes, doorway arches, baskets and abstract shapes. We share many cups of tea and eat tasty food that has just been picked. It's incredible what the collaborative, creative collective can bring to life.

As we learn new skills, find mindfulness and create beautiful woven loveliness, we more often than not find a gentle (and usually silent) rhythm with those around us and with the pieces that we are creating. Incredibly, after just a few hours in one another's company, we form a bond that feels fuller than it should, and we marvel at the sense of connection we have to one another.

Weaving is an ephemeral art that we bring to fruition in an unhurried, nourishing pace created by women being women. We are supportive, curious, open-minded and open-hearted, working together without the stress of competition, judgement or expectation.

Grow

PLANNING THE EDIBLE GARDEN

Winter gives us enough time to consider the complexities of crop rotation, to assess what worked well or not during the previous growing season and to think about trialling new crops this season. But now it's time to actually mark out how you want to plant up your garden beds.

Planning is important to minimise disease risk, to be sure that you grow the right quantity and succession of plants to get you through the season, and to rotate crops (see page 103). Here are a few considerations when planning and propagating:

+ Propagate 10 per cent more plants than you think you'll need to account for seed failure.
+ For a higher success rate, use seeds that are fresh and acclimatised to your region.
+ Rotate everything in the same direction (for example, clockwise) each year, so you rotate consistently.
+ Aim for a minimum two-year rest between a repeat planting in the same bed.
+ Aim for a green-manure crop in each bed at least every four years to replenish soil nutrients.
+ Aim to rest each bed for at least one season (winter or summer) every two years.
+ Only plant 50 per cent of your seedlings up front, with the following 50 per cent planted successively over the following 8–12 weeks.
+ Be realistic about how much you will need of different vegetables. After 15 years of growing, we now only plant two zucchinis (courgettes) and two eggplants (aubergines), and we only use broad beans as a manure crop – the kids dictate this mostly, which makes me sad but it's the reality.
+ Consider your winter garden needs when planting your summer garden layout (you may need access to some beds earlier than others to get your winter crops going).
+ Consider the time each vegetable needs in the ground (garlic and brussels sprouts require six months, yet radishes only need two months) – this can impact rotation.
+ Plant short-cycle crops later in the season, when there's no chance of frost.
+ Plant long-cycle crops further from the house, as they require less attention.
+ Plant pick-and-come-again crops closer to the back door, where you can visit them regularly.

Short on space?

Growing food between the buildings and in the concrete cracks of cities is more important than ever before, but it can be challenging. Space might be tight, but don't be fooled into thinking that you don't have enough room – look

Right: We sow the
seedling trays early
to ensure a long
growing season,
and leave them
in the protected
hoop house.

up, out, over, under, inside and outside.
Here are a few suggestions:

- Place pots on sunny windowsills.
- Choose dwarf varieties.
- Consider growing plants whose every
  part is edible (such as carrots and celery).
- Build frames on walls for espaliered
  plants or climbing vines.
- Only grow what you will actually eat.

PATCH AWAKENING

Now is the time to get your propagation mix
made up and your seedling trays raring to go,
so you can lift your mulch as soon as the days
are warm enough and get your seedlings
into the ground. We use the hoop house
for all of our propagation, as it's significantly
warmer than the open air. If you don't have a
hoop house, then an old window straddling
hay bales, some clear plastic stretched over

some poly pipe or even a sunny spot on a
windowsill will do the trick just as well.

Propagation mix

To get your seedlings going, you need more
than just any old dirt. However, it can't be
too nutrient-dense, as the seeds are delicate,
and it can't get waterlogged or the seeds will
rot – it needs to hold enough nutrients and
moisture to keep the seeds growing. Mix as
much as you need using this 'per part' recipe:

- two parts fine-sieved compost (see pages
  294–5), to feed the seedlings as they grow
- two parts pre-soaked coconut coir, for
  moisture retention
- one part fine sand, for drainage
- one part good-quality topsoil, to give it
  some body.

Mix well to ensure an even distribution of all
of the ingredients.

WHIP AND TONGUE GRAFTING TECHNIQUE

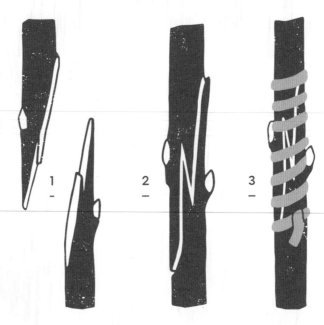

1
—

2
—

3
—

GET YOUR GRAFT ON!

For us, grafting is on our early-awakening to-do list. What we use may look like simple 'sticks' to some people, but they are precious 'scion sticks' to those of us who understand the magic of creating new fruit trees that are true to their variety.

It's thought that the Chinese discovered the art of grafting in the second millennium BC. Put simply, it's the technique of inserting a piece of wood from one tree into the stem of another. We do this to give the new tree dwarfing traits and disease resistance, and also to guarantee that it produces the fruit variety that we promise on the tag. While this particular technique is a relatively simple one, there are a few different ways to achieve this same outcome – we stick with the bench-grafted 'whip and tongue' approach for the 1500-odd trees we graft each year for our own orchard and for the tree nursery.

While we love and grow cherries, quince, pears and berries, mostly what we grow are apples. In early winter we meticulously clip, label and band each of our heritage varieties before burying them in wet sawdust. We leave them to sleep while they're in their deepest dormancy. At the first sign of new warmth in late winter, we pull out the tightly bundled bags of scion wood from the fridge, and we get our graft on!

It's a ritual that involves daily starts before dawn in the shed. We layer up, light the fire, boil the kettle and put on our head torches. Grafting can be a slow process, but you soon get into your rhythm, and by the time the teapot is empty, you have a bucketful of newly grafted, neatly labelled trees that are ready to be planted out.

Other orchardists often remark that we could just whip out the grafted trees in a few days if we 'just got stuck in', but for us, it's part of a yearly cycle that moves more slowly. It means that, alongside the seasonal change, we also have the chance to slowly awaken ourselves with daily sunrises, early-morning activity and a full day still ahead to get the rest of life tucked away.

FIVE-YEAR ROTATION PLAN

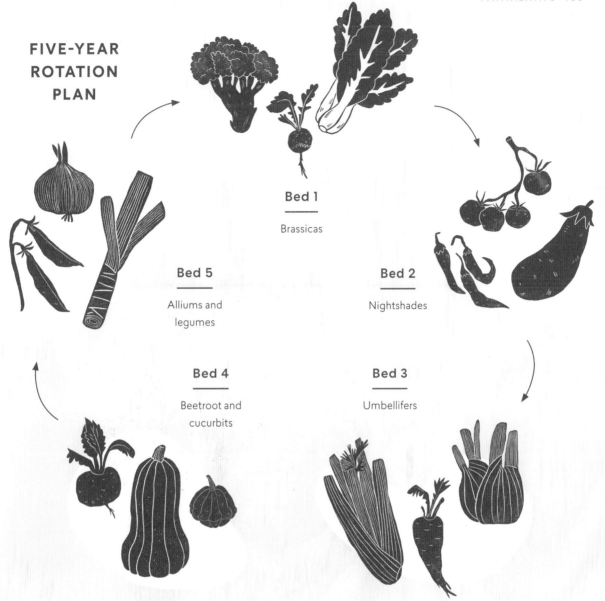

Bed 1

Brassicas

Bed 5

Alliums and legumes

Bed 2

Nightshades

Bed 4

Beetroot and cucurbits

Bed 3

Umbellifers

CROP ROTATION

While it might seem fiddly, crop rotation shouldn't be underestimated. It helps you manage soil nutrients, minimise disease and support the structure of soil, which can then be planted into each year with great food-growing results. This is relevant for everyone, from farmers with enormous paddocks to someone with a single garden bed and even those juggling garden pots on a small balcony.

It's not overly difficult, but you do need a little basic knowledge about the different families of vegetables (see the chart on page 105). Vegies are divided into their basic varieties, and some of these categories can then be rotated with each other. If space is tight, keep in mind that each vegie type doesn't need an entire garden bed to itself, but it does need to move each year. Using a five-year rotation plan is best if you have the room.

CROP ROTATION CHART

Alliums can be rotated with legumes, while cucurbits can be rotated with amaranths. Brassicas, nightshades and umbellifers should each be rotated on their own. The other vegies can be rotated with members of any other category.

ALLIUMS

chives

garlic

leek

onion

shallot

walking onion

LEGUMES

beans (all)

peas (all)

BRASSICAS

broccoli

brussels sprout

cauliflower

kale

kohlrabi

mizuna

pak choi (bok choy)

radish

rocket (arugula)

swede

turnip

NIGHTSHADES

capsicum (pepper)

chilli

eggplant (aubergine)

potato

tomato

UMBELLIFERS

carrot

celeriac

celery

coriander (cilantro)

dill

fennel

parsnip

CUCURBITS

button squash

cucumber

pumpkin (squash)

zucchini (courgette)

AMARANTHS

amaranth grain

beetroot

perpetual spinach

silverbeet (Swiss chard)

OTHER VEGIES

corn

endive

lettuce

witlof (chicory)

PLANT A POLLINATION GARDEN

If you ever needed a reason to plant pretty flowers, this is it! With a simple sprinkling of seeds into the soil or the planting of some hardy annual seedlings, you can feed pollinating insects and in turn increase the pollination success of all your food-producing plants. We discovered the power of this simple act in our paddock patch when, after a few years of growing cucumbers, melons and pumpkins (squash) with very limited success, we realised that we had a pollination issue.

With insect populations at enormous risk due to the overuse of pesticides, rising temperatures and increasing agricultural monocultures, it's important to plant flowers that re-create habitat for our unspoken heroes, the pollinating insects. A pollinator garden can be as big or as small as you like, depending on your available space. In our case, we interplant into every area of our property that produces food: the hoop house, the kitchen garden, the paddock patch and between the rows in the orchard. Since doing this, our production rate has increased tenfold, and the number of insects and small birds (that feed on these insects) has also risen noticeably.

Not only do pollination plants play a key role in producing good food, but some of them *are* food and some are *also* medicinal, so they do double duty. Most importantly, these flowers provide food for insects during summer, when the days are hot – having a ready source of pollen minimises their travel in such harsh conditions. Another potential double purpose for a pollination garden is to plant things that make excellent forage crops for your chickens.

Handy growing tips

Let our experience be your guide:

- Be on high alert for fruit fly this season, and use all of your preventative measures. Once pollination is complete, net your trees and susceptible vegetables (such as tomatoes).
- Use abundant 'weeds' such as stinging nettle to make nitrogen-rich compost teas, and apply them to fast-growing plants such as vegetables and other garden annuals.
- Use large jars (such as Fowlers jars) as mini glasshouses to give your tiny seedlings a little extra warmth when they first get planted. Be careful not to leave the jars in place during hot days, though, or the plants will cook.

With insect populations at enormous risk, it's important to plant flowers that re-create habitat for our unspoken heroes, the pollinating insects.

POLLINATION CHART

These are some of our favourite pollination plants at Black Barn Farm.

PLANT	PLANTED AS A SEED OR SEEDLING?	APPROXIMATE POLLINATION PERIOD	MEDICINAL PLANT?
alyssum (*Lobularia maritima*)	seed	early spring to late autumn	yes – for a wide range of uses, but mainly for bleeding gums, gonorrhoea and fluid retention
amaranth (*Amaranthus* species)	seed	autumn	yes – for ulcers, diarrhoea and high cholesterol
bee balm (*Monarda* species)	seedling	late spring to late autumn	yes – as a diuretic
borage (*Borago officinalis*)	seedling	mid-spring to early autumn	yes – for fever, cough, adrenal fatigue and depression
chamomile (*Matricaria recutita* and *Chamaemelum nobile*)	seed	late spring to mid-autumn	yes – for calming the nervous system and soothing skin irritation
chives (*Allium schoenoprasum*)	seed	late spring	yes – for bone health, blood clotting and its high vitamin K content
clover (*Trifolium* species)	seed	mid-spring to early autumn	yes – for fever and cough
comfrey (*Symphytum* species)	neither (it is planted as root stock)	late spring to mid-summer	yes – short-term use for sprains, swelling and bruising, but not open wounds; long-term use can cause liver damage
cosmos (*Cosmos* species)	seed	early summer to late autumn	yes – for its high vitamin C content
fennel (*Foeniculum vulgare*)	seed	summer	yes – for digestion, bloating and heartburn

CHICKEN FODDER/ FORAGE PLANT?	WEED POTENTIAL?	PERENNIAL OR ANNUAL?
no	yes – spreads easily from seed but is easy to manage	annual, but can be a perennial as it self-seeds
yes – they produce seeds en masse, and chickens love them	yes – prolific seed producer	annual
no	no	perennial
yes – chickens will pick it to the ground in minutes, so guard it well if not intended as chicken food	yes – but it can all be used as mulch or chicken feed	perennial
no	yes	annual (*Matricaria recutita*); perennial (*Chamaemelum nobile*)
no	no	perennial
yes – chickens like the new plant growth and the flowers	yes – if it's in garden beds, but it's okay in the paddock	annual
yes – it is excellent for chickens	choose sterile Russian comfrey to control the spread; it divides only by its roots, not its seeds	perennial (totally dormant in winter)
not while in flower, but yes once it has gone to seed	no	annual
yes	yes	perennial (requires a full cut-back in winter)

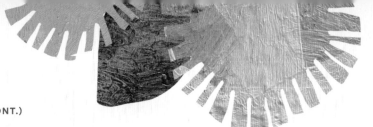

POLLINATION CHART (CONT.)

PLANT	PLANTED AS A SEED OR SEEDLING?	APPROXIMATE POLLINATION PERIOD	MEDICINAL PLANT?
feverfew (*Tanacetum parthenium*)	seedling	mid-winter to mid-spring	yes – for fever, headaches and migraines
lavender (*Lavandula* species)	seedling	mid- to late spring	yes – for anxiety, stress and insomnia
lovage (*Levisticum officinale*)	seedling	mid- to late spring	yes – for UTI and kidney-stone prevention
pea (*Pisum sativum*)	seed	spring	yes – as a fungicide on the skin
pot marigold (*Calendula officinalis*)	seed	mid-spring to early winter	yes – for stomach upsets, skin irritation, inflammation and wound healing
rosemary (*Rosmarinus officinalis*)	seedling	mid-spring to early winter	yes – for muscle pain and boosting memory and circulation
sage (*Salvia officinalis*)	seedling	mid-spring to early summer	yes – for digestive problems such as diarrhoea and bloating
sunflower (*Helianthus* species)	seed	mid-summer to early autumn	yes – as a diuretic and fever treatment
vetch (*Vicia* species)	seed	summer	no
wild carrot (*Daucus carota*)	seed	mid-summer to mid-autumn	yes – for hangovers and gastrointestinal support, but mainly to assist the body's waste elimination system
wormwood (*Artemisia absinthium*)	seedling	late spring to mid-summer	yes – for parasite control, especially worms
zinnia (*Zinnia* species)	seed	mid-summer to late autumn	yes – for a wide range of uses, but also as a natural dye

CHICKEN FODDER/ FORAGE PLANT?	WEED POTENTIAL?	PERENNIAL OR ANNUAL?
no	no	perennial
no	no	perennial
no	no	perennial
yes – chickens appreciate the green leaves as well as the seeds	no	annual
no	no	annual
no	no	perennial
no	no	perennial
yes – it can be dried and fed to chickens during winter	no	annual
yes – chickens like the soft new plant growth	yes – if it's in garden beds, but it's okay in the paddock	annual
no	yes – some areas have masses of plants; some cultivars don't seem to have as much inclination to spread	annual
yes – it's good for parasite control	no	perennial (requires a full cut-back in winter)
no	yes – they're prolific seeders that will withstand extreme conditions and still produce	annual

Left: Upside down jars provide added warmth and insect protection for new seedlings.

Over the page: Hoop house (left); woven frames will hold frost netting over potatoes in early spring (right).

MULCHING MISSION

If you want any chance of staying on top of the weeds, then you need to start your mulching mission right now! Your choice of mulch will depend on what you are growing, what you have access to, how much you want to spend and how long you want the mulch to last.

At Black Barn Farm, our mulching process takes up the centre weeks of spring every year. It's all done by hand – including our commercial-scale orchard and our three food-growing gardens. It's a bloody big job, and the days are long and physical, but the return is a productive plot that is nutrient-dense, biologically alive, free of synthetic chemicals and free of weed competition around our fruit trees, nursery trees, herbs and vegetables. We use well-composted woodchips for just about everything except our smaller kitchen garden and hoop house, where we use pea straw or lucerne straw.

Be careful with your mulch if you don't generate it yourself. We've been caught before with bulk-bought pea straw that was supposedly spray-free but was, in fact, laden with a chemical desiccant used on a neighbouring wheat crop. This residual spray impacted our legume plantings in the kitchen garden for the following two years. We have also been assured that straw mulch was free of seeds, only to be faced with a wild, overgrown crop of germinated wheat anywhere we had mulched.

A few more words on mulch

Are you constantly at war with slaters (also known as woodlice)? Keep straw mulch away from new seedlings, and lay simple traps of beer in saucers. It works every time.

Take care! Black mould – which can hide in mulch – can have seriously detrimental health consequences, such as neuroinflammation, which can lead to fatigue, migraines, nausea,

Mulching is a big job, but the return is a productive plot that is nutrient-dense, biologically alive, free of synthetic chemicals and free of weed competition.

dizziness, skin tingling and gut-health issues. When handling mulch (straw or woodchips), be sure to wear a mask and gloves, and wash your clothes afterwards to minimise the spread of spores.

Don't be tempted to use black plastic or old carpet under mulch in food-growing areas, as they may contain synthetic chemicals that can leach into produce.

FROST PROTECTION

We know the dreaded late frost all too well. As the saying goes around these orcharding hills, the latest frost could be New Year's Eve and the earliest could be New Year's Day – so we are always alert to a quickly plunging temperature gauge.

We've developed a few handy tricks to combat sudden frosts, though, as we can't let them spook us away from growing at all. Yes, you can buy all sorts of beautiful, Insta-worthy frost guards, but they are quite expensive and don't always work. Try these ideas instead:

◆ jars – you can use any jars really, but Fowlers jars with size four (4-inch) lids make perfect little greenhouses and frost protectors over each seedling.

◆ woven arches – we use left-over materials from our weaving workshop to make archways that cover an entire bed; we then drape a sheet or frost wrap over the archway.

◆ straw bales – bank them up around fragile seedlings with an old glass window over the top to work like a hoop house during the day; cover the window with a towel at night.

◆ pruning late – often we leave woody perennials looking scruffy until well into spring to protect fragile new growth from frost; it's an easy solution to just wait a little longer to prune.

◆ woven cloches – these are whimsical and gorgeous, cathartic to make and effective for smaller individual plants that are yet to harden off; they're as cute as buttons when dotted all through the garden in spring.

◆ recycled glass bottles – we have loads of these because we sell apple juice, but if you don't have an abundance, simply buy your liquids in glass and keep the bottles when empty. A glass-cutter is inexpensive online and can turn all of your bottles into mini cloches with breather pipes by making short work of cutting off the bottoms of the bottles.

Feast

SPRING HUNGER GAP

This is the season of the spring hunger gap, sometimes called the 'six weeks of want', so named because jarred preserves and root-vegetable stores are now low, the garden offers slim pickings of fresh food, and new seedlings are only just being planted. For those trying to minimise their reliance on the industrial food system by committing to CSA (community-supported agriculture) schemes, local food co-ops or growing and swapping their own, you'll already know that these are the hardest months. Most people, however, are blissfully unaware that spring is the leanest time, because supermarkets and magazines begin their marketing of fresh spring food and maintain full shelves. Look a little closer at the labels, though, and you'll see that the fresh food on offer has clocked some serious food miles in order to feed you.

While eating locally is absolutely an ethical decision, it's also about honouring our evolutionary need to provide our bodies with certain foods at certain times of the year while offering ourselves the widest range of foods available within a geographic area, foods on which our gut biome has evolved to thrive. Consequently, while filling the spring hunger gap with imported wonders from the supermarket might be an option, so is getting closer to understanding what is actually available in your area at this time of year – both in the patch and in the broader natural environment. This is where foraging enters the picture.

Foraged food, anyone?

If you've never foraged, then the idea may seem strange – but you'd be amazed by how much nutritional food abounds. If you're serious about living locally, in a way that connects you to place and is in harmony with the natural world, then it's time to consider rustling up a foraged salad or looking at mallow weed in a whole new light.

There are many wonderful reference books describing what and how to forage, and I'm not going to improve on their efforts. I will, however, list a few of spring's easiest-to-find foraged foods to kick you off on your journey into the world of nature's abundance. To find these, prepare to travel outside the confines of your backyard patch and into the wild: perhaps the local park, nearby back lanes, local school grounds, community gardens or the native bush. Wherever you go, foraging is as much about exploring, having an adventure and being outside as it is about the feast that you put in your basket.

All foragers need some basic equipment to maintain the habit, such as gumboots, sharp secateurs and containers with lids. Gloves and pocketknives are handy but not compulsory. It helps to have prior knowledge about what to forage, but starting simple will build your confidence. Just have an adventurous spirit and be open-minded about what your 'food' should look like. And don't forget to ask for permission to take the food if it's on private land (such as over a fence or on a nature strip).

Top left: 'Tis the season for a field-mushroom forage with the family.

Bottom left: A simple spring pick fills the hunger gap with asparagus, garlic scapes (shoots) and broad beans – great for omelettes and stir-fries.

A TASTY CHECKLIST

Start your spring forage with this wealth of wild goodies.

Blackberry (*Rubus* species)
From late spring, it is abundant all over and in many common places, so go for your life. Only pick those berries that have not been sprayed with chemicals.

Dandelion (*Taraxacum officinale*)
This is the quintessential spring foraging plant, as you can use the flowers, leaves and roots. It is easy to find in any nature strip, park, garden and schoolyard, and easy to identify. You don't have to worry about look-alikes, as all are edible and medicinal as well. Make tea with the roots or the flowers, and pesto with the leaves.

Violet (*Viola sororia* or *V. odorata*)
My dad recalls collecting a bunch of these for his mum at just five years old; there's something utterly delicate and colour-drenched about them that makes them irresistible. The pretty flowers and leaves are both edible and medicinal. They come up as full carpets in early spring, but love cooler temperatures and may grow through winter in frost-free locations. Use the flowers in salads, violet-infused vinegar or popsicles. Use the leaves in salads just like lettuce. Both the leaves and flowers 'cool' the body internally and are used as a remedy for respiratory illness and as a lymphatic stimulant.

Clover (*Trifolium pratense* or *T. repens*)
The two species are beneficial to us in many ways. The blossoms are sweet and edible. I recall spending hours as a kid, lolling in the paddock and eating these. They are perfect for salads, adding to baked goods or infusing in honey or vanilla essence. Red clover (*T. pratense*) is especially high in

vitamins and minerals, and makes a wonderful tea that is delicious either hot or cold.

Mint (*Mentha* species)
There's an old wives' tale that alludes to mint as the ultimate fertility plant. Perhaps that's why it's now abundant in every drain, ditch and other soggy area you can find. There are many varieties of mint: peppermint, spearmint, banana mint, orange mint, apple mint, Asian mint, basil mint and chocolate mint are just a few of the commonly found wild mints. All are medicinally 'cooling' and used to calm the nerves, minimise nausea and induce sleep. They all have variations on the same spicy, fresh flavour that is beautiful in salads and tea infusions.

Nettle (*Urtica dioica*)
It's not great to touch, but a gift when cooked in soups, made into a green sauce, baked as chips or simply steamed with butter and salt. My grandad used to steep it in hot water and drink it as tea. I think this was for gout, but it's also used for the treatment of arthritis, eczema and anaemia, and to assist with urinary problems during the early stages of prostate cancer. It has a ferocious sting that makes you curse (childhood memories, sheesh), and this condemns the plant to a life of being slashed and burned, but it actually plays a key role in feeding foragers and providing food for bees. Additionally, ladybirds feast on the aphids that nettles attract, and other insects such as caterpillars use nettles as food. Don't forget a pair of gloves when harvesting these extremely prickly customers!

Chickweed (*Stellaria media*)
While we don't have this in our patch, it's a favourite of foraging friends in warmer climes. A low, ground-covering winter annual, it usually proliferates towards the end of spring. The fine leaves can be eaten

in salads, and taste similar to grassy corn silks. Like most foraged greens, it has medicinal qualities ranging from relieving scurvy and psoriasis to easing constipation and bowel irritations.

Bracken fern (*Pteridium esculentum*)

This exists in abundance right at our back door, so in theory we could consume loads every spring. That's not ideal, however, as there are mixed reports about how safe it is. For every article I read telling me that it's carcinogenic, I find another telling me that it's only dangerous when it's raw or when consumed in high quantities. Regardless, eat this one in small doses and with caution. The act of fiddlehead foraging is a lovely one, and the taste is nutty, earthy and satisfying. We use the fiddleheads when they are young, tender and just opening, popping them into stir-fries, cooking them in butter or lightly pickling them.

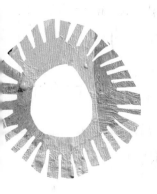

Mallow (*Malva neglecta*)

This weed is found in abundance almost everywhere. With its five- or seven-lobe geranium-like leaves and petite soft pink flowers, it's easy to spot. The magic lies in the roots, which have a large quantity of mucilage that is high in protein and carbohydrates. Traditionally, the roots were used to treat urinary tract infections, heal digestive irritations and calm inflammation. They can also be used as a poultice to soothe bites, wounds and swollen muscles. You can definitely eat mallow, although the flavour is pretty bland, and it is nutritious enough to include in a weed salad. It contains very high levels of vitamins A, B and C, calcium, potassium and magnesium.

Wild asparagus (*Asparagus officinalis*)

We have a hearty wild asparagus planting in our vegie patch, which is just as well,

because in Victoria it's considered a weed and is exterminated. But this isn't the case in many other parts of the country, and in cooler climates you can readily find wild asparagus. In early spring, you will find it pushing out of the ground just like the ones you grow at home. It can be eaten (the closer you are to the tip, the sweeter it will be) as long as it hasn't turned into a fern frond, when it becomes too woody to eat (pretty in a vase, though). You will only find wild asparagus in open, sun-filled places, not in woodlands or scrub. Once you've found a patch, commit it to memory, as it will double in size each season. Eat it just like store-bought asparagus.

Morel (*Morchella* species)

So prized are these small, earthy, meaty fungi that their locations are well guarded. They are not widely available but certainly inclined to reappear in particular locations if left undisturbed. Unlike lots of fungi, they appear in spring rather than autumn. We were lucky enough to buy land that produces them but, even so, our foraging success is sporadic year after year. They are best cooked or dried whole, and butter is their best friend.

Purslane (*Portulaca oleracea*)

We spent years cursing this plant, but little did we know that it's tasty, healthful and abundant, and people actually grow it in their vegie gardens. It's a succulent that is not particular about its soil, although it prefers dry conditions. Renowned for its incredibly high levels of omega-3 fatty acids, it's also super high in minerals and vitamins as well as antioxidants. It can be eaten cooked – steamed like broccoli, or stir-fried with Chinese greens – or raw in salads. It reportedly plays a medicinal role, supporting those with type 2 diabetes and even uterine bleeding.

SPRING BRUNCH

The days are just a little warmer, and the sun has a kick. Mornings are still cold, though, so breakfast outside is a while off … brunch, however, is ON!

Keep in mind that the spring hunger gap still haunts us, so the feasting options for fresh fare in spring are limited to kale, asparagus, eggs, winter greens and new herb shoots. How good does that sound? Without even trying, the ingredients come together to create the perfect brunch tart!

Now … Fill a bowl with winter greens, kale and fresh herbs, and top with creamy dressing (see page 192). Open a jar of pear chutney (see page 230), which is probably getting close to being the last one for the year. Make a pot of fresh herbal tea (see page 186), and add a dash of honey. Spread the paper open, and voila – you've got yourself a spring brunch!

This must be the simplest 'feast' that you can ever prepare, but there's something enlivening about being outside again, with the sun on your back, eating a freshly picked and prepared meal straight from the garden. It fills you with hope, delight and anticipation of things to come.

Asparagus and eggs

Given that, at this time of year, the asparagus patch is on perpetual growth mode and the egg basket is never empty, you'll need some easy ideas to use them up. As well as the recipes on page 124, try these:

+ roasted asparagus with grilled almonds and bacon
+ cream of asparagus soup
+ fresh asparagus with a squeeze of lemon
+ preserved asparagus
+ poached eggs with hollandaise sauce
+ soft-boiled eggs with toast soldiers
+ scrambled eggs with wilted greens
+ hard-boiled eggs for picnics.

EGG TIPS

If you keep chickens or geese and stumble on the inevitable hidden nest of eggs in the garden, pop them all in a sink of water. If they float, then discard them because they're bad; if they sink, then feast away on the delicious gifts.

You can use the eggs of numerous birds in your cooking, and they will each add a unique flavour. Here is a size-comparison scale:

+ 1 goose egg = 2–3 chicken eggs
+ 1 duck egg = 2 chicken eggs
+ 2 bantam eggs = 1 chicken egg
+ 4 quail eggs = 1 chicken egg.

A MEAT-EATER'S REALITY

The reality of a 'boots-and-all' futuresteading life is that you produce the majority of the food you consume. For us, that also means meat. While we don't eat a lot of meat, we're not vegetarian – so instead we commit to producing as much as we can in a way that aligns with our values of ethical production. We don't keep cattle or pigs, but often trade for beef and pork; when the water is warm, we stock our dam with silver perch that the kids love to catch; and we eat the non-essential roosters (sorry, boys!), so we have a good variety. But the mainstay of our meat stores is lamb. We pasture-raise six lambs each year for our own freezer. They come to Black Barn Farm during the awakening and live their life in a paddock full of food and shade until their one bad day at the end of autumn.

Nutty rusks from South Africa

Bridge the spring hunger gap by filling the cupboards with something that lasts for ages and is not reliant on the vegie patch. A gorgeous WWOOFer called Margot introduced us to this pantry staple that is found in just about every South African home. We simply pop the tray of rusks into the Rayburn stove (see page 296) for their slow overnight cook (most people don't own a Rayburn, so my advice is to make this en masse to take advantage of having the oven on overnight). This base recipe can be altered by using anything you like – stewed fruits, honey, less sugar … whatever takes your fancy. You can make the rusks gluten-free by replacing the wheat flour with your preferred combination of almond meal, chestnut flour, coconut flour or tapioca flour. All of these are 'thirstier', so you'll need more liquid – we add stewed apples.

Makes approx. 50 rusks

Oil, for spraying

2 teaspoons salt

2 teaspoons bicarbonate of soda (baking soda)

1 kg (2 lb 4 oz) white bread flour

½ cup (75 g) finely chopped dried fruits of your choice (for example, cranberries, apricots, apple)

½ cup (85 g) seedless raisins

½ cup (75 g) sesame seeds

1 cup (145 g) sunflower seeds

1 cup (150 g) coarsely chopped nuts of your choice

2 cups (400 g) coconut sugar, or 2 cups (180 g) desiccated coconut if you prefer it less sweet

2 cups (150 g) bran

500 g (1 lb 2 oz) unsalted butter, melted

2 large eggs

2 cups (500 ml) milk (goat milk is fine but cow milk is better and buttermilk is best – those on a dairy-free diet can just use nut milks, see page 297)

1. Preheat the oven to 180 degrees Celsius (350 degrees Fahrenheit).
2. Spray a large roasting pan with oil (the bigger the mix, the bigger the pan – or you'll have to make multiple batches).
3. Sift the salt, bicarbonate of soda and bread flour into a large bowl.
4. Add the dried fruits, raisins, seeds, nuts, coconut sugar and bran, and stir thoroughly.
5. In a separate bowl, stir together the butter, eggs and milk until the liquid is smooth. Add the wet ingredients to the dry ingredients.
6. Stir the mixture with a wooden spoon until it is well blended.
7. Press the mixture into the pan, and slice it into cubes or rectangles with a sharp knife.
8. Cover the pan with foil, and place it into the oven for 60 minutes or until you can stick a skewer into the mixture and it comes out clean. Remove the pan from the oven.
9. Reduce the oven heat to 60 degrees Celsius (140 degrees Fahrenheit).
10. Allow the rusks to cool before placing them onto trays and into the oven, where they will spend the entire night really drying out and going rock hard. Store the rusks in an airtight container for 12 months (if they last that long!).

Scrambled eggs with asparagus and salami

This will kickstart your spring days.

Serves 2

5 eggs, whisked

Dash of dairy milk or nut milk

Sprinkle of celery salt or nutritional yeast

½ brown onion, diced (or 4 walking onions, which we have growing in our perennial bed)

1 garlic clove, diced (2 garlic cloves if you like it strong)

6 thin salami slices

10 asparagus spears, discard woody ends and slice if desired (the average store bunch has 6–8 spears, which is enough for this recipe)

Handful of Alexanders (see page 251)

Thyme or parsley sprig

1. Pour the eggs, milk and celery salt or nutritional yeast into a frying pan over medium heat, and scramble the egg mixture. Be careful not to overcook the eggs, as you want them to remain light and fluffy.
2. In a second frying pan, cook the onion, garlic and salami over medium to high heat until they have browned.
3. Add the asparagus to the second frying pan. Cook for 2–3 minutes, tossing regularly.
4. Just before the asparagus has finished cooking, add a handful of fresh Alexanders (which thrives at this time of year) and a little thyme. Parsley is a good substitute.
5. Divide the scrambled eggs between two plates, and serve with the asparagus and salami.

Pickled picnic egg

Seriously, this is such an incredibly simple yet wondrous combination of pickled tang and creamy hard yolk. The eggs will change colour depending on what you add to your mixed spices (for example, turmeric will turn them yellow, while mustard seeds will turn them purple). This is just fine and can actually look quite gorgeous if you make a few different batches and serve them all mixed up in a bowl.

Makes 600 g (1 lb 5 oz)

10 eggs

1 cup (250 ml) apple cider vinegar (see page 221)

1 cup (250 ml) water

1 tablespoon mixed spices (my favourite blend is peppercorns, mustard seeds, dill seeds and fennel seeds, all roughly crushed using a mortar and pestle)

Crushed fresh garlic, to taste

1. In a saucepan of water over high heat, boil the eggs for 4 minutes. Peel the eggs, and set them aside.
2. In another saucepan over high heat, boil the apple cider vinegar and water for 8–10 minutes.
3. Add the mixed spices and garlic, and stir well.
4. Reduce the heat to low, and simmer the liquid mixture for 10 minutes with the lid on to avoid evaporation. Allow the liquid mixture to cool.
5. Place the eggs into a sterilised jar, and pour over the liquid so the eggs are fully submerged. Store the eggs in the fridge for up to six months (if they don't get eaten before that!).

Can you feel it? The abundant life, the verdant green, the bursting energy around us. Having gently woken over the past month or so, life vibrantly ups its pace. So strap yourself in before you whip your way through this jaunty season, grabbing it with both hands and squeezing it for all of the fabulous inspiration that it offers.

Seasons slip by quickly at this time of year, from gentle sun-kissed spring days to scorching summer heat. Provided that water is abundant, the green leaves don't seem to mind. In a blink, everything suddenly feels alive.

New life abounds and with it a sense of hope. The days are longer, the earth is warmer, and the buds on every tree that slept through winter are now competitively tumbling new leaves outward, offering shade in spades. New fruits are setting, and the spring hunger gap is now behind us in the vegie patch, where we see an inkling of the abundance soon to come.

The summer solstice marks the climax of the season, alongside festivities that push into your psyche. A momentum builds behind your 'making, baking and growing' gift efforts, which need to begin in earnest.

Hang on for the ride this season! Enjoy the pace, the outdoor thrumming and the forthcoming summer days.

THE ART OF NOTICING

Of course, the art of noticing is not just for this season, but it's a brilliant time of year to adopt or reinvigorate the practice. The rate of change is palpable, and it encourages us to observe keenly.

In a world where the virtual, physical and social spheres constantly dominate our attention, stepping outside the expected realm of consumptive message absorption is as simple as breathing deeply and noticing. It's an act so profound that it can change your paradigm entirely, yet it is so discouraged that few of us are aware that we've lost the inclination to do it. Instead, our days are filled with

advertising, curated messaging, timetables, spreadsheets, family calendars, appointments, commitments, consumption and general busyness. This leaves little time to simply sit back and notice ...

- the strength of the sun on your back
- the swelling of the blooms
- the colour in the leaves
- the smell of the wood smoke
- the chill in the air
- the taste of the just-picked tomato
- the frost on the car
- the lengthening of days
- the warble of a magpie.

To actively notice is to take ownership of your senses, to seek vitality over monotony, to be taken by the moment and to reap deep rewards from the simplest of things.

Not only is the art of noticing available to each of us, but it is also ever-changing and evolving – so the story never becomes dull. Noticing offers the opportunity to reinvigorate our intuitive capacity to observe and interact, in turn heightening our experience of the everyday, where the subtlest changes offer the most profound insights and rewards.

To notice is an act of rebellion – you undoubtedly feel more untouchable by mainstream messaging once your desires are focused on the tiny yet magical moments that are available to us all the time. There's an anti-authoritarian satisfaction that comes with this, for you've stepped outside the expected patterns of the modern Western world. You've diluted your desire for bigger, brighter, shinier interactions, and replaced them with actions that cannot be manipulated, taken or influenced.

Try a daily exercise right in your own backyard. Notice the same few things each day, observing how they change. Be curious about their path, ponder their destiny and delight in the evolution. It's a powerful process!

Ritual

FESTIVE SEASON

At Black Barn Farm, we try our hardest to keep the festive season simple and meaningful. It's not an easy task, but we fight to make sure it remains a season of joy, not stress.

What is Christmas really about? Family ... togetherness ... gratitude ... ritual ... pudding ... handmade things ... wonderment ... dishes ... generations ... feasts ... stories ... naps. (And for those in the southern hemisphere like us: summer ... cicadas ... cherries ... flies.) Shiny things don't fill our cup; they only distract from what's real.

Being a martyr isn't joyful, though, so invest in a good dose of balance. We are dedicated to a Christmas that is tinsel-free, plastic-minimised and feast-focused. Homemade presents are glorious, upcycling is a winner, using what you've got is more fun, and a dose of annual ritual encourages the momentum to build, making it magnificent not melancholy. When our favourite day of the year arrives, Boxing Day, we let it all go, eat leftovers for as long as they last, and allow the summer in front of us to unfold as it pleases.

Advent activities

An easily adopted festive ritual is our homemade clutch of fun advent activities. They're whimsical verging on ridiculous, and completely doable regardless of where you live. Use little boxes hanging from ribbons (which can be re-used every year), and add a note to each with an activity to tackle each day. The activities could include:

- going on a bike ride
- having a twilight picnic
- singing carols
- wearing dress-ups to dinner
- taking a night walk
- making green and red jelly (jello)
- baking a Christmas cake
- decorating the dog
- creating teachers' presents
- donating to either a food bank or op shop
- painting your nails green and red
- writing and performing a charming Christmas play
- collecting outside treasures to decorate presents
- eating an ice-cream after school
- having a swim at the lake.

The activities on our first four days are always the same, as this consistency is reassuring and builds anticipation.

On 1 December, we all (including the dogs) pile into the back of the ute, the chainsaw at our feet, and drive around the hills on the hunt for a 'wildling' to be this year's tree. You can't legally cut down plantation pines, so we look on the sides of the road, in nearby native bush and on farmland verges for the unwanted wild pine trees that would otherwise be poisoned. It's a long-winded task, as we rarely agree on which one is 'perfect', but eventually – usually in the dark – we trundle home with a tree, or sometimes a few smaller trees to tie together.

In recent years, we've implemented the simple rule of something to wear, something to read, something that grows and something they need. It keeps a lid on 'stuff', excess and expectation.

On 2 December, we decorate our tree. Each year, I give the kids an ornament. They are things that I've found throughout the year on my rambles and have retrofitted with ties for hanging. Each ornament is different and chosen specifically for each child. These ornaments have no theme but plenty of nostalgia, and we pile them on the tree until it looks like it might faint under the weight. It's a sentimental night, as we inevitably relive life through each ornament that was given 'at this house' or 'when I was this old'. Each child will take their box of ornaments when they begin life in their own house, and I'll be left with just the ones that my mum has gifted me over my 43 years.

On 3 December, my kids write to Santa Claus. There's no easier way to remove the guesswork from the Santa sack than by writing a letter. In recent years, we've implemented the simple rule of something to wear, something to read, something that grows and something they need. It keeps a lid on 'stuff', excess and expectation.

On 4 December, we make cards for the grandparents. We pull paper and old cards from the craft cupboard to create cards for the generation that prefers snail mail to email. To be honest, the kids often groan loudly about creating the cards from scratch, but we include this activity because it sets the intentional tone of Christmas being about others. Even in a house of conscious-living folk, the chaos and consumption of Christmas can grab us by the short and curlies.

MAKE-IT, BAKE-IT, GROW-IT PRESENTS

Okay, hands up who feels like a scrooge when they turn up with homemade presents? I hear you! This bugged me for a really long time. I'd turn up clutching creations that had taken months of consideration and careful planning, only to feel like my effort was the lesser on the offering table. But my stubborn commitment – and inspiration from the magnificent contributions of a few others in my world – led me to continue in my efforts.

The reality is that homemade gifts don't actually save you money or time. Food is a common homemade gift, but by the time you save the seed, propagate the seedling, nurture the plant, and harvest and cook the jam/cake/dehydrated chips, it actually costs you more and takes more time than buying something from the shops. So, with this knowledge in your pocket, hold your head high and be proud that the less shiny, less perfect, wholly loved, individual, one-of-a-kind personalised presents have your name on the tag.

There's an endless range of gifts that you can make with ease. The bonus is that once you set the tone, you'll have the favour returned. Some of the best homemade presents that we've received are:

- a voucher book of activities and time offered for redemption (cleaning the house, picnic day out, day at the beach, night off the dishes, night in together, being read a story)
- potted plants or herbs taken from their garden
- poetry
- stories and photos of our childhood together
- a packed picnic with thermos, real china and a tablecloth or picnic rug
- a garlic or chilli string that is ready to be hung straight up in my kitchen
- an upcycled box brimming with hot-chocolate ingredients, including a mug, marshmallows and vanilla-infused cacao
- a meal in a jar – all of the dry ingredients plus handy instructions on how to complete the meal by simply cooking it in a pot
- dried homegrown herbal tea in an upcycled container
- saved vegie seeds
- a second-hand collection box – goodies purchased in op shops throughout the year with me in mind.

The clincher to your homemade present is the wrapping. Again, it's a chance to get super creative, so why not try using:

- fabric instead of paper
- pages from an old street directory or atlas
- newspaper or brown paper decorated with natural finds
- string or a fabric ribbon.

You can make your own simple gift tags using leaves or layered paper, and add a fresh flower tucked under the corner of the wrapping for a lovely finishing touch. Did you know that spruce is traditionally considered a sign of gratitude and hope? When you next wrap a homemade gift, why not add a little spruce sprig if you can?

WEAVE A HOMEMADE CHRISTMAS WREATH

In the heat of the day, I march through the bush with secateurs in hand. I refuse to return home until my arms are full of aromatic gum leaves, interesting sticks, speckled leaves and precocious vines (but no flowers – I leave them in the bush) to weave into a wreath.

Actually, the creation is more about the process itself. The smell of the Aussie bush, the hour on my own in the dappled light, the meandering walk with purpose, and the cathartic, in-the-moment brain puzzling of the weaving process. The bonus is the finished magic, which is always different from the previous year's wreath and always lovely to hang.

There's no one to pass judgement, no waste for the bin, no theme to follow and no expectation from a soul. It simply hangs on its hook until the festivities pass and then unravels straight into the fire pile, representing another Christmas celebration that is simple but no less special for its lack of tinsel.

GET CRACKING!

Originating in London to boost sales of boiled lollies, the beloved Christmas cracker has only been around since the 1800s. But it's now a mainstay on most Christmas tables, with its daggy paper hat, dad jokes and cheap plastic toy. Years ago, when I had just started living out of home, I was cleaning up the flood of wrapping paper and packaging, and realised that half the rubbish was cracker debris. Figuring that it would be sad to eliminate them altogether, I took to making them.

Now it's a family activity, often on the advent calendar, and the theme changes each year depending on what I've got in the recycled wrapping box, or the leaves, stamps, ribbons and so on that we've found outside or in op shops. The simple challenge is to use nothing new except the strip that makes the 'bang', which we often do without. While sometimes it's a stretch, making crackers is always doable. You'll need:

◆ toilet paper rolls – save them as the year ticks past
◆ bad jokes – save these as you hear them
◆ second-hand wrapping paper or tissue paper
◆ old ribbons, stamps, newspapers and stickers, plus collected leaves and petals
◆ gifts – gathering these is the most time-consuming part; perhaps use seeds, miniature handmade soaps, hand-painted rocks, collected shells, tiny origami animals or homemade toffee/caramels.

WASTE-FREE CHRISTMAS

Challenge yourself to decorate your Christmas tree without using plastic. Stained-glass orange slices are a great starting place. These take me a few days to dehydrate, as I pop them in the cooling oven after I bake bread each day, but they are worth the wait. I first used these as tree decorations when I was nineteen and living in London with no money. I also used the balls from the abundant plane trees that lined the streets. Get the creative juices flying, and give this challenge a go!

However you spend the day, set the intention for it to be one of small moments of magic, intimacy, memory-making and joy. The richest of days are those that leave you with a full cup, a full belly and a full heart. Going without the shiny stuff won't leave you wanting more – it actually feels a little virtuous.

A BOOK A DAY

When the kids were little, I'd visit an op shop a few weeks before advent and buy 24 second-hand storybooks. I'd wrap them in newspaper and place them under the tree. Each night we'd choose one of the books, snuggle up under the covers and read the book together. It's a simple yet beautiful ritual that still plucks at my kids' memories. If you have older kids, perhaps you can try this ritual with read-aloud chapter books each night.

BELTANE BONFIRES

With its origins in Gaelic Ireland and Scotland, Beltane marked the beginning of the pastoral season, when livestock was driven out to the summer pastures. There were rituals to encourage growth and to protect crops, dairy products and people. The name means 'bright fire', which refers to the symbolic, enduring ritual of lighting bonfires, and it is perhaps a salute to the sun as the acknowledged force behind abundant food production.

Above: Honour
the new season by
lighting a bonfire.

In the northern hemisphere, Beltane is held around 30 April, while in the southern hemisphere it kickstarts the summer growing season on 31 October. Here in Australia, the timing is perfectly suited for bonfires, as the burn pile is dry after winter but fire restrictions are yet to begin. (You may still need a permit to light a fire, so check with your local rural fire service.)

We really don't delve too deeply into supernatural symbolic rituals at Black Barn Farm, but we absolutely relish the chance to gather our people, light a fire and celebrate. Beltane is a time to honour the knowledge of our pagan forefathers, raise a toast to the abundant growth surrounding us and consummate our own unique rituals and understanding of food production.

PATCH TO PATCH

At the beginning of spring, we rally a cohort of green thumbs to open their vegie gardens to the public. Visitors ride from patch to patch, gathering a clutch of knowledge and sowing the seeds of motivation to plant their own backyard food-garden beds. Gardens of all shapes and sizes are on show, and visitors take the day to ponder their own needs, seek out solutions to their problems, share stories, drink cups of tea, swap seeds and buy seedlings.

We began this annual event on a whim, but it's now a spring ritual that inspires, offers solidarity and practical advice, and gently invites us back outside after the winter months indoors. It's an event that requires a little from a few, so if you've got a crew of food growers nearby, consider getting your heads together and opening your gates on the same day. Throw in a fundraising sausage sizzle for the local school, plus some seedling sales, and with a hand-drawn map, away you go!

LAVENDER-INFUSED OIL

It's that time of year again when you get to play with flowers in the name of creating something useful. This method for producing lavender-infused oil is super simple and gives you enough to last you for an entire year.

1. Cut some lavender sprigs, or purchase them dried. Any variety of lavender will work. Use 1 cup of lavender for 1 cup (250 ml) of oil.
2. If you have fresh lavender, dry it for a couple of days on a sunny windowsill.
3. Using your fingers, lightly crush the lavender into a bowl.
4. Pour the oil over the flowers. Use whatever oil you like; try macadamia or almond oil to make massage oil or cooking oil.
5. Pour the lavender and oil mixture into a bottle (it's preferable to use a dark brown bottle so the mixture doesn't go rancid). Allow the lavender to soak in the oil for up to four weeks in a sunlit room.
6. Strain the oil, ready to use.

Voila! I rub the oil on the kids' wrists and temples to calm them at night, or on my own wrists if I'm a bit wound up. I also use the oil in salad dressings and light stir-fries.

MAKE A SCARECROW

Scarecrows have been a mainstay in rural life for centuries. They guarded wheat crops in ancient Egypt and vineyards in ancient Greece as early as 2500 BC; they have also long been used to protect rice crops in Japan and other grains in Germany and the United States.

Until recently, they were almost always humanoid, oversized and really scary. The Germans carved wooden ones, and the Americans stuffed theirs with straw. Some scarecrows were made to look like witches, while others carried bow and arrows. Now there are alternatives such as reflector ribbon tape, automated drones and bird-of-prey kites. All are designed to do the same thing – protect your food production!

The odd friendly scarecrow can be found in school gardens these days. Creating the scarecrow is usually about getting the creative juices flowing and inviting the kids to get involved in the vegie patch.

If you are short on space, or have a rooftop garden or balcony, you could make a child-sized scarecrow, or a small woven or wooden one. Change their clothes, move them around, give them a name and embrace the intention of those food-growing centuries before ours.

Far left: Gently hand-water new seedlings with a watering-can.

Left: The annual artichoke haul always includes plenty from 'volunteer plants' (see opposite page).

CREATE A RAIN RECORD

While turning on a tap with clean, flowing liquid is now expected in Western countries, it has not always been this way. Sadly, the ease with which most of us now expect and receive this resource has eroded our appreciation for and desire to understand its passage. Getting familiar with your water source is as valuable as knowing where your food comes from, how it was grown and by whom.

Understanding your annual rainfall, where your water is stored (do you have a tank?) and where the watershed pathways flow is important and fundamental. It connects you to the natural world in an inextricable way that will reshape your comprehension of this precious, life-giving resource.

An easy way to rekindle this love affair is to measure your rainfall. Nothing is quite so forthright in making you take notice of the outside world as the immediacy of a rain gauge. It leads you to observe more, ponder beyond the now and consider others.

A rain chart can be as simple as a single page with a little rectangle for each day of the year, in which you note the amount of each downpour as shown on your rain gauge. While this will capture your annual rainfall, what's even more intriguing is to compare data from year to year. So why not set yourself up with a book that not only stores information from the current year, but also includes data from previous years and has space for future years? Understanding your long-term rainfall patterns is a grounding way to connect you to place.

FIGURE OUT A FIRE PLAN

Do you have a comprehensive fire plan? Apartment and inner-city dwellers are largely safe from the threat of bushfires, but everyone else should have a fire plan in place. Now is the time to make a new plan or to revisit your old one, before the high heat of summer hits.

Grow

HOOP-HOUSE HAPPINESS

If, like us, you live in a tough climate, hot or cold, consider extending your growing season with the help of a certain Miss Polly. Polytunnels or hoop houses are worth their weight in gold. Our hoop house has revolutionised our growing. Without it, we struggle to grow tomatoes, capsicums (peppers) and eggplants (aubergines), because we simply don't have enough warm days to raise them in time. Equally, we can't grow things such as lemongrass or sweet potatoes because of late and early frosts. With the addition of a plastic covering and some second-hand 44-gallon drums filled with water to act as a thermal mass, we have artificially created a nine-month growing season.

Our hoop house is both a production house – where we grow the food plants in dedicated garden beds – and a propagation house for all of our seedlings, sick plants, cuttings and over-wintering needs. Because of this space, we now maintain year-round crop rotation – we can get seedlings going in the tunnel and not have to wait for beds to be clear of summer vegies before we plant out winter vegies. This was always problematic, because often our summer vegies were not ready to harvest until April, and if we missed getting the winter vegies in by the end of January, then they didn't have time to grow before the harsh winter weather kicked in. Our polytunnel has

allowed us to double our production simply by giving us three more months of guaranteed warmth.

If you don't have the room (or the need) for a full-scale greenhouse, a simple but effective solution to the problem of protecting new seedlings from frost and bugs is to place a glass jar over them in the early stages of growing. Use recycled jars, the bigger the better. (If the daytime weather is extremely hot, remove the jars or your plants will cook.)

VOLUNTEER PLANTS

Self-seeded plants are to be congratulated with gusto. Any plant that volunteers for free to fill a gap in the garden deserves serious celebration! Some common self-seeded plants in our garden include:

- Alexanders (*Smyrnium olusatrum*)
- alyssum (*Lobularia maritima*)
- borage (*Borago officinalis*)
- Californian poppy (*Eschscholzia californica*)
- cosmos (*Cosmos* species)
- fennel (*Foeniculum vulgare*)
- globe artichoke (*Cynara scolymus*)
- leek (*Allium ampeloprasum*).

GARLIC GOODNESS

After six to eight long months of growing, garlic is ready for harvest. First check that it has 'bulbed', which means that it looks like the ones in the supermarket, not like a spring onion. Harvest garlic after a period of no watering, so the green tops (scapes) have yellowed and wilted – this forces the bulb to finish forming and begin the process of drying off. Be sure to remove the scapes before storing; you can feed them to your chickens.

Without a doubt, garlic is one of the most easily grown culinary spices and most important medicines in the home arsenal. It's flavour-packed and nutrient-rich, and because it's easy to grow, simple to prepare and safe to use, it's a perfect option for home herbalists who want to develop their skills and confidence in herbal remedies.

Garlic is a firm favourite at Black Barn Farm! It's a versatile source of food, flavour and herbal medicine for both the humans in the house and the animals in the paddocks and pens. It's also a crop that doesn't interfere with other crops, because it grows in the off-season when everything else is waiting for warmth. In our subalpine climate, we plant it in mid-autumn when the soil is still warm. We sow 400 cloves each year. That sounds like a lot, I know – but once you learn garlic's myriad uses, you'll find that you soon get through it. They plant pretty tightly, and once they're harvested we knot them together and loop them over the rafters in the packing shed or on the verandah to dry before storing them in a cool, dry place.

Garlic is not only great for dealing with human and animal pathogens, but also for soil pathogens. We plant it after our potatoes in our crop rotation to help break up pest and pathogen cycles. Given that the soil is heavily loosened when harvesting potatoes, no additional work is needed before planting garlic.

Garlic is great at gleaning nutrients such as nitrogen, phosphorus and potassium that

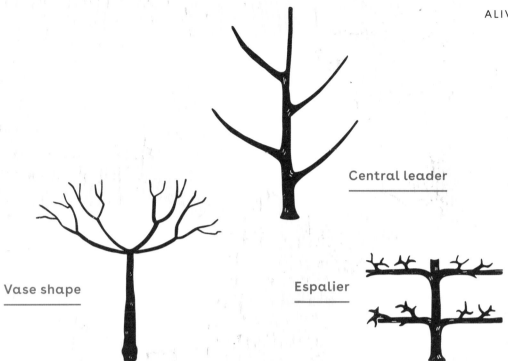

Central leader

Vase shape

Espalier

were left over from spring and summer plantings. Other than adding a little blood and bone to the roots to encourage bulb development – and some well-broken-down woodchip mulch to beat weeds – garlic makes for a low-maintenance addition to your garden.

FRUIT-TREE TRAINING

Baby apple trees need shaping, just like baby humans. But unlike humans, we can do this with the help of string, pegs and bamboo stakes. Our orchard has been pruned into 'central leader' trees, with one main trunk up the centre and laterals that produce the fruits coming out in a series of layers. These layers begin at about knee height, so we can still have nutritional under-plantings beneath the trees. This also allows the pick-your-own visitors to access the bottom three rows, while we pick the fruits from the top layers using ladders.

Training is a critical process, as it sets up these trees to produce fruits sooner and on a framework that will form their foundation for life. The other common growing method for fruit trees is called 'vase' pruning, which is a series of five or six branches that begin at thigh height and then sweep upwards, so the tree looks like a vase. This method allows for more airflow and sunshine, but it requires more ongoing pruning each year.

If space is tight in your garden, then try espaliering your trees – tying the branches to a frame or lattice that is attached to a wall. Although this requires a serious ongoing pruning commitment, espaliered trees add quite a stunning structural element to any garden and can be just as productive as other fruit trees. You do need to be sure that you have a dwarfing rootstock for this method, though, or you'll be forever trying to tame the precocious branch growth.

'I think we consider too much the good luck of the early bird and not enough the bad luck of the early worm.'

Franklin D. Roosevelt (1882-1945), former US president

GET WOODY

Although the wood stack is appreciated during the deepest, darkest winter days, chopping wood is actually a ritual that begins once the days lengthen and the grass dries out. The rationale is simple: wood requires sunlight and heat to transition from a once-living green organism to a burnable, carbon-trapping heat source. So, as odd as it feels to be planning your winter warmth at the beginning of your summer days, it really does require forethought to ensure that next winter's wood gets enough time in the sun to dry out. Now's the time to get chopping!

If you've got the space, consider planting out your own firewood source; eucalypts are generally the most effective. We planted 300 indigenous gums when we first arrived, and now we plant 10–15 each year in the gaps caused by those that have lost a limb or died completely. It's a sustainable approach to providing your own heat.

WORM FARM REBOOT

If we rationalise that the earth is our foundation, then soil is more precious than gold – it forms the basis for all things. It grows our plants; even the production of synthetics is reliant on fossil fuels that are plant-based. In light of soil's importance, we must surely consider the worm and its movements through soil as critical.

These small, pink, wriggly creatures have probably never been fairly acknowledged for their role in our collective lives. One way of offering a nod is to create a worm farm and care for it well.

Worm farms can take many shapes and sizes, and can be made from various materials. You could use small or large buckets, IBCs (intermediate bulk containers), polystyrene boxes or plastic pots. Whatever you choose, be sure to follow a few basic principles:

- The worm farm must be well drained, as worms can't sit in water.
- The worm farm needs to stay cool.
- The worms should have enough space to allow them to get into a cool, dark place if necessary.
- You need to keep the worms well fed and moist (but not waterlogged).

Worm farms are worthwhile for everyone wanting to grow plants.

Why own a worm farm?

There are plenty of excellent reasons to have a worm farm:

- Worms make short work of all of your kitchen scraps.
- Worm castings (i.e. poo) are a magnet for water and nutrients, so they make a great addition to any newly potted plants.
- Using worm juice (i.e. the liquid that drains from a worm farm) is the cheapest and easiest way of adding biological entities such as helpful microbes and bacteria to your garden beds.
- If you create an in-ground worm farm, it will help to aerate your soil.

Top right: The woodheap is in constant flux, and it is nearly always on our to-do list.

Bottom right: The reward for creating a worm farm is healthy soil.

- If your friends have a worm farm, you can take a handful of their worm castings (which are full of eggs) and populate your own farm for free.
- Kids love worm farms.
- Worm farms are self-contained and require next to no attention.

For us, the little care that worm farms do require is completed just before the heat of summer hits. Our worms are housed in big old IBCs, as we require this size for our orchard. This means that the maintenance job takes about an hour. However, if you are using a small-scale worm farm, then the job could be something quick that you do every now and then throughout the year. All you need to do is observe, respond to and nourish your worms:

- **Observe** – A worm farm reboot is as simple as lifting the mesh cover off the now depleted scraps and giving the farm the once-over: is it too wet, too dry, too hot or full of mould? Does it have visible signs of worms, weeds growing in it or cooler areas? Ask all of these questions, and take the time to really observe before you rectify any shortcoming with your next steps.
- **Respond** – In general, if the worm farm is too wet, then drill more holes in the base; if it's too dry, then add some wet compost and commit to increasing your watering. Remove any weeds, and move the worm farm if it's too hot.
- **Nourish** – Feeding worms is as simple as refilling the farm with what you have on hand: kitchen scraps, straw, woodchips, grass clippings, some leaves (although not too many) and wind-fallen fruits (again, not too many). I layer our farms until the containers are about two-thirds full, and then water them in gently before I place the mesh cover back on.

Avoid making the worm farm another job! We've placed our potted seedling trays on metal shelves directly over the worm farms, so when we water them each day, the worm farms catch stray drops and stay moist but not soaked.

Note that if you're using worm juice, it's important that the juice be properly aerated before it's applied to plants, just in case it's anaerobic and contains pathogens. Use a small pump (like the ones in fish tanks) to aerate the worm juice for 12–24 hours.

FEATHERED FRIENDS

Chickens are one of those evocative creatures that scream 'self-sufficiency' and 'homemaking goodness'. They live up to their romantic reputation by delivering eggs, entertaining with antics, letting kids cart them around and clucking their day away while scratching your mulch and making the yard feel 'lived in'. Chickens are definitely worth considering, as they're easy to look after and they teach kids responsibility, pet care, where their food comes from, how to repurpose kitchen scraps and a whole lot more. However, if you live in a town, check your council regulations, as they usually have quantity limits, and most don't allow roosters.

Chickens are low maintenance, but they do still require daily care. You need to give them food (kitchen scraps and layer pellets) and water (fresh every morning), provide shade and dust (for bathing), make sure their roosting space and nesting box are fox-proof, and have a plan for when they get sick. Will you whip off their head, apply herbal medicines or take them to the vet? You should think about all of these things before leaping straight into chicken ownership.

If you're tight on space, quails might be a better option than chickens. Although

Right: Spreading the weekly straw ration in the pens is a messy but necessary job.

Far right: We collect 'googies' from the nests every day.

their eggs are half the size of those from chickens, quails lay all year, they don't go clucky, and they require much less space.

Annual chicken-house care

Okay, it's a lousy job, but someone's got to do it. On the bright side, the inmates are absolutely hilarious, they cover your breakfast and baking needs for most of the year, and the result of mucking out their house is literally wheelbarrows full of partly decomposed manure that – with a little further decomposing in the compost or, in our case, the woodchip pile – can add incredible nutrients to garden beds. So the chicken coop pays you back tenfold. There are three key steps to the overhaul:

1. a fortnightly nesting-box clean-out
2. a twice yearly full-coop clean-out
3. the addition of a rotational wheat crop to coops.

NESTING-BOX CLEAN-OUT

We clean our nesting boxes every two weeks to be sure that the chickens don't get mites or lay their eggs in poo, and that the birds stay clean. The discarded nesting material just gets flicked onto the ground so it can begin the process of breaking down the piles of chicken poo in the roosting shed.

We use straw to line our nesting boxes, but you could just as easily use woodchips (the smaller, the better) or sawdust from non-treated timber. Ensure that whatever you use is dry. If any chickens are roosting in the box at night, it will quickly accrue manure, so discourage the habit and clean the box more regularly. Equally, if an egg breaks in the nesting box, replace the straw.

FULL-COOP CLEAN-OUT

We clean out the chicken coop twice each year: once just before winter, and once just before summer. Chicken poo is high in

Left. Our chickens
are free-range,
so they can help
manage bug
populations.
Right: Regular
handling makes for
very placid chickens.

nitrogen, so it's gold for the vegie patch or for fertilising lawns. But be mindful that it's also high in phosphorus, so it must be well composted before use. Four to six months in the compost pile is all it takes. Even then, it's worth knowing that some native plants – such as banksias and grevilleas – won't love you for it, and long-term use could actually kill them. So stick with using well-composted chicken poo only on the vegie garden, just to be safe.

Once our orchard trees are bigger, we'll move the chickens into portable chicken tractors between the tree rows. They'll turn any potential bug problems into fertiliser under the trees. It's a win-win situation!

ADDITION OF ROTATIONAL WHEAT CROP TO COOPS

As a general rule of thumb, allow 0.25 square metres (2½ square feet) per chicken inside the chicken coop, and 1 square metre

(10½ square feet) per chicken in an outside run. More space is always better. Ideally, there should be no more than 15 chickens to a coop, as they are reported to only have the capacity to recognise that many other chickens before the natural order (the pecking order) is compromised by confusion. Limiting space for your chickens will cause stress, pecking and sometimes even death.

Based on this, it's ideal to run your chickens free range if you can. While we do this for nine months of the year, during breeding season it's harder. We need to keep individual breeds separated, so they cannot all be roaming together. To overcome this, we have an additional coop, which we sow with wheat and rotate the chickens through. In addition, we have sprouted wheat 'trays' that we feed to the birds that are not ranging. It stretches our wheat further, provides the chickens with

Far left: Rotating our pens allows us to grow wheat crops for the girls.

Left: Insect hotels in food-growing gardens enhance pollination.

green pick (new plant growth) and means that they have something other than scraps and layer pellets every second day when they are still locked up. It's a really simple solution to a problem that we only have during spring.

INSECT HOTEL

This creative work of art allows you to use what you've got, to be inspired by outside activity, to be mindful and to keep little hands busy – and that's just while you make it. Once it is hanging in the garden, you'll all be lured outside to soothe your curiosity about who and what now calls it home.

There's no particular formula for creating a successful insect hotel. It can be any size or any shape, and made using whatever you have on hand. There are a few things to consider, though:

+ Natural materials should be used.
+ A diverse range of materials extends its appeal.

+ A timber frame won't last as long as a metal one.
+ Expect to give it a refresh each year.
+ It is ephemeral, so don't expect it to last forever.
+ It takes longer to create than you think.
+ The more small crevices and cracks, the more guests you'll get.
+ A metal 'cap' will extend its life.
+ It can be designed to hang or sit against a wall.
+ It makes a great present.

Some perfect materials that are easily sourced include:

+ hay
+ bamboo (cut to size)
+ wood rounds with drilled holes
+ mud packs with drilled holes
+ bark
+ sticks (cut to size)
+ dried hard flower heads, such as banksias.

Feast

LUNCH BELL

Remember those old movies where the cook clangs the lunch triangle to bring the workers in from the paddock? Well, that isn't a romantic notion – it's bloody practical! When you're way up in the back paddock, entrenched in a project, you lose track of time. The sharp, silence-splitting clang of metal on metal is definitive and cuts through any work-induced haze.

This ritual isn't really season-specific, although it's handy during our spring and autumn WWOOFing seasons, when we have multiple projects being undertaken all over the property. It's great to have a definite prompt to down tools and walk back to the house. The ritual isn't so much the banging of the triangle but the invitation that this offers – which is to come together to enjoy a pre-laid lunch table: a mishmash of freshly dug carrots or picked tomatoes and cucumber, homemade chutney, left-over rice or pasta, simple green sauce and boiled eggs.

Obviously, lunch evolves throughout the seasons, but mostly it sticks to a pattern: it's hearty, quick to prepare and homegrown, and anyone can create it – so the kids, the WWOOFers or we can whip it up. Lunch is a big thing in our house, mostly because much of our work is physical, but also because it's the time when we all come together to tell a yarn, solve the problems concerning the morning projects, share the podcast knowledge learned by those who had them in their ears, and plan the afternoon.

Clearly, city folk can't adopt the loud triangle, but what about having a special lunch that brings you all back to centre and sets some structure for the day, even if it's just once a week? I realise that a home-based life is a much easier environment in which to do this, but what if you could make it work?

GLOBE ARTICHOKE GLUT

Globe artichokes are delectable roasted, marinated or boiled and then dipped in butter. They are equally glorious if they are left to burst into beautiful bloom, but if you are eager to feast on them, they are surprisingly simple to prepare and store:

- Use a super-sharp knife to cut off the stem, outer layers and tops. Scoop out the 'hairy choke' from the centre.
- Boil the globe artichokes in a pot of salted, lemony water for 15 minutes or until they are soft. Drain them very well, and allow them to cool.
- While the globe artichokes are cooling, place fresh rosemary, black peppercorns, fresh thyme, fresh garlic cloves, mustard seeds, fennel seeds and salt into a sterile, dry jar (make your mix to suit your taste).
- Pack the globe artichokes into the jar, and top with olive oil.
- Seal the jar with a tight-fitting lid, and store the jar in a dry, dark, cool place for up to six months.

Gran's Christmas pudding

My grandmother has made the family pudding using her mother's recipe for as long as my mum can recall. Gran usually tackles the job at the tail end of winter, as by then she's had time to buy the ingredients bit by bit throughout the year, and the kitchen is cooler. She makes one pudding for each of her daughters. To avoid being overwhelmed, Gran measures out all of the ingredients on day one; the mixing and cooking occur on day two. Mum often pulls her pudding from its hiding spot in the depths of the following winter; if she didn't use it as an excuse to host a family dinner, I'm sure she'd eat the lot in one sitting.

Serves 12–15

350 g (12 oz) raisins, chopped

350 g (12 oz) sultanas

220 g (7¾ oz) currants

6 prunes, finely chopped

170 g (6 oz) chopped mixed peel

Grated rind of 3 lemons

½ cup (125 ml) brandy

½ cup (125 ml) milk

1 cup (250 ml) orange juice

120 g (4¼ oz) soft white breadcrumbs

1 large carrot, grated

1 cup (220 g) sugar

220 g (7¾ oz) suet flakes (use Copha [white vegetable shortening] if you can't find suet)

⅔ cup (100 g) plain (all-purpose) flour

½ teaspoon salt

½ teaspoon nutmeg

1 teaspoon mixed spice

4 large eggs

1. Place the raisins, sultanas, currants, prunes, mixed peel and lemon rind into a large bowl, and pour in the brandy, milk and orange juice. Allow the fruits to soak in the fridge for 24 hours.

2. Remove the soaked fruits from the fridge (do not drain them), and add the remaining ingredients to the bowl. Stir the mixture until it is well blended.

3. Place the mixture into the centre of a 50 x 50 cm (20 x 20 in) calico fabric square. Gather up the fabric corners, and tie tightly with string as close to the mixture as possible.

4. Place the wrapped mixture into a saucepan of water, and boil it for at least five hours or 'as long as you can be bothered'. The longer you boil the pudding the better, but be careful not to let the saucepan boil dry.

5. Hang the pudding to drip-dry for a few days and to dry out the cloth. Gran used to let it hang until Christmas, but it would go mouldy on the outside. Freezing it after it has drip-dried causes less worry.

6. Defrost the pudding early on Christmas morning, and boil it just before you want to serve it. You can also boil it right after defrosting – simply wrap it in a towel so it stays hot.

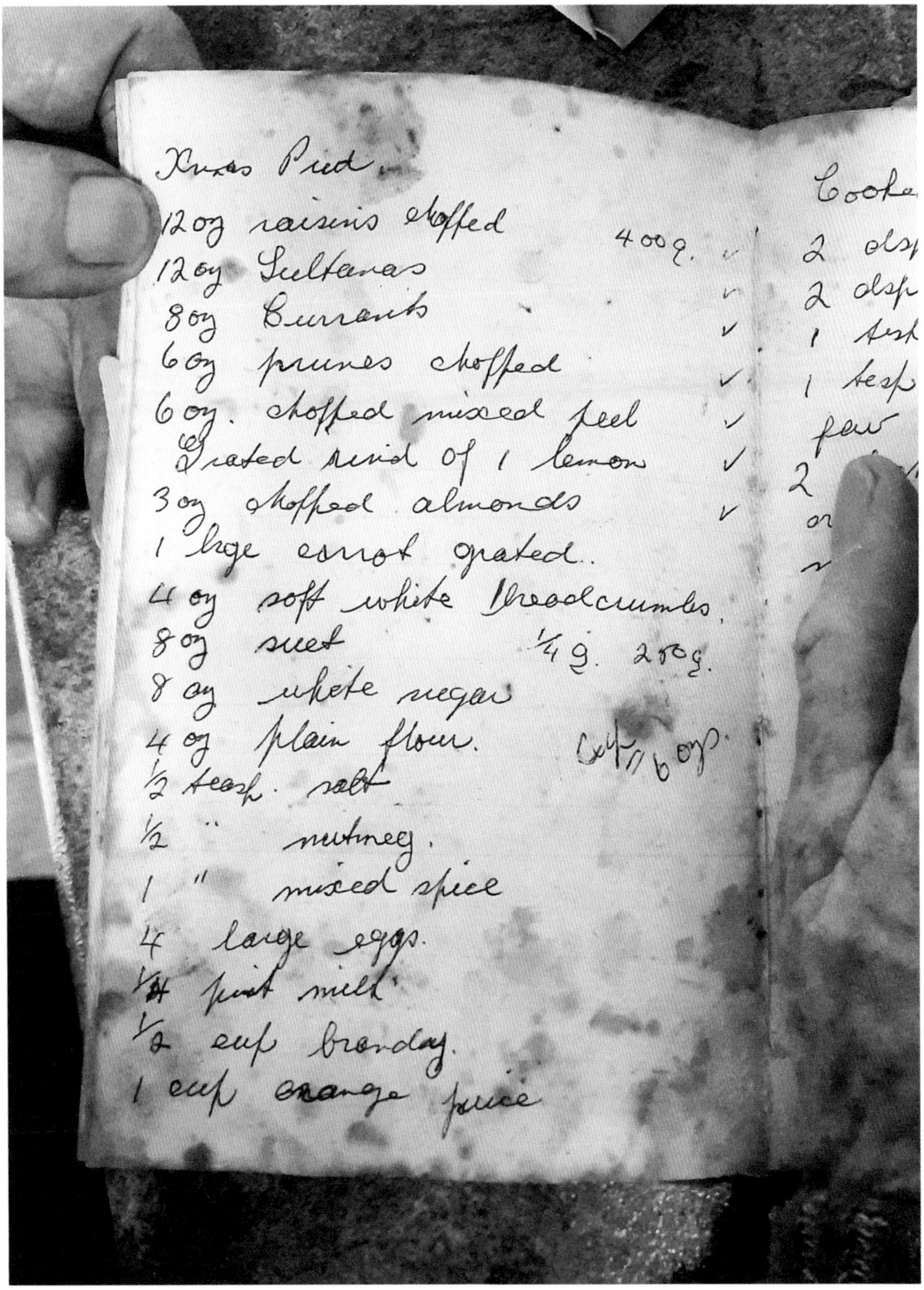

Xmas Pud.

12 oz raisins chopped   400g. ✓

12 oz Sultanas   ✓

8 oz Currants   ✓

6 oz prunes chopped   ✓

6 oz. chopped mixed peel   ✓ ✓

Grated rind of 1 lemon   ✓

3 oz chopped almonds   ✓

1 lrge carrot grated.

4 oz soft white breadcrumbs.

8 oz suet   ¼ g. 250g.

8 oz white sugar

4 oz plain flour.   cut to 6 oz.

½ teasp. salt

½ "   nutmeg.

1 "   mixed spice

4 large eggs.

¼ pint milk

½ cup brandy.

1 cup orange juice

Cooke...
2 dsp...
2 dsp...
1 teak...
1 tesp...
few
2
or

Easy pesto

Basil is abundant by mid-summer. But if you get some growing earlier in spring, it's not unrealistic to be feasting on the decadent flavour by early summer. We plant it en masse, because it grows easily and we like to use it fresh for months – then we make enough pesto for the rest of the year.

We make about 50 serves of pesto each summer and freeze them in recycled glass jars or re-used sandwich bags (I get about four uses out of each bag before they get holes in them). I make some without cheese and some with less garlic to be sure that we have all of our visitors covered.

This delicious pesto can be used in rice and pasta dishes, on pizza bases and swirled through roasted vegies. Simply multiply the ingredients for bulk freezer stores.

Makes approx. 750 g (1 lb 10 oz)

4 cups (200 g) fresh basil leaves

1 cup (160 g) almonds

½ cup (125 ml) olive oil

½ cup (50 g) finely grated parmesan cheese (or nutritional yeast, if you require dairy-free pesto)

1 tablespoon roasted garlic

Juice of 2 lemons

Salt, to taste

1. Place all of the ingredients into a blender and whiz until smooth. If someone in your family can't eat dairy, leave out the cheese or replace it with nutritional yeast at half quantity.
2. Place portions of the pesto into clean containers of your choice. Store the pesto in the freezer for up to 12 months.

Homemade lemonade cordial

The good old lemon tree is a planting staple in many backyards, and at different times of the year it can be abundant. Our citrus trees do not produce many edible fruits, so we are often given baskets of fresh lemons or oranges. While we try to make them last for as long as we can, sometimes we get a gifting glut and need to preserve them, freeze the juice in ice-cube trays for our drinks, or whip up a batch of homemade lemonade cordial. It's the stuff of childhood memories – perhaps because it's simple enough for children to make themselves.

Makes 8 cups (2 litres)

2 tablespoons finely grated lemon rind

2 tablespoons finely grated lime rind

2 cups (500 ml) lemon juice

1 cup (250 ml) lime juice

3 teaspoons citric acid

3 teaspoons tartaric acid

3 cups (660 g) caster (superfine) sugar (you can use rapadura sugar if you run it through the blender first, but your cordial will be more brown than yellow)

8 cups (2 litres) boiling water

1. In a bowl, mix together the lemon and lime rind, lemon and lime juice, citric acid, tartaric acid and sugar.
2. Add the boiling water. Stir well until the sugar has dissolved.
3. Strain the liquid into a heatproof jug. Pour it into hot, sterilised bottles and seal. The cordial will keep unopened in a cupboard for up to six months; once opened, store it in the fridge for up to two weeks. I use small bottles, so I don't have to use too much once opened.
4. Serve super cold, perhaps with a little fresh mint.

Rustle up your swimsuit from the bottom drawer and ponder what to pack in your picnic basket, for the season of twilight swimming and riverbank picnics is here!

Days start early with sunrise walks and the must-do chores of feeding the chickens and watering the garden, before we bunker down in the cool of the house for the heat of the day, where we escape the deafening drum of the cicadas. There is no better excuse for reading a few chapters, sucking on homemade popsicles and making slushies with just-picked fruits.

Other than the odd dash out to the garden to turn on drippers or to whip the sun-baked washing off the line, our days are slow and mellow.

The days flow languidly as we enjoy endless jugs of water filled with fistfuls of mint (we have so much mint that we might go mad, although we won't tell Mum as she warned us not to plant it at all). Long evenings are warm enough to swim by moonlight, and the water feels like milk against our skin.

It's the season of 'high heat'. Harvest has begun, but it isn't yet in full swing.

Cockatoos circle relentlessly in search of their next feed, tomatoes and corn reach skyward, and seed heads are beginning to appear. As a kid, it was my favourite time of year; as a homesteading adult, it's the season that tests your mettle and your commitment to the cause.

This season sears you on both sides, but the advantage is that it leaves you tender in the middle and best served with a glass of wine or cider, while holding the hose in the other hand.

Once the baking sun has dipped, it's back outside for more bustle and antics. More watering, patch picking and barbecue dinners where the kids bounce on the trampoline and kick the soccer ball while the grown-ups turn the chops. The early produce is beginning to flood the kitchen, and we feast on foods that need to be used.

IT'S GETTING HOTTER

In Australia, even in temperate climates, the season of high heat is increasingly hard to manage. This applies not just to humans, who are becoming accustomed to air-conditioned environments, but also to animals, which simply cannot adapt fast enough to cool themselves in the height of summer. Plants also react badly, by wilting, self-thinning, bearing sunburnt fruits and splitting.

This impending climate calamity leaves us feeling like the proverbial 'frog in a pot', which when heated slowly does nothing to save itself from being boiled alive. As climate change creeps insidiously across our world, those in a position of influence are unable to move governments quickly enough to enact change before we are faced with an unresolvable situation. This is a complex subject that I cannot go into here, but I will draw attention to the impact that this climate emergency is having on one of the most fundamental requirements of human existence: food.

It affects not just backyard producers, but all agricultural enterprises. Increased temperatures, changes in rainfall patterns, the regular occurrence of extreme weather events and the overall reduction in water availability are wreaking havoc on our ability to reliably and efficiently maintain a stable state of food sovereignty. Even those of us who are committed to regenerative growing and living practices are finding that the unruly climatic conditions are making homesteading increasingly harder to manage.

Ritual

NEW YEAR'S RESOLUTION

As we enter the new year, the previous year sits in our head and heart, and is left to gather dust without the pressures of expectation. That baton is passed to the new year.

My greatest shortcoming is to build expectations beyond the realm of reality and then push with all of my might to make them happen to avoid disappointment. While this kind of thinking can help us achieve much on our to-do list, it doesn't allow us to savour the magic moments, intriguing ideas and beautiful distractions that appear unexpectedly and contribute to a well-lived life. A simple internet search tells us three oft-repeated New Year's resolutions:

I will 'exercise to get in shape'.
I will 'diet to lose weight'.
I will 'save money'.

These commitments feel like punishments. They don't inspire hope, encourage joy, evoke excitement, embrace reality, consider our place in the world or contribute to anything bigger than ourselves.

A number of years ago, I reshaped my resolutions. Creating hard and fast rules with black and white deadlines only set me up for failure. Life has shades of grey and is a complex yet wondrous journey. Let's not avoid reality by creating a single resolution that leaves no room for being human, experiencing the unexpected, seeing the evolution of thought, and feeling desire. Instead, let's use this ritual as an opportunity to build hope, confidence and a path filled with purpose.

The commitment at the beginning of each and every new annum now follows a very simple mantra:

Expectation – Realisation = Happiness

I set a themed focus for the year that is broad and open to interpretation, such as 'Family, Farm, Food'. I note 'desirable outcomes' related to these themes; this leaves room for a to-do list that is still substantial but is absolutely 'desirable', not 'expected'. I allow the year to unfold as intended by life, seasoned with the salt and pepper of new ideas that celebrate our humanity. That in itself is worth getting excited for another year of life!

Allow the year to unfold as intended by life, seasoned with the salt and pepper of new ideas.

Take a rug and pillow outside, find a flat patch and plonk yourself down. It's time to get serious about what's out there.

STOP AND LOOK UP

High heat is the time to stop ... really stop. I know it's hot and the days are long, but there's no time like right now to take a breather. If you ever wanted to feel humble, then connecting to the earth and looking at the sky stops you in your tracks and makes you breathe. Some call this earthing. It doesn't really matter what you call it – what matters is that you actively make the decision to lie on the ground and look up.

Are you a cloud watcher or a stargazer? Take a rug and pillow outside, find a flat patch and plonk yourself down. It's time to get serious about what's out there. Let your childlike imagination soar as you seek out faces, animals and stories in the clouds or wait patiently for an elusive shooting star. Your breathing will slow, your mind will empty and, just for a while, you can be little more than a tiny speck floating in space.

At this time of year, it can take until midnight before the darkness is complete and the odd shapes on the horizon are no longer seen. If you can stay awake that late, it's the perfect time to be blanketed by the blackness of the night.

DINNER AT THE LAKE?

On many nights each week during summer, we often end up at the lake. It's a couple of degrees cooler than home, our toes wriggle in soothing sand, and we eat a mishmash of whatever is pulled from the fridge. The food is put on a communal table to share with whoever else turns up. It is unplanned but feels ritualistic, is without ceremony but feels decadent, and is free of the mundane but couldn't be simpler as we banter, laugh and debate. The big ones take a quick dip to rinse off the day, while the little ones refuse to leave the water until their digits are pruny, not even to eat – sausages in bread are inhaled mid-game. Despite the hours on fluffy towels as twilight descends, darkness always comes way too soon. We scramble to pack up, giving hugs and saying goodbye ... until the next day, when a picnic just might happen again.

A lake is not crucial – it could be a park or a nearby laneway. The point is to gather with others at a neutral place that serves you all. It is a place to be together, to extend your family and to share. Where's your meeting place?

Nourish

DAYTIME SIESTA

Need I say more than DO IT! Embrace the Spanish summer tradition of 'the sixth hour'. Since the hours of the day begin at dawn, the sixth hour is noon, which is when siestas often start. Avoid the worst of the heat and wipe the list clean … at least for an hour or two. When the heat of the day has passed, you can venture back out into a world less racked with rays, and explore the cooler evening.

LOVE THE SKIN YOU'RE IN

We are the custodians of our own integrity, intention, deepest desires, greatest fears and personal strengths. We are so much more than the job we hold, the children we parent, the culture we come from and the dreams we hold. Our paths are complicated and evolving, and each passing decade brings clarity to what we want and who we are.

If you're anything like me, your youthful summers were vibrant and bustling. Each day was full to bursting with as much activity as the sunlight would allow. But as I've grown older, summer has now become a time for making the most of the low light at the beginning and end of the day, and for taking the heat cue as a time to be slow. Because the days are long, they are inevitably filled with more, so I've learned to make them more 'nourishing' rather than 'bustling'. It's a lesson that I've welcomed along with the wrinkles on my forehead.

OBSERVATION

Be still.
Be still for long enough to really see.
Really see what's around you. What's around you is what you've created.
You can own that. The good, the so-so, the wonderful!
Own it, celebrate it, learn from it.
Change, adapt, chew it over and make it matter.
Only you can make it mean something.
Does it?

SUNRISE YOGA, SUNSET WALK

A yoga session doesn't need to be set around challenges, but can be restful, intentional and nourishing. You might only achieve ten sun salutations and some slow, simple stretches before sitting with your face to the rising light, feeling the warmth of the day peek over the treetops. But if you keep your breath deep and your gratitude strong, your awareness of the world around you will be piqued. For me, this is as beneficial as a hard-hitting game of tennis or 50 laps in the pool.

Summer walks at twilight are much the same. They are most nourishing when they're focused on observing the slowing activities of the animal life around us. When I now visit the city and pace the streets, I notice the song of cicadas, the spit of garden sprinklers and the smell of barbecue dinners.

START AN OBSERVATION DIARY

Some people call these 'writing journals', others call them 'garden diaries' or 'handbooks'. The title is not important; it's just somewhere you can note your observations about the things you see that tickle your fancy. It's like a journal but less esoteric and more practical, so you can refer back to it in coming years to compare, evolve, plan and reference.

I make note of what I've planted and where, so I can manage crop rotation for the next season. I make notes about insects, birds, breeding times (for chickens and geese), first/last frost, mulching and compost. There are notes on cuttings, so I can measure success or failure, plus tips from gardening friends, records of seed varieties, methods of nutrient spreading, names of plants that I'd love to grow ... the list goes on.

You can journal your emotional state alongside each activity during the evolving year. You could draw diagrams, sketch whimsical images, press flowers ... you get the drift, I'm sure. In the suburbs, your diary could even include what your neighbours are growing, scrumping locations and where to find edible weeds. It's a beautiful way to track your seasonal experiences and reflect on patterns, weather and successes.

Left: Sunflowers are a multipurpose crop – they are pretty, help with pollination and make great chicken food.

Grow

SMILING FACES

There is a powerful pull during a seasonally evolving year. The impending divorce from long days and warm nights is always marked by the harvest and hanging of our sunflowers. When their buoyant petals are no longer bobbing warmly, it's time for them to take on a new role in the garden.

For lots of reasons, sunflowers are our favourite flower crop. These blooming beauties are easy to grow, make beautiful picked flowers and are the gift that keeps on giving. Their perky, smiling faces are joyful beyond measure, but once their petals drop, we hang them in the packing shed and feed them to the chickens throughout the winter months. Any left-over seeds are used for next year's crop. It's a perfect closed-loop cycle.

The wonder of seeds

It's time to get your seed-saving skates on. Although the glut of seeds holds off until after the autumn harvest (see page 246), it's one of those jobs that beats you if you don't start early. If this task gets the better of you, then it's an all-out state of chaos: piles of seeds all over the shed floor, mixed-up seeds and plenty of waste. So start now.

Slow summer days are the perfect time to do some seed saving. It is almost unbelievable that every one of those tiny seeds is already imbued with the knowledge that allows them to create something beautiful, edible or capable of producing even more seeds to ensure that the process repeats forever.

Humans, too, contain powerful coding: the multigenerational seeds of knowledge.

The dirt under our feet is not ours to own. We can dance on it, grow from it, be part of it and rely on it, but we cannot own it.

Australia's First Nations people have rich cultures and complex connections to the natural world that have allowed their continuation for longer than any other known group of humans. Arrogantly, we have obliterated our ability to call on the profound and intuitive knowledge held and passed on by our First Nations people. Their understanding of our land, its cycles and its capability to adapt and nurture is 60,000 years old, yet our colonial approach to ownership and control has ensured that this deep knowledge is a skeleton of its former self.

The dirt under our feet is not ours to own. We can dance on it, grow from it, be part of it and rely on it, but we cannot own it.

WICKING BEDS

Hotter summers make for harder growing conditions, and the poor vegie garden beds can suffer the most. One way around this is to set yourself up with wicking beds.

The basic theory behind wicking beds is that the water is stored in an airtight reservoir underneath the soil, and it 'wicks' up through the soil to the roots that are growing down from above; the plants then transpire the wicking moisture through their leaves. Depending on the size of the reservoir, it can keep the soil moist for up to ten days. It virtually eliminates evaporation from the soil and removes the chance of leaf scald, which can occur when watering from above.

To create your own wicking bed, you will need:

◆ a raised garden bed that features a firm frame
◆ brickies sand (very fine sand), enough to cover the base of your garden bed to a depth of 50 millimetres (2 inches)
◆ food-grade plastic, enough to line the entire garden bed
◆ 50-millimetre (2-inch) slotted ag pipe (agricultural pipe), enough to reach one-third of the length of your garden bed
◆ sealant to seal the ag pipe in place
◆ 25-millimetre (1-inch) poly pipe, enough to reach half the height of your garden bed
◆ a poly elbow, to join the shorter piece of 50-millimetre (2-inch) slotted ag pipe to the 25-millimetre (1-inch) poly pipe
◆ 14-millimetre (½-inch) aggregate (blue-metal gravel), enough to fill the bottom half of your garden bed
◆ 50-millimetre (2-inch) slotted ag pipe (agricultural pipe), enough to reach along the length of your garden bed
◆ 50-millimetre (2-inch) poly pipe, enough to reach from the top to the bottom of your garden bed
◆ geotextile fabric, enough to cover the entire base area of the garden bed
◆ high-quality topsoil, enough to fill the top half of your garden bed
◆ mulch (pea straw or lucerne straw), enough to cover the top of your garden bed to a depth of 50 millimetres (2 inches).

Step 1: Set up your raised bed

It can be made from anything; however, ideally it needs to be a minimum of 50 centimetres (20 inches) high, with a solid frame and base (such as a corrugated-iron container, timber box or old bathtub). Ensure that it is placed on a level site. Also make sure that it is on a stable, even surface (laying a bed of sand first is a good idea).

Step 2: Add the liner

Ensure that the base of the garden bed is clear of anything sharp. Consider covering the base with a layer of brickies sand, just in case (you could also use some old carpet). Spread the food-grade plastic evenly across the base and up the sides, ensuring that it reaches almost to the top of the garden bed. If your plastic is thin, consider doubling it over before using it.

Step 3: Insert the overflow pipe

On one of the short sides of the garden bed, cut a hole just a little larger than the ag pipe you are using. Also cut through the liner. Install the shorter piece of ag pipe so that it pokes out of the hole, and then seal it on both sides to ensure watertightness. Attach the poly elbow and the 25-millimetre (1-inch) poly pipe, so that the top of the pipe will sit at the same height as the top of the stones in your bed. This poly pipe can be used to indicate when you have enough water in the garden bed, and it can be swivelled to release the water from time to time to avoid stagnancy.

Step 4: Form the water reservoir

Add the gravel. Lay the longer piece of ag pipe across the centre of the gravel from one side of the garden bed to the other. At the end of this ag pipe that is closest to the overflow pipe, place the 50-millimetre (2-inch) poly pipe so that the top of the pipe is higher than the top of the garden bed (you will need something to hold it in place until the soil is added). This is the inlet pipe, which you will use to add water to the garden bed (with a hose or narrow-spouted watering-can). The gravel between the inlet and overflow ag pipes prevents water from rushing through and out of the garden bed before the reservoir is filled, and it allows you to fill the reservoir quickly without backflooding the garden bed, which is really important.

Step 5: Check for leaks

Add water to the garden bed through the inlet pipe, and leave it overnight to see if there are any leaks.

Step 6: Insert the geotextile fabric

If you don't have access to geotextile fabric, then you can use a piece of shadecloth that has been doubled over. Whatever you use, ensure that the material allows water to move up but stops soil from going down.

Step 7: Add the soil

Pour in the topsoil. To keep your soil rich and healthy, ensure that you add approximately 10 centimetres (4 inches) of fresh compost to the garden bed each year before planting.

Step 8: Start planting

Treat this like a normal raised garden bed, with the tallest vegetables in the centre and the shortest or creeping species on the edges. Note that the driest soil will be located at the surface, which helps to stop weeds from growing. But you will need to hand-water seedlings from above for a couple of weeks until their roots get going. When you have finished planting, add a layer of mulch.

Left: Hand-feeding geese is a daily ritual that tickles my fancy and my fingers.

Right: Self-seeded fennel grows en masse at Black Barn Farm.

FLOWERS EN MASSE

The season of high heat is also the season of flowers growing en masse at Black Barn Farm. So we wouldn't compete with the few small-scale, ethical flower growers nearby, we made a decision to only plant flowers that are either edible or used for pollination between the orchard rows. It means that we have loads of fennel, zinnias, leek, comfrey, echinacea and globe artichokes. They send the bees into overdrive, are self-propagating and don't need high-quality soil, so they have been great for providing ground covers while returning a crop – and a pretty one, too. For anyone who threw seeds around their backyard a few months ago, this is the time to reap the rewards.

TAKE A GANDER AT GEESE

Hand-feeding my geese (and I say 'my' geese intentionally) is a daily highlight. More than any other activity on the farm, this job assaults your senses and demands that you are in the moment. Some days I get into a bit of a dazed rhythm, but this changes when I bob down with a handful of wheat; the cacophonous noise of the geese smashes the daze, while their impatient beaks roughly tickle my fingers and their expectation for more closes in. They all let me pat them, but two are happy to press right up close so I can feel their soft downiness. They are Toulouse geese, which are notoriously hard to breed but reputedly gentler than most geese despite their enormous size.

Geese are excellent guards in the garden, making an enormous racket when anything is out of the ordinary. They keep the grass down in our bottom garden, and spread their waste nutrients through the orchard paddock; during spring, they lay eggs that are around three times the size of a chicken's. However, they also nip off seedlings and ringbark young grafted fruit trees if the gate is left open.

Feast

SUMMER IN A JAR

There's something virtuous about bottling sweet summer fruits for a rainy day. There's something even more virtuous when they are foraged fruits from the side of the road. If you have the inclination, there's nothing better than a spontaneous leap into the car for a scrumping mission – the alluring art of gathering your food from roadsides and empty blocks all over the countryside. It smacks of seasonal connection, offers a thrill-of-the-hunt adrenaline burst and provides an abundance of beautiful food that would otherwise go to waste.

You'll stand on your tiptoes, stuff as many fruits into your mouth as into the box, and marvel at how much food exists on the side of the road, free for the feasting. In Victoria, scrumping season starts just after Christmas, with early-season peaches, apricots and nectarines plus blackberries galore. It picks up pace in February, with the addition of plums; by March, there are apples on offer, too. If you get into the scrumping swing – and I promise that the chance of addiction to this activity is high – you'll eventually build a mind map showing where all of the best trees are located, and the time of year they offer their bounty.

Be sure to always have good fruit-carrying vessels in your car at this time of year, as you never know when a laden tree will beckon. You'll want to pull over straight away and pick fruits until your arms ache.

Clockwise from top left: Removing pits from apricots; foraged hawthorn berries; preserving apricots for winter stores; basil, ready for making pesto.

Preserving stone fruits

Once you are home with your harvest, gorge until you can no longer eat and then bottle the rest of the fruits. I do loads of preserving, so I keep my stone-fruit process pretty simple:

- Wash and halve each fruit, and then pack the pieces tightly into sterilised jars. I use Fowlers jars, but you can use anything that has a sealable lid.
- Add a few small chips of vanilla bean to each jar.
- Make a light sugar syrup, enough to fill each jar to the top. I use a ratio of 1 cup (220 g) of sugar to 6 cups (1.5 litres) of water. I use rapadura sugar, which has a caramel flavour that I love; however, it does make the water brown, which some people don't like.
- Fill each jar with syrup, making sure that the fruit pieces are completely submerged.
- Slap on your rubber rings, lids and clips if you are using Fowlers jars, or just normal lids if not.
- Place the jars into a pot of water, and let them simmer gently at 60 degrees Celsius (140 degrees Fahrenheit). I use a Fowlers stovetop pot, but before I found it at a garage sale, I just used my big soup pot. Be careful not to let the water go past the lid, and to simmer the jars for just one hour. Keep your eye on the temperature, or the fruits will turn to mush – then they have to be eaten with ice-cream straight away.

ENJOY A PICNIC

Picnics are our go-to for lots of meals and snacks. Often it's just our family plonking down outside under a tree, but sometimes we meet mates at the local lookout for dinner or enjoy a lunchtime meal on the riverbank.

Picnics are more fun and less work than an inside meal. By their true essence, they need to be simple to prepare, easy to carry and quick to eat. We create food depending on what we have available, so the following recipes contain ingredients that can be swapped out if you have different items in your fridge, pantry, garden or community plot. Have a little fun experimenting with your picnic foods, and consider any time of day perfect for picnics, especially in summer.

Our picnic plates nearly always include cut-up carrots, tomatoes and beans straight from the garden. However, if we're feeling more fancy, some of our favourite picnic foods include:

◆ summer vegie tart (see page 191)
◆ chia pudding (see page 192)
◆ greens with flowers and the best dressing ever (see right)
◆ roasted vegie and black lentil salad with fresh herbs and goat cheese (see page 188)
◆ dill pickles (see page 187)
◆ pear chutney (see page 230)
◆ apple and custard tart (see pages 264–5)
◆ pickled eggs (see page 124) with green tahini paste and sourdough bread
◆ a jar of fresh medjool dates – we buy these in bulk, straight from the food co-op (they make a perfect picnic dessert or sweet treat with a morning or afternoon cup of coffee)
◆ cold left-over chops with chutney
◆ zucchini (courgette) fritters (great for the mid-summer glut)
◆ pikelets with homemade jam.

GREENS WITH FLOWERS AND THE BEST DRESSING EVER

We make this salad as a side for nearly every meal, including breakfast, during summer. It is easy to make enough for everybody by using a mixture of whatever greens are on hand, such as Tuscan kale, Red Russian kale, butterhead lettuce, mignonette lettuce, red-veined sorrel, lemon sorrel, rocket (arugula) and spinach. It's worth stretching the salad with some foraged weeds, such as broadleaf plantain, marshmallow, nasturtium, dandelion and fat hen (but make sure you have correctly identified the plant). You can also add fresh herbs for extra zing, such as parsley, coriander (cilantro), Alexanders, basil and mint.

The edible flowers you add are entirely up to you. This list is certainly not exhaustive, but readily available flowers that are edible and easy to grow include:

◆ chamomile
◆ chives
◆ cosmos
◆ dill
◆ fennel
◆ fruit blossoms such as apple, cherry, pear, plum, apricot, nectarine and peach
◆ marigold
◆ nasturtium
◆ rosemary
◆ sage
◆ thyme
◆ violet.

Simply mix the greens and flowers together, and add a few roasted seeds and nuts. Pepitas (pumpkin seeds), sunflower seeds, almonds and hazelnuts are my favourites. Top the salad with creamy dressing (see page 192) and serve. If you're heading off on a picnic, hold the dressing until you're ready to eat so the leaves and petals don't wilt.

SUMMER WATER INFUSION

I've somehow made it through life drinking very little liquid at all, and only discovered the sensation of thirst in recent years. However, if you're anything like me, drinking eight glasses of water a day leaves you feeling drowned and uninspired. I have tried all sorts of tricks to keep the liquid flowing, but this must be the simplest and most interesting. It can vary depending on what you've got in the fridge, freezer and garden, and you can add to the infusion throughout the day – the flavour gets stronger the longer the ingredients sit in the water.

Inspire your lacklustre commitment to the wet stuff by adding:

- apple slices (although these go brown quickly, so the water doesn't look flash)
- berries
- cooled herbal tea
- ginger slices
- honey
- kiwi-fruit slices
- lavender
- lemon slices
- mint
- orange slices
- rose petals
- rosemary
- stone-fruit slices (such as plum or peach).

There's no formula and no rules. Play around with your favourite flavours, and get your body hydrated. Infusions are perfect for an interesting picnic drink.

HOMEMADE SUMMER POPSICLES

Although these are easy to make and taste like sugary treats, they are actually good for you! Made from the freshest of seasonal ingredients, these popsicles evoke summer months spent by the beach.

I encourage you to explore new flavours, experiment with new textures and trial new combinations. There are no rules – your success is limited only by your imagination. You really can't go wrong for your belly, your tastebuds or your commitment to using fresh, local and waste-free foods – especially if you follow just a few general principles (not rules!):

- Anything juice-based will freeze faster than anything cream-based.
- Juice is packed with fructose, so don't overdo the sweetness by adding sugar to fruit-based combinations.
- Don't be lured by the desire to own and use specially created popsicle containers or fancy-pants ice-cream makers.
- Keep it super simple and fun – shun the multistep process that many of the glam mags will have you believe is the only way to create such special desserts.

For creamy popsicles, we use a base of either natural yoghurt or coconut milk; banana works well, too. For icy popsicles, we use apple juice – but that's because we have it in never-ending quantities. It's super sweet, so we have to dilute it. We actually love to use pineapple and orange juice, too, as they are not quite as sickly sweet.

Right: Boost your fluid intake with water infusions.

Far right: Get imaginative with summer popsicle ingredients.

How to make these treats

For creamy popsicles, simply blend two parts cream with one part fruit in your chosen flavours before pouring the mixture into your chosen moulds (small drinking glasses and jars work just as well as dedicated silicon, plastic or stainless-steel ice-cream holders). You can use a spoon or metal straw as your handle if you don't have popsicle sticks. For icy popsicles, place one part solid fruit into your mould and pour one part liquid over the top. Here are some tasty blends to try:

- apple juice + peach pieces + mint
- coconut milk + banana + choc chips
- coconut milk + banana + nutmeg
- lime juice + coconut + raspberry
- mango purée + banana slices + strawberry pieces

- natural yoghurt + puréed strawberries (swirl them together in the mould)
- natural yoghurt + mixed berries
- orange juice + coconut + lychee
- orange juice + kiwi-fruit slices + lemon balm
- pineapple juice + mint + coconut
- watermelon juice + strawberry slices + mango pieces.

Play with colours, textures and flavours. Try adding edible flowers to the edges. If you want striped popsicles, simply freeze them in multiple stages. No matter what you do, you can't go wrong!

Far left: The sight, feel and smell of dried herbs for tea are heady.

Left: Pickling cucumbers is a daily job at this time of year.

GROW, DRY AND BLEND YOUR OWN TEA

Herbal tea blends smack your senses on all fronts. The smell is heady, the colour is like a vibrant oil painting, and the temptation to plunge your fingers into the crunchy petals and crispy leaves is not worth fighting.

We grow all of our own tea herbs in the garden: chamomile, lavender, peppermint, spearmint, chocolate mint, lemon balm, lemon verbena, rosemary, basil, fennel and sage. You'll also find other tea ingredients in our garden: lemon and orange (we use the peel), dandelion, rose, mountain pepper, elderberry and viburnum.

We dry the leaves, berries and peels during the high heat of summer on our drying racks before we store them all separately so we can mix our own blends throughout the year. Each tea blend has its own glorious flavour and packs a seriously aromatic punch.

Fennel, lemon balm and mint are firm favourites at Black Barn Farm. These herbs are fast growing, require little help to reproduce and are fantastic for soothing frayed nerves when used fresh in boiling water with a dash of lemon juice and a little honey. They are delightful hot or cold, fresh or dried.

CUCUMBER GLUT

Our kids eat cucumbers like apples, so we use up to 15 each day. For this reason, I plant them in our paddock patch, our kitchen garden and our polytunnel. This works perfectly at the beginning and end of the growing season, but not so much when the ripening pace picks up in the heart of the season. I hate to waste food, so once I have more than 20 cucumbers coming in each day, it's time for pickling (see the dill pickles recipe opposite).

Hawthorn berry sauce

This is a great way to use foraged berries. Just remember to remove all the seeds (see step 3), as they contain cyanide.

Makes approx. 600 ml (21 fl oz)

500 g (1 lb 2 oz) hawthorn berries

300 ml (10½ fl oz) apple cider vinegar (see page 221)

300 ml (10½ fl oz) water

170 g (6 oz) sugar

½ teaspoon salt

½ teaspoon freshly crushed black pepper

1. Wash the hawthorn berries well. Ensure that all stalks and leaves are removed.
2. Pop the berries into a saucepan with the apple cider vinegar and water, and bring to the boil. Reduce the heat to low, and simmer for 30 minutes or until the berry skins start to split.
3. Remove the berries from the heat, and pass them through a sieve to remove any seeds and skins.
4. Pour the liquid into a clean saucepan, and add the sugar. Simmer over low heat, stirring until the sugar has dissolved.
5. Bring the liquid to the boil for 10 minutes or until it has reduced to a syrup consistency. Remove the liquid from the heat.
6. Stir in the salt and pepper, and then pour the liquid into sterilised bottles. If the bottles are properly sealed, the sauce will keep in the pantry for up to a year. The sauce works well with roasted meats.

Dill pickles

This recipe varies for each batch, depending on what I have in the pantry, and the quantities are to taste. Batch sizes are also entirely dependent on what's coming in from the daily harvest. I tend to do a batch when I get overrun with the daily pick and need to process large quantities quickly. It's not a hard process, but it can be fiddly – so I do a batch of seven 1 litre (35 fl oz) jars each morning. This recipe is based on having a full pot of seven jars.

Makes 700 g (1 lb 9 oz)

½ teaspoon mustard seeds in each jar

½ tablespoon dill seeds in each jar

½ teaspoon coriander seeds in each jar

1 garlic bulb, peeled, in each jar

½ teaspoon very lightly crushed black pepper in each jar

2 teaspoons sugar in each jar

1 teaspoon salt in each jar

Enough cucumbers, whole, sliced or quartered (I use all three), to fill each jar

4 cups (1 litre) apple cider vinegar divided between the seven jars

Fennel or dill flowers, if desired

1. Place all of the ingredients except the fennel or dill flowers into each jar.
2. Top up each jar with water if necessary.
3. Finish each jar by pressing fennel or dill flowers into the top of the mixture if desired, but ensure they are submerged beneath the liquid.
4. Place the lid on each jar, and boil at 60 degrees Celsius (140 degrees Fahrenheit) for 45 minutes (don't boil for any longer or let the temperature get any hotter, or the cucumbers will turn to mush).
5. Store the jars in the pantry for up to three years. The dill pickles are ready to eat immediately, but the flavour improves if you wait a few days before opening each jar.

Roasted vegie and black lentil salad with fresh herbs and goat cheese

I've chosen this recipe because it's a great way to make use of 'fridge stores'. These are the things that we often make en masse and store in the fridge for use in a whole range of different meal options. They make snacking healthy, easy and waste-free, and they use the food from our garden in an appealing way. They also use wholefoods that we buy from the co-op, and they make midweek family meals a fun activity, not a drawn-out mission. Making this particular meal is an exercise in assembly rather than cooking; having pre-prepared fridge stores such as rice, lentils, greens and roasted vegies makes this super quick and simple.

Serves 5 as a main or 10 as a side

3 cups (600 g) precooked pulses or grains (lentils, brown rice … whatever you have in your fridge stores or cupboard; to get the best flavour, cook them with stock or mix them with nutritional yeast or salt after cooking)

3 cups (450 g) roasted vegies (such as beetroot, onion, potato, pumpkin [squash] and sweet potato; be sure to roast them with plenty of garlic, salt and herbs so they're packed with flavour)

1 cup (30 g) blanched or fresh greens (such as chopped rocket [arugula], spinach, lettuce, foraged greens or a mixture)

1 cup (30 g) fresh mixed leafy herbs (such as chives, basil, parsley, mint, coriander [cilantro] or a mixture)

½ cup (75 g) mixed roasted seeds and nuts (such as pepitas [pumpkin seeds], sunflower seeds, almonds, hazelnuts or walnuts)

½ cup (75 g) currants

Handful of fresh edible flowers, to garnish

Handful of fresh feta broken into pieces, to garnish

Mustard vinaigrette or creamy dressing (see page 192), to serve

1. Place the grains, vegies, greens, herbs, seeds/nuts and currants into a large bowl, and mix well.
2. Pile the salad high on a platter or in individual bowls.
3. Scatter the flowers and feta over the top.
4. Dress with mustard vinaigrette or creamy dressing, and serve.

Summer vegie tart

The most seasonal grab-and-go meal we eat in summer is a simple vegie tart. We always have eggs, but the tart changes depending on the vegetables we have in the patch. With little more than a quick dice of a few freshly picked ingredients, the tart can be whipped up for lunch or dinner. It can be eaten hot or cold, and it's perfect when served with chutney (pear is our favourite!).

Serves 5 as a main

3 cups (450 g) diced seasonal vegies

Salt, to taste

8 eggs, whisked

A few dollops of easy pesto (see page 157)

Handful of crumbled cheese (this is a great way to use up the last of the feta in the pot or leftovers from cheese platters if you've had guests)

Chutney, to serve

1. Preheat the oven to 180 degrees Celsius (350 degrees Fahrenheit).
2. Place the diced vegies into a frying pan, add salt to taste and brown over low heat. You can use zucchini (courgettes), tomatoes, fresh herbs, silverbeet (Swiss chard), kale, corn, spring onions (scallions), peas, beans … whatever you've got. If you use pumpkins (squash), potatoes or carrots, it will take longer to brown the pieces.
3. Mix the browned vegies, whisked eggs, pesto and crumbled cheese together in a baking dish, and place into the oven. Cook for 25 minutes, or until the egg is set and the tart is golden.
4. Serve with chutney. See page 230 for our favourite pear chutney recipe.

Creamy dressing

I always make more of this dressing than needed, and keep the extra in the fridge. You can make this dairy-free by using mayonnaise instead of yoghurt, but it will be oilier and not as creamy.

Makes 1 cup (250 ml)

½ cup (130 g) full-fat Greek-style yoghurt

Juice of 2 large lemons

¼ cup (60 ml) olive oil

1 tablespoon apple cider vinegar (see page 221)

2 garlic cloves, finely minced

1 teaspoon finely sliced chives

Drizzle of honey (warm it up first so it melts and blends)

1 teaspoon wholegrain mustard

Pinch of salt

Quick grind of pepper

1. Tip all of the ingredients into a clean jar, seal well and shake until combined.
2. Add the dressing to your favourite salad. Store the jar in the fridge for up to four days.

Chia pudding

This is a definite treat! We try to buy the ingredients we don't grow from our local co-op so we know their origin.

Makes 5 or 6 small puddings

400 ml (14 fl oz) organic coconut milk (you can use coconut cream, but you'll need to add a little water so it's not too thick)

½ cup (100 g) chia seeds

1 cup (150 g) fresh berries

Honey, for drizzling

Roasted coconut flakes, to garnish

1. Mix the coconut milk and chia seeds together, and pour into five or six glasses or jars.
2. Allow the puddings to sit for 10 minutes so they thicken.
3. Once the puddings have thickened, place a cluster of berries on top of each.
4. Drizzle with honey, sprinkle with coconut flakes and serve.

HARVEST

There's no denying that it's been a slog. It'd be easy to get all rosy-eyed about the virtuousness of growing your own food, but let's be real – it's a big job. However, in this 'harvest' season, you get to reap the rewards for the last six months of plotting, prepping, planting, weeding, watering, thinning and training. But not without one last job: PICKING.

Pull out the bottling jars and the pickling kit, make space in the freezer, wipe down the shelves in the shed and clear the decks – the harvest is on!

The basil becomes pesto, tomato makes passata (puréed tomatoes), and fat pumpkins (squash) rest on cool, dry shelves. There's stewed apple by the bucketful, pear chutney for days, beetroot and cucumber to pickle, and eggplant (aubergine) to roast for baba ghanoush. The corn and beans need blanching and freezing, while the potatoes and carrots can rest a little longer in their dirty beds.

Not only is it the season to harvest fresh fruits and vegies, but it's also the time to cull roosters and sheep for our annual meat needs. After a good life in the pens and paddocks, it's their one bad day – but we respectfully honour their lives and use everything they offer.

The days are shorter and cooler, but definitely not slower. They are filled to overflowing with winter preparation and productivity. What isn't stored now is never eaten, so the pressure is on. Each day is a juggle to preserve the most urgently overflowing bucket of abundance.

This is the pinnacle of the year, when we can revel in the fruits of our labour. But don't just tip your hat to prosperity: this is a significant season for those who grow food. Actually, it's significant for everyone, if you allow it to be. It marks the downward turn that is now upon us. It's the seasonal beginning of autumn, so try to actively observe the changing world around you: the turning of leaf tips, the vegie patch sprouting a few more seed heads, the air no longer holding its comfortable warmth and the lengthening shadows behind the trees.

MABON: AUTUMN EQUINOX

Our attitude to the equinox, or Mabon, is one of complete gratitude and openness. The spiritual potency of this time creates a universal balance between dark and light, masculine and feminine, and inner and outer before the steep slide into the darkness of winter.

The autumn equinox (which occurs on 20–21 March in the southern hemisphere, and 22–23 September in the northern hemisphere) is a time to acknowledge the coming darkness, to hold gratitude in your heart for the lessons that help you grow, and to let go of everything else. It's also a time to harvest both the abundant food stores and your inner awareness, finding thankfulness for the seeds that you have both sown and reaped.

Rituals at this time can be beautiful, simple and obvious – such as rustic harvest gatherings, twilight picnics, potluck feasts and bonfires – or perhaps more introverted, such as writing gratitude letters, practising mindfulness meditations, unleashing your inner child with creative activities or going for walks.

Give yourself the ultimate gift of time, even if it's only a little window each day to breathe deeply and nod appreciatively at all that's going on around you.

Ritual

EASTER RITUALS

Easter often feels like the last hurrah. It's a four-day break when the weather is usually spectacular, and the rivers, lakes and ocean are still warm enough for little kids to swim and big kids to dabble. It's a chance to loll around with friends over camp-fire fare and home brew.

It's our busiest time of year in the orchard, with the pick-your-own activity in full swing, but it's also the most beautiful season thanks to the stable weather delivering clear, warm days, no wind and little rain.

Even when the days are crazy, there is always time to make Easter special. The kids traipse around the farm for the obligatory 5 am egg hunt (their preferred time, not ours), and they return with fistfuls of brightly coloured, sweet-smelling mini eggs. They scoff these before breakfast like sugar-deprived heathens.

But their favourite Easter treat actually happens on Easter Saturday, when they pretend to be little birds and scour the ground right across the farm, collecting anything that catches their eye – baling twine, wire, fabric, feathers, stones, petals, leaves, flowers, seed heads, bark and straw. They fill their baskets with a clutch of goodies that usually forms a loose theme, select their spot and assemble their 'nests'.

These are the most beautiful creations: sometimes big, sometimes small, sometimes on a mat or perhaps the grass, sometimes consisting of layer upon layer and sometimes just made of single-layered rings. They form organically, based on what was found; colours clash, blend, bleed and complement. The nests might be feminine, soft, masculine, robust, autumnal, floral or industrial.

There are no rules on colour, materials, size, shape or time taken to create – actually, the kids can sometimes spend hours making their nests, and the care taken with the task is beautiful to watch. The only consideration given is to where the main egg will sit. There's sometimes a little clutch of sheep's wool, a handful of feathers or perhaps a fistful of straw. The early-morning egg hunt finishes back at the nests, with each now hosting a single, beautiful, chocolate egg.

A festive brunch follows the hunt, before the mid-morning activity of egg blowing. This became a family ritual more recently, as everyone can now take part in it. We all sit at the table together, and it can occur rain, hail or shine.

We prick a hole at each end of an egg with a pin, and blow hard into one of the holes (the egg white and yolk that come out of the other hole get scrambled for lunch). Out comes the box of goodies that have been gathered all year: left-over wrapping paper, paint, crayons, glue, fabric, wool, glitter, magazine pictures and more. And away we go, decorating the eggs.

Over the years, we've created many of these fragile masterpieces. We do our best to keep these ephemeral creations safe, but inevitably they return to the earth in time.

Nourish

HEALTHCARE HARVEST

This season is the climax after the previous nine months of work. Your body, mind and soul are all tired right now, and anything you have in reserve will be squeezed from you during this final harvest hurrah. It's important to stay on top of your self-nurturing during this time.

Warm yourself with earthy food

This type of food is ripe right now, and your body needs exactly what's on offer, not only for nutrition but also for energy. By harvesting and feasting on the things that are fresh, you'll help your body prepare for the workload and the dormant season soon to come. Fresh crunchy salads are so last season. Make way for root vegetables, and autumn fruits such as apples, quinces and pears. Add some warming spices such as cinnamon, nutmeg, ginger and cardamom to your dishes.

Friends and feasts

Make plenty of time to cook with the freshest of foods and the closest of friends. The madness of high-heat social antics is behind you, but just before you slip into the quieter months, gather your closest crew and take time to cook and feast together. A potluck dinner is wonderful (see page 94), but so is cooking from scratch while standing side by side.

Give your lungs a helping hand

Your lungs (which are traditionally associated with this season) need all the assistance they can get during these busy months, so respond to their call for pungent foods to protect them. Foods such as horseradish and garlic will help to relieve respiratory infections, so get stuck in.

Get spicy

The easiest way to boost blood movement is to add a little spice to your diet. Try garlic, horseradish, cinnamon, ginger, golden milk (featuring turmeric) or chai (with cardamom and other spices). Some other worthy and nourishing foods to get stuck into at every opportunity during this season are dark, leafy greens. Think kale, spinach, silverbeet (Swiss chard) and collard greens, which are rich in vitamins A, B, C and K, and packed with fibre. These greens get sweeter as the nights get colder, so revel in their crisp and nutritious deliciousness.

Right: Rinsing off vegies in the outdoor sink helps to stop mud being brought inside the house.

SET UP AN OUTDOOR SINK

I bet you never imagined that an outdoor sink could be so wonderful! In our case, an old laundry tub salvaged from a tumbledown shed has been the single-best addition we've made to our vegie patch. It is never more appreciated than during the harvest season, when buckets and baskets full of produce are coming straight from the dirt and getting dragged towards the kitchen. Before we even leave the garden, we scoot past the garden sink, rinse off all of the dirt, and top and tail any compost items (such as corn husks or outer leaves). We then arrive at the kitchen bench with fresh, clean food that is ready to prepare.

Our sink is hooked up to the house water, but it doesn't have to be that flash to be effective. As a kid, our garden sink was simply an old basin that sat below the tank and ran out onto the lawn, with a little bench either side to rest on. You could even set up a little bench right next to the garden hose (if there are no water restrictions in your area). We keep a chopping board, sharp knife and clean bucket at the sink so we minimise the hard yards in the kitchen, which takes a pounding at this time of year. Now the kitchen is a place for cooking, not making mud!

Grow

MAKE A MEDICINAL GARDEN

According to ancient Greek physician Hippocrates, 'food is thy medicine'. I'm not a herbal health expert, and I've not written this book to share extensive wisdom on the topic. But a book about connection to the natural world, ritual building, self-care, nourishment, localisation and seasonal life would not be complete without acknowledging that an ability to make and use herbal remedies would join the dots for resilience as comprehensively as food production.

Herbal health remedies are as much about the growing process and the power of pouring love into the creation of poultices and potions as they are about soothing a specific ailment. In the 'Home library' section at the end of the book, I have listed some of the most comprehensive herbal medicine books from my own home library, and, of course, online resources are abundant. However, I want to shine a light on the idea that you could in fact support your own health and vitality simply by using the plants that continue to play a critical role in the modern pharmaceutical industry.

You don't need to have an entire dedicated space in order to have a 'medicinal garden'. Many of the plants that provide goodness are readily found in lanes, parks, schools and backyards. You simply may not have realised what you have available. It's also worth reiterating that by shifting to a more homegrown, plant-based diet, you are immediately giving your own health a shot in the arm.

On the farm, we are embarking on a slow-burn project where we are growing the plants for a cluster of naturopaths, Ayurvedic specialists and holistic health professionals. We have to supply provenance-identified plants, so we actually do need a dedicated medicine garden – but even before I plotted out the area, I realised that many of the plants needed were already in my garden. Perhaps they're in yours, too. You just need to see them through the right lens!

Herbal medicine plays an important role in encouraging us to own our health responsibilities. It allows us to take charge of many of our own needs, so we're not so reliant on a publicly managed health service. Herbal health is often more focused on being preventive rather than reactionary, it is often slower to manage symptoms, and it relies on your own immune system to respond. However, it can still be powerful. So take your herbal healing seriously, be sure to do your own in-depth research and know that it can pack a punch and conflict with a pharmaceutical medicine regime, so consider your options carefully. If you have any concerns, ask your doctor before taking herbal remedies.

Top left: The herb haul sits pretty on the drying rack.

Bottom left: We tie our peppermint harvest with string before hanging it up to dry.

MEDICINAL PLANTS CHART

Of the 252 drugs considered 'basic and essential' by the World Health Organization at the beginning of the 21st century, 11 per cent were 'exclusively of flowering plant origin'. Numerous medicinal garden plants are commonly available. They are used in cooking, steeped in tea, utilised as a poultice or distilled into an oil.

COMMON NAME	LATIN NAME	COOKING (C), TEA (T), POULTICE (P) OR OIL (O)	BENEFITS
birch leaf	*Betula* species	T, P	anti-inflammatory, diuretic (anti-fluid retention)
broadleaf plantain	*Plantago major*	T, P, O	wound-healing aid, anti-ulcerative, antidiabetic, antidiarrhoeal, anti-inflammatory, antibacterial, antiviral
chamomile	*Matricaria recutita* and *Chamaemelum nobile*	T	calming, stress relief, insomnia relief
comfrey	*Symphytum* species	P, O	bone health, relieves aches and pains
dandelion	*Taraxacum officinale*	T	antioxidant, anti-inflammatory
echinacea	*Echinacea* species	T, P	immunity booster
elderberry	*Sambucus* species	O	antioxidant, immunity booster
evening primrose	*Oenothera biennis*	T, P, O	anti-inflammatory, blood-pressure support, can relieve menopause symptoms
fennel	*Foeniculum vulgare*	C, T, P	digestive aid, helps regulate blood pressure
garlic	*Allium sativum*	C, T, P, O	immunity booster, antimicrobial, cardiovascular support
ginger	*Zingiber officinale*	C, T, P	reduces nausea, relieves cold and flu symptoms
ginkgo leaf	*Ginkgo biloba*	T, O	can help boost brain health and slow cognitive decline

COMMON NAME	LATIN NAME	COOKING (C), TEA (T), POULTICE (P) OR OIL (O)	BENEFITS
lavender	*Lavandula* species	T, P, O	calming, insomnia relief, anti-anxiety support
lemon balm	*Melissa officinalis*	C, T, P, O	antioxidant, anti-anxiety, stress relief
lemon verbena	*Aloysia citriodora*	C, T, P, O	antioxidant, anti-anxiety, stress relief
mountain pepper	*Tasmannia lanceolata*	C, P	antioxidant, general wellbeing
nettle	*Urtica dioica*	C, T	anti-inflammatory, antihistamine
peppermint	*Mentha x piperita*	C, T, P, O	digestive aid
rosemary	*Rosmarinus officinalis*	C, T, P, O	antioxidant, neurological protector and stimulant
sage	*Salvia officinalis*	C, T, P	antioxidant, oral health support, menopause support
spearmint	*Mentha spicata*	C, T, P, O	antioxidant, anti-anxiety, stress relief
tea-tree	*Leptospermum* species	T, P, O	antimicrobial, good for cleaning cuts, can relieve skin irritations
thyme	*Thymus vulgaris*	C, T, P, O	immunity booster, packed with vitamins and minerals
tulsi	*Ocimum tenuiflorum*	T, P	'elixir of life', can relieve respiratory ailments and assist with some blood disorders, antiseptic
turmeric	*Curcuma longa*	C, T, P	anti-inflammatory, antioxidant

COMPOST TEAS FOR THE GARDEN

With production of food at its annual high right now, it's worth considering the nutrient depletion of the soil around the plants that produce all that food. Hailed as soil saviours, compost teas are quick, homemade tonics that replenish some of the lost nutrients, expediting plant growth and fruit ripening, and improving soil vitality. Using compost teas to increase the population of mycorrhizal fungi and encourage microbial activity in the soil helps to break down organic matter and release important nutrients for plants; some of the microorganisms also protect plants against disease.

I spent time at an Australian ashram once, where one of the daily chores was to rake up the rabbit and kangaroo poo in the paddocks so it could be soaked in big bathtubs before the liquid was strained and distributed all over the garden. Even in a suburban backyard, this is definitely an easy solution that you can create yourself without spending too much money or getting hung up on scientific complexities.

You can apply compost teas to your garden beds once a year at any time or even multiple times of the year. There are actually two different types of tea:

1. **An aerated biological tea** – Some argue that this is the true compost tea. Put simply, you take a handful of compost, wrap it in muslin, dunk it in water, feed it carbohydrates (sugar) and aerate it to develop the aerobic microorganisms before applying the liquid to your garden. I'd encourage you to research and explore this, especially the Elaine Ingham Soil Foodweb model. It is mildly complicated but well worth the invested time.
2. **A fermented infusion tea** – The greens or compost of choice are placed in a muslin bag and dumped in the water to infuse and ferment for 24–36 hours before applying the liquid to your garden. The trick with this method is to be 100 per cent sure that the greens or compost used are absolutely clean (greens should be washed first, and compost should be well broken down so it smells good and sweet, not putrid) and to ensure that they are not left to ferment for longer than 36 hours. A longer fermentation time can make the liquid anaerobic, and this can cause the proliferation of bacteria and fungi that actually hinder not help soil and plant health.

Make a tea

To create a simple compost tea, you'll need:

◆ a clean 20-litre (5-gallon) bucket or tub (or 2 x 10-litre [2½-gallon] buckets)
◆ 20 litres (5 gallons) of non-chlorinated water (if you're on town water, just leave it in the bucket for 24 hours before adding compost)
◆ 200 g (7 oz) of compost or 400 g (14 oz) of fresh green leaves from plants such as comfrey, borage or nettle (these are high in phosphorus and potassium), placed inside a muslin bag
◆ 2 tablespoons of liquid fish or kelp fertiliser (this is easily bought from a hardware store)
◆ 1 tablespoon of molasses or an equivalent, such as raw sugar or golden syrup (but not honey).

Place all of the ingredients into the bucket, and allow them to soak for 24 hours – at that point, put your senses on high alert and observe the compost tea. Does it smell clean? Is it free of a film on top? If so, aerate it by stirring gently before leaving it to infuse for longer (but no more than 36 hours in

total), If not, you will have to throw out the mixture and start again.

To apply, mix one part compost tea with five parts water, and saturate the garden beds or pots. You cannot apply too much. I often soak our pots with it before planting out, to give the plants a healthy start.

HAND-WATERING HEAVEN

How big is your garden? Is it too big to water by hand? For years I fussed about our lack of automated watering, especially in our food-production gardens. I fussed mostly because it meant that I was tied to a hose for two hours in the morning and two hours at night most days during the harvest season when actually my time would have been better spent preserving the harvest … or would it?

Now that we have automated watering for 50 per cent of our gardens, I spend significantly less time in those spaces. Yes, it's more efficient, but what I've inadvertently done is cut down on my observation time. While holding a hose in my hand, I would also weed, redistribute mulch, check soil health, observe pests and insects, notice emerging fungal or rust issues, see pollinators at work, and interact in the space with an intimacy that comes only from many hours of unrushed time. I can't believe that I'm writing this, but the hours I spent hand-watering were actually a precious gift of time, observation and intimate interaction.

WINTER VEGIE PLANTING

While it's hard to turn your head towards winter when you're up to your eyeballs in summer vegies, you need to get your winter seedlings underway now so you don't miss your window to get them into the ground

prior to the soil turning cold. Before the harvest really hits top gear, try to get these three things organised:

1. **Seedling trays** – Ensure that they're ready to have seeds dropped into them (see page 101 for the best seed-raising mix).
2. **Seed stores** – Check to make sure you have enough of what you need to get you through winter (swap with other growers to get a range of produce).
3. **Garden plans** – Check your records for what you planted where last winter, and do a preliminary sketch of where you will be planting your earliest spring vegies. Once this is considered, you can decide where to plant the winter crops. They'll be in the ground for five or six months, so be sure that they won't interrupt other plantings.

As I mentioned earlier, our growing season is often thwarted by early and late frosts, so we installed a polytunnel for the sole purpose of extending our growing ability. This gives us much more scope for our winter crops.

Seedlings will go into trays now for crops of green cabbage, savoy cabbage, broccoli, cauliflower, kohlrabi, red Russian kale and Tuscan kale. We direct-plant seeds for spring onion (scallion), beetroot, mustard greens and lettuce, and cloves for garlic (see pages 144–5 for details on growing garlic).

AN APPLE A DAY

There are more than 7500 types of apple known worldwide. However, when I run workshops for schoolkids, the most they've ever named for me is 12 – and, sadly, this number always includes 'red apples' and 'green apples'. At Black Barn Farm, we have 98 varieties of heritage apples, including cider, cooking, dessert and crabapples. We've scoured the country for them all – seeking

various pollination periods, harvest periods, tastes and usefulness. How many varieties can you list? See pages 238–41 for our favourites.

CITRUS LOVE

Citrus trees are shallow-rooted, so they're not great foragers; they benefit greatly from regular feeding (every six weeks or so). If I've let this slip before the harvest season, then it's important that it doesn't get forgotten in the peak of their flowering and early fruit-set days. The easiest thing to feed them is chicken manure. Ensure that it's well broken down so it doesn't burn the roots, and don't disturb the roots when you feed the trees – just place the manure around their drip line (the edge of their foliage). In addition to chicken poo, they also appreciate iron and an acidic soil, so using iron sulphate or anything that's high in potassium and nitrogen is good.

THE POWER OF THE CHICKEN SCRATCH

At the end of every growing season, we gut the beds, turn over the soil and re-mulch, but one profoundly worthwhile step is sometimes overlooked: the chicken scratch! It's just as it sounds. Once the beds are clear of old plants, we set up a temporary pen made from chicken wire, pop a chicken or two in and let them work over the ground.

They diminish the immediate insect problem by eating them, and they disrupt the next cycle by disturbing or eating the larvae. Their scratching breaks up the topsoil, they add some nutrient-rich poo to the mix, and they do a marvellous job of churning it all over. Soon the garden bed is ready for the mulch, a green-manure crop or to be left fallow until the next planting season. Why use a pitchfork when you can just add chickens?

Feast

PANTRY FOOD

We call our harvested food stores 'pantry food'. The acts of preserving, dehydrating, bottling, freezing, fermenting and salting our food stores during the harvest season occur purely with our winter bellies in mind. No method is more correct than another. The technique you choose depends on your preference as well as your space, time, needs and uses – but don't let your 'skills' be the determining factor in how you store your excess food.

During winter, the vegie patch is bare save for the odd brassica, so most meals rely on our squirrelled stash from the height of the harvest. Providing we have a normal growing season without unexpected pests or extreme weather events, we can generally store enough in the cupboard and freezer to get us through to early spring.

For a family of five (and our WWOOFers), our pantry list is quite extensive. Homesteading at this scale has taken 15 years of rhythm building, as well as trial and error to get to these quantities, so it's by no means an overnight success. All of the jars that I use are recycled from op shops and differ in size, shape and quantity. I sometimes use Fowlers jars, but more often I use whatever I can source. You can do this, too, if you're eager to start preserving your own food.

This is what we store for winter, because we've restructured our life to do so. You don't have to commit to such a long list to be working towards your own food sovereignty.

Perhaps to begin you could consider what you might put into the pantry to kickstart your winter stores. Here's our list:

- 100 x 250 ml (9 fl oz) bottles of tomato sauce (see page 228 for recipe) or tomato passata (puréed tomatoes)
- 12 x 1 litre (35 fl oz) bottles of pickled olives
- 20 x 1 litre (35 fl oz) bottles of stewed apple
- 80 litres (20 gallons) of apple cider vinegar
- 200 garlic bulbs (see pages 144–5 for growing and storage tips)
- Around 60 pumpkins (squash; see page 222 for storage)
- 50 jars of dill pickles (see page 187 for recipe) and preserved beans
- 20 jars of pickled beetroot
- 20 jars of pear chutney (see page 230 for recipe)
- 15 jars of zucchini (courgette) and eggplant (aubergine) relish
- 8 jars of dried tea herbs/flowers: chamomile, peppermint, lemon balm, lavender, rose petals, lemon verbena
- 6 frozen sheep
- 12 frozen chickens
- 5 jars of dehydrated spring onions (scallions)
- 10 jars of marmalade or jam
- 6 jars of pickled green tomatoes
- 10 kg (20 lb) fermented Jerusalem artichokes (see page 302 for recipe)
- 40 kg (90 lb) potatoes (see page 222 for storage)

- 30 kg (70 lb) carrots (see page 222 for storage)
- 12 kg (25 lb) frozen sweet corn (no husks)
- 3 kg (6 lb 12 oz) broad beans
- 3 kg (6 lb 12 oz) dried podded beans (mixed varieties)
- 2 kg (4 lb 8 oz) dehydrated mushrooms (8 kg [about 20 lb] pre-dehydration)
- 100 softened and dried persimmons
- 5 kg (10 lb) frozen cooked spinach/ silverbeet (Swiss chard)
- 35 sticks of salami
- 10 kg (20 lb) frozen mixed berries
- 50 x 300 g (10½ oz) bags of pesto, frozen (see page 157 for recipe)
- 40 kg (90 lb) stewed stone fruits (either bottled or frozen)
- 12–15 x 250 ml (9 fl oz) bottles of plum sauce
- 2 kg (4 lb 8 oz) dehydrated apples (skin on)
- 24–48 x 250 ml (9 fl oz) bottles of home-brewed beer

In addition to this, we pick fresh citrus fruits by late winter/early spring, eggs and asparagus appear on the menu once the days lengthen, kale and silverbeet (Swiss chard) keep us going with greens, kimchi is always fermenting in the pantry, and we make a daily loaf of bread to satisfy the carb craving.

We buy anything that we don't grow from our local food co-op. Grains, seeds, nuts, flours, oil and coconut milk are the main things we have to purchase.

Preserving season

Yes, it's harvest season, but perhaps a more accurate name would be the harvest and preserving season. It's an eternal quandary. You can only eat so much, and even when you cleverly plan your garden, utilise succession planting and give away some produce, an inevitable glut is still the reality. That's when you start the preserving process.

TOMATO TIDE

Without a doubt, our biggest preserving effort involves the tomatoes. We plant 80 heritage varieties, so the range on offer over this season is huge. Our favourites are Black Russian, Mortgage Lifter, Yellow Oxheart, Tommy Toe, Green Zebra and Grosse Lisse.

We usually harvest 100–120 kilograms (220–260 pounds) of tomatoes per season. Sometimes we're not so successful (as the weather was too hot, too dry, too wet or too humid, or there was low pollination), but even in a bad year we still pick 50–60 kilograms (110–130 pounds) of tomatoes over a three- to four-month period. We aim to fill 80–140 x 375 millilitre (13 fluid ounce) bottles with either tomato passata (puréed tomatoes) or tomato sauce to use throughout the year.

Making passata is as simple as whipping some tomatoes through the automatic sieve to remove the skins and seeds (these hold the bitterness), and then funnelling them into sterile jars before water-bathing them at 60 degrees Celsius (140 degrees Fahrenheit) for 40 minutes. Nothing else is added and the process is fast, but the flavour is nothing special. Passata is used in winter soups and as the base for slow-cooked stews.

Our tomato sauce (see page 228) is much more exciting. It uses more tomatoes as it is simmered for longer, so its flavour is enhanced.

SAVE THE SEEDS

We save tomato seeds by smearing the seed pulp onto paper towel and letting it dry in the sun. I spread the seeds out, so I can simply cut or tear the paper and drop it into the pots when it comes time to raise the seeds. I usually plant two or three seeds per pot, later discarding the weaker seedling(s) so the stronger one can thrive before we plant it out.

Left: We ripen the last of the green tomatoes by hanging them upside down for a week or two.

For dehydration, you don't need any fancy
equipment, and it's the perfect solution
to dwindling space in the fridge or freezer,
as most dehydrated foods can be stored
on a pantry shelf.

THE DELIGHT OF DEHYDRATING

This might be the oldest-known preservation
method in the world. Humans have been
dehydrating food for as long as we've had
the sun. There's evidence of Middle Eastern
and Asian peoples dehydrating food as early
as 12,000 BC.

You can dehydrate just about anything.
(My brother once tried dehydrating pizza,
which wasn't so flash ...) Depending on your
preferred level of chewiness, the process
can be surprisingly quick. The bonus is that
it's a bit 'set and forget', as the sun or warm
air does most of the work. You don't need
any fancy equipment, and it's the perfect
solution to dwindling space in the fridge
or freezer, as most dehydrated foods can
be stored on a pantry shelf.

If it's early enough in the season and the
sun still has plenty of kick, then we use our
homemade timber frames with fine-mesh
chicken wire stretched across them. This
works especially well for tomatoes, apples,
kale (see page 228), grapes and fruit leather
(puréed fruits spread thinly on baking paper
and placed on the mesh). When using the
sun to dehydrate food, you need to do a
few things:

- Make sure the food is cut into small,
  consistent pieces that will dry as evenly
  and as quickly as possible.
- Give the food as many hours of sunlight
  as possible. If the nights are cool, then
  move the food inside so it doesn't
  absorb moisture.
- Protect the top of the food with fine
  netting that still breathes.
- You can speed up the process by making
  a 'hot box'. This could be as simple as
  placing the mesh frame into an old
  bathtub lined with foil, or using an old
  meat safe with perspex on the outside
  and wire shelves on the inside. I've seen
  an old perspex display box decked out
  with mesh shelves that has been used
  effectively, too.

Once the sun's bite softens, we change our
process a little. We revert to only using the
sun to get the bulk of the work done, and
then finish off the process using an electric
dehydrator. It's not an expensive one (it
only cost us about AU$100), but it has
six stacking shelves and five different
temperature settings. It's pretty quiet, and
we put it on at night when our electricity
is off-peak. It costs about 6 cents an hour

Right: If possible, we dry our tomatoes on wire in the sun.

Far right: We utilise the dehydrator for mushroom stores, as it's too cold now to sun-dry them.

to run at night, and a full load of semidried tomatoes takes about six hours to dry on a low setting.

It's also possible to dry things using the ambient air temperature by stringing them up in a breezeway, hallway or door arch for a few weeks. Of course, you can also use the oven on a very low temperature; however, we only use this as a last resort, because the oven is expensive to run – even with a roof covered with solar panels.

Dehydrating using an electric dehydrator

While there are great guidelines you can apply to your dehydrating, there are no hard and fast rules simply because there are so many variables to consider:

+ How efficient is your dehydrator?
+ How chewy or dry do you like the finished product?
+ What is the water content of the food?
+ How thick is each cut piece? (Thicker food takes longer to dehydrate than thinner food.)
+ How many shelf layers will you use at the same time? (The more you use, the longer it takes.)
+ What brand of dehydrator are you using? (Wattage and temperature settings are important factors.)
+ What is the humidity level at your place? (Dehydrating any type of food will take much longer if you are in a humid environment.)

The best piece of advice is to actively get to know your equipment, processes, taste preferences and food varieties. For example, some of our apples dehydrate quickly, while other varieties are much slower. Keep a record book as a prompt for next year, when it's time to get it all out again.

DEHYDRATION CHART

This information will help you on your dehydrating journey. Use it as a starting place, and adapt it to suit your equipment, needs and preferences. Our preference is to use the sun.

FOOD PRODUCT	PREPARATION	TEMPERATURE	APPROXIMATE DRYING TIME	NOTES
apples	peel (or not) and slice	60°C (140°F)	12–14 hours	We leave the skin on and prefer them chewy to crunchy, so we call it quits at 10–12 hours.
apricots	pit and halve	60°C (140°F)	16–18 hours	Be sure they're free of moisture before storing, to avoid them going mouldy.
bananas	peel and slice	60°C (140°F)	16–18 hours	As for apricots.
berries	––	50°C (122°F)	7–9 hours	
cherries	pit	50°C (122°F)	6–8 hours	They are like little cranberries in size.
chillies	string	––	2–3 weeks	We string them above a doorway.
citrus peel	––	50°C (122°F)	12 hours	As well as using the sun, we also pop these on top of the wood box for 24 hours.
herbs	cut off stalks	––	1–2 weeks	We string them up around the verandah in bunches, and let them dry in the wind and sun.

FOOD PRODUCT	PREPARATION	TEMPERATURE	APPROXIMATE DRYING TIME	NOTES
kale	marinate (see page 228)	60°C (140°F)	10–12 hours	We use the Rayburn stove (see page 296) for this.
mushrooms	peel and slice	40°C (104°F)	6–8 hours	These can become paper-dry very quickly, so be sure to check them regularly.
nuts and seeds	use post-activation	40°C (104°F)	10–12 hours	See page 290 for activation details.
persimmons	peel, pit and slice	50°C (122°F)	4–6 weeks for the astringent variety; 10 hours for the non-astringent variety (fuyu fruit)	We peel, string and hang them for 4–6 weeks, and massage them each day to encourage the softening process. They get a fine white sugar all over them and will store for 12 months.
pomegranates	split and free the 'jewels' (seeds)	50°C (122°F)	6 hours	The 'jewels' dry much like sultanas and can easily dry in the sun, but the fruits often arrive too late in the season to catch hot days.
spring onions (scallions)	wash and slice	40°C (104°F)	6–8 hours	They dry fast. We avoid using the 'slimy' tops of the greens.

Far left: The weekly kombucha batch is always on the go in the pantry.

Left: A scrap apple vinegar batch sits in our 'kitchen buckets', which we use for all sorts of food production.

FABULOUS FERMENTATION

This must surely be one of the world's oldest methods of food preservation. Not only does it make your food stores last longer, but in many cases it also extends the nutritional value of the food. There are fat books on just this topic that I encourage you to explore, but if you are eager to dip your toe into the water, then the simplest activity that is most easily incorporated into family life is the single-ferment kombucha, a type of fizzy tea.

Single-ferment kombucha

This really is very easy to make at home. What's more, the homemade version is much healthier than its store-bought cousin. Here are the step-by-step instructions:

1. Place a scoby* into a clean, 1 litre (35 fl oz) jar with a wide mouth.
2. Brew 4 cups (1 litre) of medium-strength organic black tea with ¼ cup (55 g) of sugar, and make sure the sugar has dissolved.
3. Leave the tea until it's completely cool.
4. Pour the strained tea into the jar that contains the scoby.
5. Cover the jar with muslin cloth, and leave it in a cool, dry, dark place for three to five days.
6. Strain the tea into a clean storage jar with a tight-fitting lid, and refrigerate it for three days before consuming.
7. Wash the scoby, and repeat the process.

*The word 'scoby' is actually an acronym. It stands for 'symbiotic culture of bacteria and yeast'. It's a living, growing mass, and it needs to be cared for even when it is not actively fermenting tea. Don't get overwhelmed, though, as it's really as simple as feeding it with a little sugar and fresh tea every few days to be sure that it doesn't die. The easiest place to secure a scoby is from a friend who is willing to cut some of theirs off for you. There are plenty of online fermenting forums, so these can also be a starting place in your search for a scoby.

Scrap apple vinegar

Alongside pantyhose and bicarbonate of soda (baking soda), it seems that apple cider vinegar has become the new waste-free, chemical-free whiz-kid on the block. It is used for just about everything, from washing hair and balancing your gut to cleaning floors and keeping chickens healthy.

Don't be fooled into thinking that you need to buy organic apple cider vinegar from a shop. It is one of the easiest brews to make at home, using little more than the peels and cores of eaten apples (we also make it en masse in 20-litre [5-gallon] buckets using the last of the apples from the autumn season). Here are the basic step-by-step instructions for making scrap apple vinegar:

1. Add two tablespoons of raw sugar and two tablespoons of boiling water to a 1 litre (35 fl oz) jar.
2. Stir the sugar until it has dissolved, and allow the mixture to cool.
3. Add apple scraps from four apples (peel and core – no rotten or mouldy bits). You can freeze these during the week until you have enough for the quantity you plan to brew.
4. Fill the rest of the jar with cool water.
5. Stir vigorously, and cover the jar with muslin cloth. Store the jar in a cool, dark place.
6. Stir the mixture four times each day for a week.
7. Strain and bottle the liquid. Store the bottle in a cool, dark place.
8. Every day for more than a week, turn over the bottled liquid a few times and release the cap to let out gas.
9. The scrap apple vinegar can be stored in a cool, dark place for up to two years.

You may find that you get mould on top of the vinegar – this is harmless and can just be scooped off prior to use. You may also find that you have grown a scoby mother – this can be used to make more apple cider vinegar and speed up the process. It can also be fed to chickens, which will love you for it.

Apple cider vinegar has a multitude of uses:

- liquid cleaner – dilute it in hot water for benchtops, floors and bathroom surfaces
- hair conditioner – for a thick, soft hair feel (for an easy shampoo recipe, see page 284)
- aiding gut health – take a daily dose
- salad dressing – balsamic is sweeter and thicker, but that's from added sugar and actually doesn't have the same health benefits as apple cider vinegar
- washing clothes – throw a capful into the space where you would normally place your detergent
- foot soak – it's said to have antibacterial qualities, so mix it with Epsom salts and soak your toes for soft, clean feet
- deodoriser – its antibacterial qualities mean that it's an ideal base for your room spray; mix it with water and use it in problem areas
- sore-throat soother – simply gargle it intermittently with a salt gargle
- skin toner – mix one part apple cider vinegar with two parts water, and use as you normally would as part of your face-cleaning regime
- fruit-fly traps – pour some apple cider vinegar into a cup, add a few drops of dish soap (so that any trapped flies sink), and you're good to go (be sure the flies are dead before you dispose of them, as they are a serious pest with the real potential to devastate fruit-growing regions – so we need to take our fruit-fly management seriously)
- weed killer – spray undiluted apple cider vinegar with added salt (1 cup [130 g] to 4 cups [1 litre]) on unwanted weeds in your garden to get rid of them.

ROOT-VEGIE STORAGE

Storing your bounty takes time and creative solutions. But considering the number of months it has already taken to grow the vegies in the first place, it's worth making a superhuman effort to nail your storage solutions. Root vegies are a sought-after addition to your winter pantry, but they can take up loads of space. There are a few basic things to know:

+ You need a space that is no cooler than 4 degrees Celsius (39 degrees Fahrenheit) and no warmer than 10 degrees Celsius (50 degrees Fahrenheit).
+ The temperature needs to be relatively consistent.
+ Keep the root vegies in the dark.
+ Store each variety separately if possible.
+ Keep the root vegies in breathable containers.
+ High humidity is NOT the root vegies' friend, so remove moisture from the storage space.
+ Fridges are not ideal storage solutions.
+ Use what you've got!

Your solution might be to pop them on a shelf inside, into baskets under the house or in the roof, into a straw bed on an old gate and hoisted high into the rafters, under the stairs in your house, or into a purpose-built cupboard next to your hot-water unit outside. The ideas are endless and so, too, are the experiments to discover what works best for you.

Pumpkins (squash)

These get harvested as late as possible but before the first frost. When you cut each stalk, be sure to leave some of the vine intact on either side. Don't carry pumpkins by the stalk, as they will rot if this breaks off. However you store them, keep a few things in mind: they can't touch each other, they are best stored on their sides so they don't pool water in their centre, they can't fall below 4 degrees Celsius (39 degrees Fahrenheit), and they need a stalk.

Potatoes

The humble spud is a foundational mainstay in our house, so we plant loads of them. To harvest them, we gently hand-fork along the planting rows once the green part has died back, just after the first frost. We brush the potatoes to remove clods of earth, but we leave them unwashed as the soil helps to preserve them through winter. We leave them in the (now weak) sun for a few hours, so they dry off and won't turn mouldy. Once we are confident that they are dry, and we've removed any that are split or forked (these get mashed that night), we store them in hessian bags in the harvest pantry, which has a steady temperature and is quite dark.

Carrots

The easiest way to store them is to leave them tucked in the earth where they grew, and simply pull a bunch out when you need them. They can be kept in temperatures as low as minus 5 degrees Celsius (23 degrees Fahrenheit), and they actually get sweeter with the cold. They won't continue to grow once the soil cools, so don't panic about them getting woody until spring – when it's best to harvest any you've got left and either pickle, blanche or freeze them, or cook them in a variety of dishes that can be frozen for later consumption.

Beetroot

These earthy magenta baubles also stay happily in the ground, but their growing habit tends to pull them from the earth. Any part that sits above the ground will get nipped by cold winters, so if you're in a frost-prone area, be sure to tuck them in with more soil and mulch around them.

They will also turn woody if they're left in the ground once the soil warms again in spring. Our preference is to harvest them before the depths of winter and bottle them, which is as simple as washing, steaming, slicing and getting the beetroot into a 20 per cent vinegar and 10 per cent sugar brine before water-bathing the bottles and sticking them on the pantry shelf.

Parsnips

These are treated much the same as carrots, although they're not as easy to use raw. Other options include cooking them up into mash that you freeze, adding roasted parsnips to prepared frozen meals, or pickling them.

Jerusalem artichokes

They can be stored in the ground if you want to use them fresh during winter, or they can be pickled (see page 302).

Turnips

They will keep just like potatoes once they've been trimmed of their greens (which you can use in a wilted green stir-fry or green sauce).

Fennel

Although it's considered a 'root vegie', it's not great for storing over winter, so it's best to keep it in a paper bag and in the fridge on a low-humidity setting. Use fresh if possible.

Sweet potato

Store these as per potatoes.

ETHICAL MEAT-EATING

On our farm, the rooster-culling and sheep-slaughtering day really does happen, and it's really hard. It's hard despite it being one of my earliest memories: helping my mum cut off chickens' heads, and helping my dad drive cattle to the local abattoir on the back of the tractor. I've always known that this is where my meat comes from, but it doesn't get any easier with experience and understanding. But as meat-eaters, we're committed to knowing that the animals we eat were given the best life they could have had. They didn't suffer unnecessarily, and we are respectfully grateful that they gave their life for the sake of our nutrition.

A licensed friend butchers our sheep for us before we pack and label all of the freezer-bound pieces. We cull our roosters in a culling cone, and pluck and dress the birds before freezing them. The muster and cull day is as hard as you'd imagine it to be. No one likes to face the reality of this, even those of us who do it regularly. But as omnivores who prefer to follow our evolutionary path, we opt for real meat rather than synthetic or vegetable-based substitutes, and this requires us to own the responsibility for where our food comes from, how it's produced and what it's actually like to take the life of something living.

We use as much of the carcass as we can. Anything that can't be eaten we bury in our woodchip pile to enhance breakdown. As with all of our food, we are considered in our actions and honour those giving up their lives. Our kids are involved in every part of the process, too, so the education opportunity is vast and they can make up their own mind about eating meat.

Also, it wouldn't be an integrated farm – echoing a natural ecosystem – without animals. They scratch, forage, upturn, poo, wee and pasture-manage just as they would in an unfarmed habitat. This is important for us, as it mimics natural growing patterns. As a meat-eater, I'm happy that it's the most humane, respectful, nose-to-tail and waste-free approach we could take!

HONEY HARVEST FEAST

Nothing says 'harvest' like a pot of freshly spun honey. Humans have been lured by the wonder of the bee for 9000 years. Not only do bees deliver golden nectar that our tastebuds love, but this sticky purity has also long been recognised as a medicinal marvel and revered for its external use on wounds and internal use for diseases of the gut. Hive wax can be utilised in many of the same ways as plastics: lubricants, seals, leather and wood polishes, glass and metal casting, waterproofing agent, candles and cosmetics.

Bees have unique hive structures with a complexity that resembles the human world. As a primary pollinator required for food production, they are rightly celebrated for what they do. Yet the dance between bees and humans is a delicate one, because they need a world that is free of synthetics, disturbance and climate change. Despite the centuries of reverence and celebration of bees, they could become collateral damage during the current industrial age. Although, given their central role in the food system, we would be wise to consider them like the canary in the coalmine and heed their warning about the way we are impacting their world. And ours!

We keep bees at Black Barn Farm, not only for their golden gift but also because they're a potent, living reminder of why we farm the way we do, with the intention of returning our surrounding land to a place of balance and diversity. They remind us of why we live with consideration and lightness, and in step with the seasons.

The kids love the antics of beekeeping, and happily suit up to stand by their dad's side while he inspects the hive and slips out the frames for a honey raid. They willingly volunteer to whip the honey spinner into a frenzy of gravity-assisted honey removal, and they scramble over one another to dip their finger in the liquid gold and suck on the sweet, sticky treat.

With just one hive that has two supers (frames where the bees store their honey within their own honeycomb), we harvest about 16 cups (4 litres) of honey each year. It's less than we need, but given the winter temperatures here, we are tentative about disturbing our bees' carefully harvested food stores. We have no interest in feeding our bees just so we can raid greater quantities of the sticky stuff for our morning porridge. Instead, our preference is to take and use significantly less, leaving them with what they need to get their hive through the months when they lie low. This is a healthy balance, and one in which we're more than happy to partake.

Our harvested honey changes each season, depending on where these winged creatures have danced. The nearby nectar stores greatly influence the taste and colour of the honey; it ranges from light yellow with a simple sweetness to deep tan with complex tones on your tastebuds. Spinning this gift of honey is like bottling the brilliance of the sun.

THE FRUIT OF THE GODS

Apples, pears, bananas and oranges are the mainstays in most fruit bowls. However, for those who are a little more daring, you'll find magic in the fruit of Eve: the quince.

In late spring, the quince tree performs its best show when it's covered in flouncy, delicate, soft pink blossoms. In the blink of an eye, as we round the corner to summer, the misshapen, furry-skinned fruits hang on the tree as big as apricots, taunting the birds, late frosts and potential fungal spores to try their best to knock them off. For those fruits that withstand the elements and make it to the finish line, the result is tart yet sweet, mouth-puckering heaven. On the outside

Right: Black Barn tomato sauce is a favourite (see page 228 for the recipe).

Far right: Our sweet honeycomb haul is a once-a-year treat.

they are knobbly, furry, yellow fruits that look somewhat oversized; however, they have a heady and sweet aroma. With the right preparation, quinces can become a mainstay of the winter feasting experience. Try the tasty recipe for slow-roasted quince on page 229.

PARTAKE IN SOME POMEGRANATES

My kids split the fruits and pop the little jewels (the seeds) into their mouths until they've demolished the lot, leaving the pithy carcass to fling to the chickens. Eat the fresh seeds on their own or in fruit salads and green salads, or sprinkle them on curries. They contain antioxidants, fibre, folate and vitamins C and K.

SNACK PLATES

I'd love to say that snack plates are only a weekend thing, but really they're an anytime-we're-too-busy-to-create-something-else thing. They are especially easy during harvest season, as much of the picnic can be plucked from the ground (such as carrots), rinsed and stuck on a plate. We raid the pantry for nuts and seeds, boil some eggs and pop open a jar of pickles or olives that has been lurking in the pantry since last season. It's pretty wild, with no real theme or consideration for flavour combos, but it's quick, healthy and waste-free, and it takes zero brainpower.

Black Barn tomato sauce

Kale chips

We mix different tomato varieties together, so we can regularly cook the sauce in small batches; we don't want to wait until we have enough of one variety. Charlie sieves the tomatoes to remove the seeds and skins, but I tend to just dice them up and throw everything into the saucepan without sieving. I quite like the added body this offers, and I don't find the resulting sauce bitter at all.

One of the most delicious ways to get the kids eating kale is to make kale chips. It sorts out the kale abundance problem, too – but don't expect the chips to last long, as they are seriously good! I use Tuscan kale, as the leaves are like big, flat surfboards that hold loads of the marinade, which makes these chips even better. Adjust the measurements so you make enough to fit your storage space, and use the left-over marinade on meat, rice … anything really.

Makes approx. 12 x 350 ml (12 fl oz)

Makes 40 chips

2 onions, diced

6–8 garlic cloves, diced

1–2 chillies (deseed if you prefer a milder sauce)

½ teaspoon garam masala

½ teaspoon Moroccan allspice

Coconut oil, for frying

5 kg (11 lb) tomatoes

½ cup (110 g) rapadura or coconut sugar

1 tablespoon Worcestershire sauce

1 teaspoon black pepper

1 teaspoon salt

1 cup (250 ml) apple cider vinegar (see page 221)

Juice of 2 lemons

3 heaped tablespoons tahini

1 tablespoon olive oil

½ cup (60 g) ground cashews

1 tablespoon honey

1 teaspoon crushed garlic

40 kale leaves, washed and dried (that's how many fit in our dehydrator)

1. In a frying pan over medium heat, brown the onions, garlic, chillies and spices in the coconut oil.
2. Place all of the ingredients into a large saucepan. Simmer over medium heat for 1 hour.
3. Place the mixture into a blender, and whiz until smooth.
4. Return the mixture to the saucepan, and simmer for a further 2 hours or until it has a sauce-like consistency.
5. Pour the sauce into sterilised bottles, and water-bath the bottles at 60 degrees Celsius (140 degrees Fahrenheit) for 1 hour. The sauce can be stored in a cupboard for up to two years.

1. In a large bowl, mix together the juice, tahini, olive oil, cashews, honey and garlic to make a marinade.
2. Toss the kale leaves through the marinade, and ensure there's a good coating on them all.
3. Gently (so you don't lose the marinade), place the kale leaves into the dehydrator. If you don't have a dehydrator, preheat the oven to 50 degrees Celsius (120 degrees Fahrenheit). Place the leaves onto a baking tray, and leave them in the oven for 12 hours.
4. Once the kale leaves are completely crispy and dry, store them in an airtight container for up to three days. (But I bet they're all gone within hours!)

Slow-roasted quince

While quince paste is a favourite autumn staple, it can be fiddly. If you're prone to easy distraction like me, then it's easily burned. Rather than making paste, I prefer to cook masses of slow-roasted quince. This can be done with any variety of quince; if you're short on time, you can get away with not peeling or cutting the fruits. You will need to core and wipe them, though, as they are furry on the outside, and the core is quite bitter. While it feels like a lot of ingredients, you can simplify the recipe and change the ingredients to suit your taste.

Makes approx. 500 g (1 lb 2 oz)

5 quinces

2 star anise

½ teaspoon freshly grated nutmeg

½ teaspoon ground cinnamon

5 cloves

1 teaspoon ground allspice

2 tablespoons rapadura sugar

1 cup (250 ml) orange juice

1 cup (250 ml) apple juice

½ cup (125 ml) red wine

125 g (4½ oz) butter, melted

Thick (double) cream, to serve

1. Preheat the oven to 120 degrees Celsius (235 degrees Fahrenheit).
2. Prepare the quinces as you prefer – I peel, core and cut them into eighths.
3. Toss the quince pieces into a baking tray, and sprinkle them with the spices and sugar.
4. Pour the juices and wine over the quince pieces, and then the melted butter.
5. Cover the baking tray with foil or a lid, and place it into the oven for 4 hours. Toss the quince pieces every hour to ensure they remain moist.
6. Serve the quince pieces with the cream.

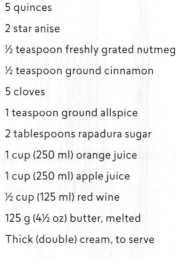

Pear chutney

Recipes and eating rituals often come from excess food that needs a creative solution. We rented another apple orchard once, and ran it as a pick-your-own business. During this time, we also accessed their Beurre Bosc pear trees ... but so did the birds! We managed to harvest nearly a tonne of saleable pears, but for every good one, we struck a bird-pecked one. Hating waste, we filled our quiet moments between customers by cutting the bird-pecked pears into tiny pieces. At the end of each day, we carted the diced fruits back to our kitchen. Some were freezer-bound, some went to friends, and all the scraps went to the worm farm, chickens and geese – but we still had crates and crates of diced pear. So we made chutney!

The slapdash, off-the-cuff recipe used only what we had in the cupboard. We ended up with 40 x 750 ml (26 fl oz) Fowlers jars full of seriously delicious pear chutney. When you eat three meals a day at home with ingredients that you've grown yourself, it can get mildly dull – so the best way to liven things up is with a hit of sweet, sticky chutney. We scraped out our last jar from our original batch 18 months later and missed it! Pear chutney is now a pantry mainstay.

You can change the recipe with ease, so experiment with what you've got. Scale the measurements up or down to suit your pear quantity and taste.

Makes 6–8 x 375 ml (13 fl oz)

15 pears, cored and diced (they can be any variety; we use half-ripe, unpeeled Beurre Bosc pears, which hold their shape)

1 brown onion, diced

1 cup (220 g) brown, rapadura or coconut sugar

¼ cup (40 g) sunflower seeds

¼ cup (70 g) flax seeds, ground lightly using a mortar and pestle

1½ cups (200 g) finely chopped fennel, including the fronds

¼ cup (30 g) dill seeds

2 teaspoons salt

3 chillies, deseeded and finely sliced

Roughly ground pepper, to taste (I love pepper; it balances the pears' sweetness exceptionally well, so I use up to 1 tablespoon)

1½ cups (375 ml) apple cider vinegar (see page 221)

4 cups (1 litre) water

1 cup (250 ml) apple juice

1. Place all of the ingredients into a large saucepan over low to medium heat. Simmer for 2 hours, stirring regularly. Add more water if the mixture looks too dry.
2. Once the solid ingredients have softened and mixed together, spoon the chutney into sterilised jars and use a water bath to seal the jars. The chutney can be stored in the cupboard for up to 18 months.

THE
TURNING

Picking
Soon

Meet Jonathan

One of the world's favourite eating apples, most people agree that Jonathan's sweet and tangy taste is damn-near perfect. Its origin, however, is more contentious. Mrs Digby of Queensland says it was her teething, carved after a local lad, that grew up to be the famous Jonathan. But Philip Dix of somewhere generally gets the credit.

Meet Snow

When you've got 20 different nicknames, you're certainly loved. A very old heritage eating apple (think 1730s Europe), Snow is interchangeably called King in the Snow, Fameuse, Chimney Apple and more. People adore her pretty looks and fragrant, snowy colouring, with snow-white flesh to die for.

Almost overnight, the days change their stripes and begin spruiking the virtues of autumn. Warmth only lasts while the sun is high; it burrows deeply as soon as the sun drops behind the trees. The evenings shroud us in a dark blanket that is heavy and cold.

Slowly, we begin to understand that it's time for summer fun to fade away, which leads to a change of pace in our daily patterns. Instead of clicking our heels at a clipped trot, we plan less and expect less; we cover our shoulders with scarves and drop into a more relaxed and gentle season.

As our rhythm slows, we turn our attention inwards, away from the demanding harvest that has steadily moved from abundance to subsistence.

Our vibrant social antics wind back to our core tribe, and we spend more time with our internal monologue. This allows more mindful contemplation in readiness for the planning phase of the year, which is fast approaching.

We find tasks that are monotonous yet cathartic, such as swinging the axe. Spreading blankets on beds of fallen leaves during the day, we feast on the bounty that the season has produced. We also pack baskets in our kitchen and take them fireside in the paddock for an early dinner with neighbours – so early that we are tucked up inside by 7 pm before darkness engulfs us and the sharp chill of the air invades our bones.

The leaves pack their green crayon away for another year and replace it with ochre, burnt orange, deep red and egg-yolk yellow. It's a heady mix of colour that punches the visual senses and stamps the arrival of 'the turning'.

Ritual

PICK-YOUR-OWN APPLES

This book wouldn't be complete without some hefty love offered to the humble but glorious fruit of my heart: the apple. Lucky for me, it fits snugly into the season of harvest, and it ticks all of the boxes: as a *ritual* (apple picking), a *feast* (apple pies and tarts), a chance to *create* (making stores of dehydrated rings and mushy sauce for winter) and a source of *nourish*ment (apple cider vinegar).

As one of the world's oldest food heroes, the apple has starred in stories since biblical times – and for good reason. 'An apple a day keeps the doctor away' is far from an old wives' tale, with abundant evidence showing that the high pectin and fibre levels in apples help to lower cholesterol and fat in the blood, and there is even a suggestion that their skin is excellent as an anti-inflammatory. These health attributes are due to their high levels of phenolics; interestingly, these are more prevalent in the old heritage varieties. Not only are the heritage varieties better for you, but they also serve up a complex range of flavours to suit every apple whim, from slow-baked stuffed apples to crisp fresh apples – there are even a few that are so tart and rough-skinned that it takes a real connoisseur to appreciate their individuality.

Black Barn Farm is home to 98 varieties of apple. This means that we pick them fresh from mid-summer until early winter. Apples such as Esopus Spitzenburg, Yellow Huffcap, Eagle Point Star, Blenheim Orange and Summer Strawberry sit alongside the bomb-proof Granny Smith and everyone's favourite (except mine, as I find them too sweet), the Pink Lady.

You don't need a pick-your-own orchard in your backyard to make a tradition of the apple-picking season, where multiple generations of the family gather in one place, picking, peeling, chopping and pie-baking, before drowning the pie slices in cream and feasting on them around an impromptu backyard fire as an afternoon treat with a pot of chai tea. With as few as three trees of your own, the apple harvest can be bountiful. You would have freshly picked treats for five months, and be set up for the rest of winter.

When we were in the United States, we visited an exhaustive number of small, family-owned orchards, as we were learning how to make a small orchard viable within today's commodity-centric world. We saw organically grown orchards offering reliable picking for six months, disease resistance and open farm gates, which provided the chance for people to fall back in love with a fruit that has long been tarnished by being an overstored, underappreciated, flavourless commodity that lacks appeal. What we saw elated us beyond measure.

Our top apple picks

This is a little like choosing your favourite child, but – let's be honest – some are just better than others. We haven't included Pink Lady, despite knowing that it's everyone's favourite, because that's like taking the highway instead of the old dirt road that wanders through forgotten country towns. These varieties have been chosen for their reliability, consistency, flavour and quirkiness.

MUTSU – Both of us claim that this is our undisputed single-best apple ever. It's big, juicy, split-in-your-mouth crunchy and aromatic; it's a massive cropper and disease resistant. It's a Japanese apple whose mum is Golden Delicious. It can be picked mid-season but gets sweeter and sweeter if it's left on the tree, so hold off picking it until late season.

SUMMER STRAWBERRY – Doesn't that name sound so utterly evocative? This little darling is an early- to mid-season apple that is strawberry red on the outside and snowy white on the inside. It's boxy in shape, sweet but not sickly and a consistent cropping variety. It's a beauty for fresh eating.

OPALESCENT – It really does have a luminescent quality. It's big, crisp, juicy and red. The flavour is not overly complex or overbearingly sweet. It's a great fresh apple but equally holds its own in a pie. It's resistant to black spot, too.

CAMEO – This is Charlie's equal favourite alongside Mutsu. A medium-sized, block-shaped, streaky red apple, it harvests mid-season and seems to delight the men in my life. Funny but true! Our male WWOOFers all love it, Charlie and our boys gravitate towards it and, as odd as this sounds, it even looks more masculine and handsome than other apples. The tree produces consistently, the fruit stores well, and it's versatile fresh or cooked. It's also resistant to black spot.

GALA – This little beauty is relatively well known as it still appears in supermarkets, but its real talent is its prolific production. It pleads to be picked from late summer onwards, effectively breaking the fresh-apple drought en masse. The apples are small, making them perfect for little hands to wrap around with gusto, and they fit into lunch boxes. They are happy to hang on the tree for a long time – providing you can keep the birds at bay – and simply get sweeter by the week.

EAGLE POINT STAR – It's pink in the centre and purple on the outside; even its bark and leaves are purplish. There's debate about whether it's a crabapple or an eating apple; regardless, it's undoubtedly a beauty with serious appeal given its pink flesh. It first appeared on the side of the road at Eagle Point, Victoria, and has been shared around small heritage orchards ever since. Its clusters of smaller apples can be harvested from early- to mid-season.

WINTER BANANA – What a funny name for an apple! Funny or otherwise, this one starts conversations and then backs itself with a large fruit that has an apricot yellow skin blushing pink on the sunny side. It has a pinkish flesh,

Summer Strawberry

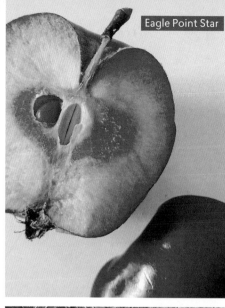

Eagle Point Star

Gala

Winter Banana

Gravenstein Red

Cameo

Jonathan

Bonza

Mutsu

Windfall Apples
Human Grade $10 crate
(cider, vinegar)
Stock feed $5 crate.

Top left: This woven basket of autumnal goodness holds tasty Gala apples.

Bottom left: We waste nothing; windfall apples are placed in crates so they can be used for cider-making or animal fodder.

which is crisp, tender and aromatic. It can be picked from mid- to late season and is great for eating from the tree or for juicing. And yes, it really does taste like a lolly banana!

GRAVENSTEIN RED – A sport of the popular Gravenstein, even the name sounds cool. Harvested very early in the season and best eaten straight from the tree, the fruit is small to medium, aromatic and beautifully red once ripe. It's not a great keeper, but when it comes this early and is the first of the season, who wants to keep it anyway?

BONZA – A heavy cropper, it has firm white flesh and is crisp, juicy and sweet. The large fruit is round, and the skin is pillar-box red. It was first discovered in Batlow, New South Wales, in 1950 as a seedling from a Jonathan apple. A clever multi-use apple, it's suitable for drying, stewing, eating fresh in salads and cooking in pies. The fruit can hang for some time without losing quality, and it stores well after picking. It's resistant to black spot.

The old favourite – Jonathan

When my grandad died, my gran came to stay. She thought that maybe this would be her last big trip away, so she wouldn't see our orchard grow to full size. But she also said that she would wait Earthside until she tasted one of our Jonathan apples, so she could be transported back to her childhood when she used to ride to the river with her sister and climb the branches of the big old Jonnie tree to feast. This recollection was vividly etched in her memory right through adulthood, and she could already imagine the sensory delight of eating a Jonnie again fresh from our tree.

FIRESIDE DINNERS

Wedged between the summer fire season and the winter snow season, there's a perfect little window to create coal-cooked feasts.

Just outside our back door is a little cluster of mismatched chairs we've found at garage sales and junk shops. A jumbled ring of broken bricks sits centrestage.

At around 4 pm most autumn days, we gravitate to this higgledy-piggledy spot, set a fire, contemplate what to eat, play a game of soccer and let the wind-down begin. Then we sit around the warmth and wait for our coal-cooked early dinner. It's dark by 6 pm at this time of year, so it's all over by then, but it's a beautiful way to wring the last joy from the day before tucking up inside a warm house.

Luckily, this window coincides with corn, mushroom and lamb-cull season, so we keep it simple and fast, with minimal dishes. We cook corn while it is still bound in its husk so it steams with a smoky barbecue flavour, pop salted, buttered and herbed mushrooms in a pan over the hot coals, and throw a little salt and rosemary on new-season lamb chops. If friends call in, we pick an extra cob of corn and thaw an extra chop. It's all considered finger food (with a napkin or two), and we can call it dinner without any fanfare! The dogs eat the bones, the chickens take the corn scraps, and we're inside by the time it's dark.

EPHEMERAL THINGS

Everything has its 'lifetime', doesn't it? Nothing is designed to last forever; it's best this way, for it allows seasons and cycles to be our rhythmic heartbeat. While the end of a lifetime is sad, it's reassuring to know that this is the natural way of things, and with it comes regeneration, vigour and life. This is true not just of people but also of places and possessions. Coming to terms with Mother Nature's endless need to rebalance – and the impact this has on 'things' – is a worthy endeavour, as it removes the angst from the ending of something and replaces it with an understanding that its time has come, and that's for the best.

Nourish

FILL UP ON OUTSIDE PLACES

Did you know that nature-deficit disorder is a thing? It's hard to imagine, but yep – it is! With autumnal days of sensorial overload and the impending winter closing in, grasp the turning with gusto. Spend your days sidestepping the apathy of nature-deficit disorder by reinventing your childlike curiosity for the great outdoors.

Each of us arrives Earthside with an intrinsic wonder of the natural world. Our senses are teased by pure sensations: the wind on our face, dappled light through the trees, the feeling of sand between our fingers or stones under our toes, and the assaulting colour of autumn leaves. Early childhood is filled with trees to be climbed, mud pies to be baked and autumn leaves to pile into ... the joy is genuine, the appreciation is unaffected and the connection is formative. Sadly for many people, during early adulthood this necessary and natural connection is replaced with sterile, curt, controlled environments that disrupt our 'knowing'.

Be nourished this season by reigniting your childlike wonder for outside places. Remove expectation and time frames, and give in to your instinctive attraction to interacting and observing without purpose. Seek wild places that lack symmetry and order, and say hello to a world rich in natural patterns and biodiversity. Develop a trust in the wilder side, and listen to your body as it grows in confidence. Outside is free, and we can be wild when we're in it – you'll see!

Get your dose of the outdoors by:

+ having a picnic in the afternoon sun
+ filling bowls with autumn leaves in every colour
+ building an outdoor fire bath, and soaking under the stars
+ setting the table with collections found during your wanderings
+ soaking foraged leaves in boiling water, and steaming your face
+ shifting your lens to see wild spaces as diverse, not messy
+ whittling without purpose; let it be more about the repetitive rhythm.

Create

BUILD WOOD STACKS

The saying goes that wood fires warm you three times: once when you cut and collect the wood, once when you bring the wood into the house, and once when you burn the wood. Spot on, that one! Without a doubt, it's a demarcation of seasonal turning when we empty the wheelbarrow of its summer garden clippings and delegate it to the woodpile for its daily haul up the hill.

If we had followed permaculture-zoning principles, our woodpile would not be so far from our house, but it's a good example of compromising between two elements of practicality. When we cut the wood during spring and summer, we need to be able to easily stack it in the sun to dry. So we do this in our 'industrial area', where piles of wood, bark and sticks can lounge around for months, drying out without inhibiting other activities. Just before the rains appear, we scramble as a family to pile it under cover, ready for the long winter burning season. It's not a long task and we all don gloves to chip in, but it's a sweaty, dirty and defining job that brings us together and reminds us that time keeps ticking – another year has passed since we united for this exact task 'just the other day'.

It's quite a skill to stack a solid pile of wood. While I'm as hands-on and capable as anyone, the ability to create a 'tucked in' end that's safe and sturdy still eludes me. My dad did this when I was a kid, and now that task is Charlie's – although I have noticed that the boys are beginning to observe this art form with more interest, and I wonder when the baton will be passed from father to sons.

START A SEED-SAVING LIBRARY

There's much to be said for the food sovereignty of those with the skill to save their own seeds. It's a ritual we take seriously, and it's something we marvel at every season. It's amazing that such a simple act can ensure food for my family, yet it's not a skill that is held in high esteem and taught to all.

The first seeds ready at Black Barn Farm are those from Alexanders, beetroot, spring onions (scallions), garlic and rhubarb. Regardless of what you grow, all plants eventually produce seed heads, so there are a few key things to remember:

+ Seeds need to be fully formed before being pulled from the plant.
+ If you want non-hybrid seeds, then you need to either separate the varieties so they cannot cross-pollinate, or you need to cover your plants during pollination (you can use fine-mesh bags or even paper bags).
+ It's easiest to dry seeds when they're still on the plant, so wait until the flower heads are dry and then hang them as a bunch.
+ The seeds need to be stored in a cool, dry place.
+ Each container needs to be marked clearly with the variety, the date that the seeds were harvested and the place where they were harvested.

We use old biscuit tins for storing our seeds. They are waterproof, airtight and dark, they stack easily, and they are things we already had, having collected them from op shops and saved them from presents over the years.

Golden rules of seed saving

These are the five rules you need to know:

1. **Ensure low humidity** – the most important thing with seed saving is the humidity. Never exceed 5 per cent humidity, and never store them in a fridge. Just store them in an airtight container.
2. **Maintain temperature** – ensure that the seeds are not too hot or cold, and minimise fluctuations. A temperature between 5 and 15 degrees Celsius (40 and 60 degrees Fahrenheit) is ideal.
3. **Label seeds clearly** – include all the relevant information from the start.
4. **Know their age** – the fresher the seeds, the higher the germination rate. Some seeds have a long life span (see the table on page 248).
5. **Share unused seeds** – do this with your local food co-op or gardening group. You can also start a seed-saving library to share with your community.

WHY SEED SAVE?

In just 100 years, we've seen the loss of 90 per cent of our seed diversity thanks to our industrial food system. Salvaging heirloom varieties is critical to food sovereignty and is a burgeoning movement at a grassroots level. Get saving and swapping in your neighbourhood – today.

Over a century ago

In 1903, commercial seed houses offered hundreds of varieties, as shown in this sample of ten crops.

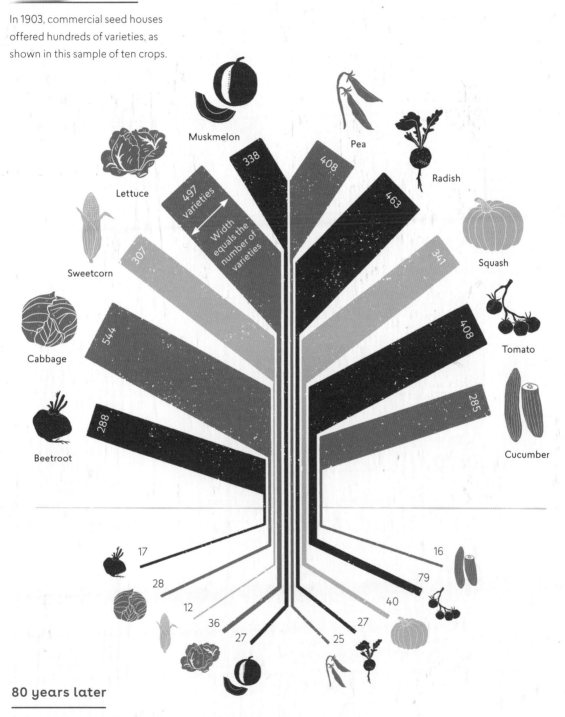

Muskmelon

Pea

Lettuce

Radish

Sweetcorn

Squash

Cabbage

Tomato

Beetroot

Cucumber

497 varieties
Width equals the number of varieties

338

408

463

341

307

544

408

288

285

17

28

12

36

27

16

79

40

27

25

80 years later

By 1983, few of these varieties were found in the US National Seed Storage Laboratory*

*Changed its name in 2001 to the National Centre for Genetic Resources Preservation

HOW LONG WILL MY SEEDS LAST?

Inevitably, even big vegie gardens run out of growing space every year, leaving you with an excess of seeds. Luckily, many seeds will last much longer than one season. If you don't have any way to share the seeds with others, then store them well and save yourself the trouble of keeping some aside the next year.

CROP	YEARS THE SEEDS WILL KEEP	CROP	YEARS THE SEEDS WILL KEEP
asparagus	3	kale	4
bean	3	kohlrabi	3
beetroot	4	leek	2
broccoli	3	lettuce	6
brussels sprout	4	mustard	4
button squash	4	okra	2
cabbage	4	onion	1
capsicum (pepper)	2	parsley	2
carrot	3	parsnip	1
cauliflower	4	pea	3
celeriac	3	pumpkin (squash)	4
celery	3	radish	5
Chinese cabbage	3	rockmelon (cantaloupe)	5
collard greens	5	silverbeet (Swiss chard)	4
corn	2	spinach	3
cucumber	5	tomato	4
eggplant (aubergine)	4	turnip	4
endive	5	watermelon	4
fennel	4	witlof (chicory)	4

Grow

PRAISE FOR PERENNIALS

In our kitchen garden, we have one big bed that is dedicated purely to perennial edibles. There's much to be said for a perennial bed, and we sing its praises loudly and proudly. Put simply, it requires the least amount of work but provides us with the most food – not to mention the earliest food for harvesting.

If the soil has been well prepared, then these perennials will stand the test of time with great hardiness, excellent production and year in, year out reliability. When you're eager to grow your family's food but are time poor, perennials are a winner!

Each year, just after the first frost, we cut the plants to the ground, feed the soil with compost and put it to bed under straw for winter, salvaging any last harvest as we go.

There the bed sits for months in complete hibernation, before – almost like magic – small but sturdy growth pushes through the straw and begins its season-long reach to the sky. This process can start at the end of winter, which is weeks or even months before we are able to plant our spring annuals.

> We can't recommend highly enough the virtues of planting a perennial patch in your edible garden, and suggest a space allocation of 50 per cent perennials and 50 per cent annuals. You'll be thankful come the spring hunger gap, when you have earlier than usual food production.

Perennial plant list

Here are some of our favourites:

ALEXANDERS (*Smyrnium olusatrum*) – a robust, frost-hardy winter-growing herb that tastes like parsley and celery combined. The leaves, stems and seeds can be eaten. The root is also edible, and has medicinal value. The flower heads can be pickled.

APPLE MINT (*Mentha suaveolens*), **LEMON BALM** (*Melissa officinalis*), **PEPPERMINT** (*Mentha x piperita*), **SPEARMINT** (*Mentha spicata*) – they're beautiful when used fresh or dried in tea or creams. These are a gift in the garden, but they come with a warning – they will take over if you turn your back.

ASPARAGUS (*Asparagus officinalis*) – it's best left for two or three years until it has established, and it will have abundant spears from very early spring. The tall, dense, weed-blocking fronds can be used in summer omelettes and salads, or picked for a vase.

FEVERFEW (*Tanacetum parthenium*) – a perennial herb that is available year-round. As the name suggests, it can be brewed into a tonic to help with headaches, fever and flu symptoms, so it's good to have on hand.

JERUSALEM ARTICHOKE (*Helianthus tuberosus*) – it's also called the fartichoke (unless you try the fermentation preparation on page 302) or the sunchoke (mostly because of its sky-high yellow and black flowers). It's a prolific producer and self-propagator, so be sure to lock the plants into their designated area with deeply dug corrugated iron to thwart their spread.

KALE (*Brassica oleracea* cultivar) – this is often grown as an annual, but in cooler climates it will comfortably produce for up to three years. It sure beats an annual sowing of lettuce greens.

LOVAGE (*Levisticum officinale*) – this perennial herb produces year-round and can be used in soups, stews and mashed vegetables.

RHUBARB (*Rheum rhabarbarum*) – offers a multi-season harvest, depending on variety. This tart, astringent vegetable can be used to make cordial, tarts, cakes and pies. It enhances the flavour of any apple pie!

STRAWBERRY (*Fragaria* x *ananassa*) – you have these for three years before they require replanting using the runners.

TARO (*Colocasia esculenta*) – grown for its starchy tuber, the plant will continue to thrive if you're careful not to pull it all out when harvesting.

WALKING ONION (*Allium* x *proliferum*) – these guys are prolific, so keep them tucked in. They replace normal onions in our house, as they require zero work and produce year-round. You can eat the bulb as well as the stalk. Their flavour is milder than regular onions, so we use a few more.

YACON (*Smallanthus sonchifolius*) – a small, sweet, nutty root vegetable that can help lower cholesterol and improve digestion.

SWEET, SWEET CORN

In our house, we play this game where we each decide what to take to a desert island forever. But we have rules. One of those rules is that you can only take three foods (tough choice, huh?). Amazingly, three out of five people in my family include corn on their list. It's heavily debated around the camp fire, but the argument for corn is strong: it's sweet, juicy, flavoursome, versatile, easy to grow, abundant, nutrient-dense and filling. What more could you want on a desert island?

For all of these reasons, corn is simply a must-have in the backyard patch and also a powerhouse in the global food-production process. In 1903, there were 307 varieties of corn available commercially, but by 1983 there were only 12. Many of the heirloom varieties of sweet and popping corn have been meticulously bred and shared by grassroots community groups, and an increasing number of small seed companies are making a wide variety of heirloom seeds available.

Growing corn

We've long experimented with corn, as it's a fresh mainstay during summer; we grow big quantities for our winter stores, too. All varieties are easily grown, and they share some base requirements: sun, heat, water and nutrient-rich, well-composted soil. You really can't scrimp on these growing conditions, or you simply won't get the full-cobbed, sweet harvest that you hoped for. Here are the growing seasons for different regions:

◆ **cool regions** – late spring
◆ **temperate regions** – early spring to as late as mid-summer, but it needs 16 weeks of warmth to reach maturity
◆ **warm regions** – early to mid-spring; if you are in a tropical zone, you can plant at any time other than early summer.

Corn is a hungry annual, so make sure your soil is nutrient-dense before you plant. Fill your beds with fresh compost or well-aged manure (cow or horse poo is preferable, as it's not as nitrogen-rich as other manure, so it won't burn the plant if it's a little 'hot' – a 'hot' manure still has a great deal of root-burning nitrogen). It's also the perfect vegie to grow after a green-manure crop, as it rapidly uses the nutrients from the rotting leaf matter.

Sow the seeds directly once the soil is warm enough: 20 degrees Celsius (70 degrees Fahrenheit) is ideal. Protect seedlings from pests by placing a glass jar over them. When the seedlings fill the jar, let them loose. Once they reach about 30 centimetres (12 inches), 'heel up' the soil (rake or shovel the soil so it sits higher around the base of each plant) and mulch with pea straw so the plants are strong and well fed. They appreciate regular compost teas, too.

Plant in blocks rather than rows, as this helps with pollination and wind protection. Aim for a minimum of eight by eight plants, 40 centimetres (16 inches) apart in your block, and create multiples of this for succession planting. Depending on the variety, corn can take between 60 and 100 days from seed to harvest. Variety also dictates the size and quantity of ears per stem.

The secret of when to pick the corn is in the silks. Once they brown right off, check the kernels inside. Gently peel back the husk, and poke the cob with your fingernail: a 'milky' not 'watery' liquid confirms that you're good to go.

THE HUMBLE CARROT

If you're anything like me, growing carrots can be elating or disheartening in equal measure. I've learned that they won't tolerate my usual approach to gardening, which suffers from a flippant dose of 'she'll be right'. Carrots are earnest vegetables and require attention.

Right: Fresh corn can be cooked in its husk on the open fire.

Far right: Carrots can be harvested fresh for eight months of the year.

A few years back, following a multi-season carrot-growing strike, I recommitted my attention to the humble orange root vegetable. I read everything that I could and dedicated a complete garden bed to the efforts. I overhauled it to become a wicking bed (see pages 173–5 for details on how to do this), topped up the soil with a sandy, free-draining mixture that was 30 centimetres (12 inches) deep and set up a watering system so the plants were automatically watered three times daily. I also scrounged some old shadecloth to cover them while in their tiniest seed state, so birds were kept at bay and evaporation was minimised. I mixed one part seeds to one part sand in a bucket, and carefully laid out the rows.

My efforts were rewarded with plant growth within days, and after three weeks they were strong enough to endure my already waning focus and thrive on their own. For the first time in my food-growing life, I had grown more carrots than any family could eat. Of course, this spurred me on to be creative with ways to use the abundance. Not only did the neighbours fare well, but also the horses and the chickens – which is criminal, really. But I still had hundreds of carrots. Rather than me tiring of them, they've become one of my favourite vegetables.

Carrot tips

I don't thin carrot seedlings as recommended by most gardeners. Rather, I add a cup of fine sand to a packet's worth of seeds and mix well before planting, which effectively separates the plants. The natural size discrepancy of the carrots actually suits me, as I'm not a market gardener in need of consistency to sell them. Also, I don't rush to pull them all up, as they actually store beautifully in the ground during winter, even in our subalpine temperatures. Use the patch as your winter vegie store, and simply pull the carrots as you need them.

CHILLI CHAMPIONS

We can only grow chillies in our hoop house, because they need a long, hot season. Any average household will only need one chilli plant to get them through the year, and it will happily grow in a pot on your bench or at your back door.

We do two things with our chillies: dry them and make sauce from them. To dry them, we string them on cotton thread and then hang them in the doorway. The chillies take about three weeks to completely dry, and then we store them in a sealed glass jar for up to three years. For our sweet chilli sauce recipe, see page 263.

RAVISHING RHUBARB

There are five varieties of rhubarb; many people would be surprised to find that some are green, and some are pink. As a rule, the green ones are the more robust growers, and despite the common belief, they are no less sweet than the red varieties. Actually, the sweetness we associate with rhubarb comes with cooking it – the distinguishing feature of this perennial is its teeth-stripping astringency and stringiness.

It's certainly an acquired taste, but when mixed with apple, pear or berries, its flavour balances perfectly with the natural sugar, and it makes a delectable treat for late-autumn or early-winter evenings. Try basic rhubarb compote or the superb fool you dessert (both recipes are on page 269).

GARLIC PLANTING

Just before night and day are equal, we prepare our garden bed with long, straight-mounded rows that are 30 centimetres (12 inches) apart. We select the biggest, healthiest-looking garlic heads, use only the outer cloves (the biggest ones), and plant them 10 centimetres (4 inches) apart. We stuff the channels between the mounds with straw, although not pea straw, as the high levels of nitrogen stimulate shoot growth but not bulb growth. As a rule of thumb, we plant 30 bulbs per person for a year and add an extra 30 for the next year's clove harvest.

Feast

TWILIGHT MUSHROOM FORAGING

On the days when you've hunkered inside, cosy at first but listless by mid-afternoon, selecting a basket each and heading outside to the nearby pines to 'hunt' for mushrooms is the perfect way to rattle the cage of claustrophobia and replace it with all things reminiscent of childhood whimsy.

At the end of our dirt road is a pine plantation. This mass-planted monoculture should feel relatively lifeless, yet there's a quiet vitality about it when you walk though the forest at this time of year. Thick layers of multigenerational pine needles muffle the sound. By osmosis, you feel calm and hushed as you meander under the canopy with your eyes focused on the ground, seeking the telltale mound that suggests a fungus is reaching for the light. Saffron milkcaps (*Lactarius deliciosus*) are the tastiest and most versatile of all, and we're confident of their identity so we feast without worry.

Of course, our paddocks deliver regular mushroom bounties, too. These usually appear a day or two after rainfall and provide just enough for a meal of buttery, salty, earthy goodness piled on top of toast, with a little goat cheese, freshly picked cherry tomatoes and fresh herbs.

While some years they're so abundant that you can fill buckets, other years they're more elusive. Also, just because they are found en masse at one location in one year,

don't expect that they'll be in the same location 12 months later. The inclination of the underground fungal network to spawn its 'fruits' is its decision alone, and it plays to its own rules – so expect to hunt for them. Actually, exploring is possibly my favourite part of the foraging experience. It's filled with anticipation and hope; the act holds promise but not a guarantee. You will feast if you are successful, but you can go home hungry if you've misread the timing or location.

There are a couple of unwritten mushrooming etiquette rules to keep in the back of your mind, too: don't take more than you need, and don't take anything that you can't 100 per cent positively identify. Because the pines near us go up hill and down dale for kilometres, we feel confident that we can fill quite a few buckets without exceeding our community quota. But what can you do with brimming buckets of mushrooms, you ask?

- Slice and dehydrate them for later use in soups, risottos and sauces. They cope with being thickly sliced and dehydrate surprisingly fast, so keep your eye on them. If they go too far, don't waste the mushrooms – simply grind them into a powder, and add it as a nutritious boost just like stock.
- Barbecue or pan-fry them. Add a dash of salt and a healthy lick of butter, and then hit them with heat. Cooked mushrooms

Right: Fresh-picked corn is popped straight onto the coals for cooking.

Far right: Baskets of foraged field mushrooms are ready for cooking and dehydrating.

will store in the fridge for a couple of days if you want to add them to risottos, sandwiches, salads and anything else that needs mushroom flavour.

◆ Pickle them. They are surprisingly easy to pickle, but not all forms of fungi have the meatiness needed to pickle (field mushrooms turn to mush – yuck). But saffron milkcaps hold their form and flavour well (see page 260 for recipe).

Fungal faux pas

Just a little word on mushroom foraging ... fungi can be a hotbox of heaven, but if you get your ID wrong, then they're a hotbox of hell. Before you venture into the woods alone, it's best to go with someone who has a proven track record of knowing their stuff. Perhaps start with one or two varieties, gain your confidence with these, and then trial new ones.

COOKING CORN

There's nothing as alluring as a cob left in its husk to steam away over a camp fire, absorbing the smoky flavours, before it is drowned in butter and salt as a succulent treat. The corn is picked fresh, cooked immediately and eaten hot ... all without plates or waste. We use the rough husk as a handle, before it goes straight to the chickens or compost.

Corn loses quality quickly once picked, so it's best eaten fresh. It will maintain quality on the stem for multiple weeks. If you have a glut and want to store it for winter, simply pick the corn, remove the kernels from the cob, blanch them for 30 seconds, place them into a bag and freeze them.

CARROT IS KING

There are three main ways to prepare carrots:

1. **Roast them** – wash them; keep them whole or halve them if they're too big; fling them into a baking dish with some coconut oil, rosemary, garlic and salt; and bake them at 180 degrees Celsius (350 degrees Fahrenheit) for 1 hour.
2. **Boil them** – use your favourite pumpkin soup recipe, but replace the pumpkin (squash) with carrots. You could leave it at that or, if you fancy a touch of Moroccan, add a well-pestled array of cardamom, cumin, cloves, cayenne and fennel. I often also add baked cashews and barley or red lentils to bulk out the soup.
3. **Pickle them** – you can do a quick pickle for immediate use or a longer-lasting pickle, which is much the same except for the finish.

Here's how to pickle your carrots:

1. Aim to use whole carrots that are small. Wash the carrots, and place them into a sterilised glass jar. You can add chilli, garlic, mustard, dill or fennel seeds at this point, depending on your flavour preferences, or you can leave the carrots on their own.
2. In a saucepan over low heat, blend together one part vinegar and one part water. We use apple cider vinegar because we have it on hand, but if you have distilled vinegar, that's good, too.
3. Add sugar and salt, and stir until they have dissolved. The sugar and salt need to make up around 10 per cent of the mixture, so if you have used 4 cups (1 litre) of vinegar, then add about 1½ tablespoons of sugar and 3 tablespoons of salt.
4. Pour the vinegar mixture over the carrots, making sure the carrots are completely submerged in the liquid.

If you want to eat your pickled carrots immediately, then allow them to marinate for at least one hour before eating. They will keep in the fridge for up to a week. If you want your pickled carrots to last longer, then seal the jar and boil it at 70 degrees Celsius (150 degrees Fahrenheit) for 30 minutes. Store the jar on a shelf in a cool, dark place for up to six months.

Note that whole, unpeeled carrots retain the most nutrients and antioxidants, so try to keep them intact. If you roast or boil whole carrots en masse, then you can store them in the fridge for the week so they're ready to add to soups, salads or snack plates.

Carrot-top greens

The tops of carrots are a nutritious leafy green that can be used in all sorts of dishes. Discard the stems and keep the fine green leaves, and then rinse and finely chop the greens. Add equal part herbs – whatever you have in your garden – and wilt them together in a frying pan with a little coconut oil, chilli, garlic and shallots or walking onions (which are perennial and easy to grow). This forms the base for any number of dishes. You might add parmesan cheese, roasted nuts/seeds, minced chicken or your favourite spices. Remember: carrot greens are gold so don't throw them away.

RAINBOW CHARD

A relative of silverbeet, rainbow chard (a form of *Beta vulgaris*) comes in five different colours – hence it is sometimes referred to as five-colour chard. This is one of the best year-round vegies you can grow. I use it in pies, pastas, quiches, stir-fries, soups, plus steamed and fried dishes; it gets served across all meals of the day. It freezes easily with a quick fry or steam first, it's easy to grow, and it tolerates baking summers and freezing winters. It grows well in pots for balcony gardeners and is pretty enough

to go in flower gardens for those who don't have a dedicated vegie patch. It really is an edible plant that everyone can grow … and the colours are just a beautiful bonus.

DAMPER DELIGHT

In the back of my dad's old yellow van, he kept a damper box. As its name suggests, it contained everything you'd ever need to cook up a damper over an open fire at the drop of a hat – even the bottle of beer to add that extra yeastiness.

On more occasions than I can name, he'd whip out the box and weave his magic. Rough hands would mix it all together (with the obligatory swig of beer for the chef) before throwing it among the hot coals. Then we waited. Finally, the charred remains would be dusted off and cracked apart to reveal the soft, fluffy innards ready to be drowned in butter and jam. Our fingers, faces and clothes got charry and sticky, but it was a pure delight that still tickles the fancy of the next generation.

Anyone can make damper, as there's little skill in that. But the existence of the box – where everything sits in waiting – in the first place is the genius that allows the ritual to become reality. Check out Dad's damper recipe on page 263.

PUFF WITH PRIDE

Rough puff pastry is a cheat's puff, but there's no judgement here! It's easy to make from scratch and can be used in lots of delicious dishes. Follow steps 1–4 from the apple and custard tart with rough puff pastry recipe on pages 264–5. The process usually takes half an hour in winter and a little longer in summer. Once made, the pastry will store in the fridge for a week or the freezer for a month. I usually make more than I need, so I have plenty of leftovers. The pastry can be used for an egg and bacon

pie, sausage rolls, or quinoa and nut-meal vegetarian rolls (see page 307).

The secret to a good puff pastry is keeping the ingredients cold while you work towards creating the 'lamination layers'. You make these by blending layers of butter into the dough through repeatedly rolling out and folding the dough and butter together. If it's cold then you can achieve this easily, but if it's warm then you'll need to refrigerate your 'in progress' puff a number of times throughout to ensure that it doesn't become a melted mass. A cold, laminated pastry will result in beautiful, paper-thin layers that steam during cooking, giving you a perfect puff.

Dessert hack

If you have some left-over rough puff pastry after making your apple and custard tart with rough puff pastry (see pages 264–5), or extra store-bought puff pastry – as well as a few apples – you can make some simple apple turnovers.

Peel and dice three apples (soft cooking apples are ideal for this). I'm usually led by whatever needs to be cooked first, cutting off any bruises from the older fruits. Toss the diced apple into a bowl, and mix in a little sugar, cinnamon and melted butter – quantities are based on taste, but ensure there's enough butter to coat the apple evenly and well (don't drown them, though!).

Roll out your pastry, and cut it into squares. Place the apple mixture onto the pastry squares, just enough so you can still fold them over and join them together. Give them some breather holes, and brush them with the same apricot jam and lemon juice mixture used for the apple and custard tart.

In an oven preheated to 180 degrees Celsius (350 degrees Fahrenheit), cook the turnovers for 20 minutes. Either eat them straight away, or store them in an airtight container in the freezer for up to three months.

Pickled mushrooms

When the foraged harvest is abundant, and you've had your fill of fresh and dehydrated mushrooms, pickling the rest is a sterling option. If you don't have a forage haunt, you can easily use store-bought button mushrooms for this recipe.

While it calls for a water bath, you can also prepare these mushrooms without a water bath by cooking all of the ingredients together (except the apple cider vinegar) in a frying pan; once the mushrooms are soft, spoon them into your sterilised jars straight from the oven. This method is just as tasty but the mushrooms won't last as long on the shelf (mould may grow on the inside of the jar), so they are best eaten immediately.

Makes 8 x 275 ml (9½ fl oz)

2 kg (4 lb 8 oz) saffron milkcap or button mushrooms

8 garlic cloves, peeled and sliced thinly lengthways

8 thyme sprigs, divided

8 dried chillies (heat level of your choice)

1 onion, sliced and pan-fried

4 tablespoons black pepper

4 cups (1 litre) apple cider vinegar (see page 221)

2½ tablespoons finely ground rock salt

1. Carefully wipe the tops of your foraged finds to be sure that they are clear of dirt and bush debris. Don't immerse them in water, as they get waterlogged and damaged easily.
2. Slice the mushrooms into bite-size chunks.
3. Into each of your eight sterilised jars, place a peeled and sliced garlic clove, a thyme sprig, a dried chilli, 1 teaspoon of fried onion and ½ tablespoon of black pepper.
4. Pack the raw mushroom chunks tightly into each of the jars.
5. In a jug, mix together the apple cider vinegar and the salt. Add a little water if necessary to ensure that you have enough liquid to cover the mushrooms in all of the jars.
6. Gently pour the vinegar mixture over the mushrooms until the jars are full.
7. Close and clip your jars before water-bathing them at 100 degrees Celsius (200 degrees Fahrenheit) for 45 minutes.
8. Allow the jars to cool on the bench, and then label them. Store the jars in the pantry for up to two years.

Sweet chilli sauce

I specifically use small jars, so I use all of the sauce within a week of opening each one. Make sure you use gloves and a chopping board dedicated to onions, garlic and chillies, to avoid painful eye contact and cross-contamination.

Makes 6 x 200 ml (7 fl oz)

30 fresh chillies, finely chopped (deseed if you want to decrease the punch)
5 garlic cloves, finely diced
½ cup (110 g) rapadura sugar
¾ cup (185 ml) water
1 tablespoon soy sauce
½ cup (125 ml) rice vinegar

1. Mix all of the ingredients together in a saucepan. Simmer over low heat, stirring often, for 1 hour or until the sauce is thick.
2. If the sauce is not thickening, mix 1 teaspoon of cornflour (cornstarch) in a little boiling water and add it to the sauce.
3 Spoon the sauce into sterilised glass jars and seal. Place the jars into a water bath for 20 minutes at 60 degrees Celsius (140 degrees Fahrenheit). Store the jars in the pantry for up to 12 months.

Dad's damper

If you fancy adding damper to your autumn meals, try Dad's tasty recipe.

Makes 1 loaf

2 cups (300 g) self-raising flour
2 teaspoons powdered milk
1 teaspoon bicarbonate of soda (baking soda)
Pinch of salt
1½ cups (375 ml) beer (you won't need it all)
Butter, to serve
Jam, to serve

1. Lightly flour the base and sides of your camp oven, and place it into the hot coals of a fire to heat up.
2. Place all of the dry ingredients into a bowl, and mix it well.
3. Add beer slowly while mixing with your fingertips until a dough is formed (ensure that it's not too sticky).
4. Mould the dough into a mounded shape, and place it into the camp oven. Put the lid on the oven.
5. Nestle the camp oven back into the coals, and add hot ash to the top of the oven.
6. Bake the damper for approximately 25 minutes before checking it. You will see that it has risen, and it has a cracked, light brown crust on top. Tap the bottom of the damper. If it sounds hollow, then it's ready to go. If not, then pop it back under the coals for another 10–15 minutes.
7. Serve laden with butter and jam.

Apple and custard tart with rough puff pastry

I bet you've already got a favourite version of this: a recipe from your granny, neighbour or favourite cafe. If that's true, then stick with a good thing – but if you fancy something different, then try this one on for size. It's a recipe that I created after looking at a picture of a tart taken during a photo shoot here at Black Barn Farm. I didn't actually see the tart being made, but it looked – and tasted – like all of my childhood memories rolled into one, even though Mum's tarts were more rustic and made from left-over preserved apple mash.

There are short cuts if time is tight, such as buying the pastry and being a little more haphazard with your apple slices, but sometimes the rewards come as much from the creating as the eating. Homemade pastry is always better than store-bought, and the tart can become a work of art if you just slow down a little. Sadly, it will still be scoffed quickly and only be pretty in your memory.

Makes 1 tart

For the tart base (pastry)

2 cups (500 g) grated very cold unsalted butter, halved and placed into 2 separate bowls

2½ cups (375 g) plain (all-purpose) flour

¾ teaspoon salt

240 ml (8 fl oz) ice-cold water

1 teaspoon ice-cold apple cider vinegar (see page 221; the acid helps to relax the gluten in the flour)

For the custard cream

3 egg yolks

3–4 tablespoons sugar (white sugar looks prettier, but I use rapadura or coconut sugar as they are slightly less sweet)

1 tablespoon plain (all-purpose) flour

1 tablespoon cornflour (cornstarch)

1 cup (250 ml) full-cream milk (coconut and soy milk are okay, too, but rice and almond milk just aren't fatty enough)

1 vanilla bean, split and seeds scraped, or 1 teaspoon vanilla essence

For the apple layer

1 tablespoon melted butter

½ teaspoon cinnamon

½ cup (110 g) sugar (again, white sugar is prettier as it doesn't discolour, but I use rapadura)

5 apples, cored and finely sliced (I love apples that are red with skin on; Gravenstein Red, King Cole and Gala work beautifully, as they hold their shape but soften perfectly)

¼ cup (85 g) apricot jam

1 tablespoon lemon juice or water

1. To make the pastry dough for the tart base, set aside one bowl of butter. Place the remaining ingredients into a large bowl, and **quickly** mix with your fingers until the dough has an even consistency, without any lumps of butter, dry flour or wet patches. Don't melt the butter to achieve this. Place the bowl of balled dough into the fridge to rest for 10 minutes.

2. Roll out the chilled dough into a rectangle that is about 5 mm (¼ in) thick. Scatter half of the retained bowl of grated butter lightly over two-thirds of the rolled-out dough. Fold the remaining third (without butter on it) over the middle third of the dough, and then fold the other third (that has butter on it) so it sits on top. You now have a three-layer rectangle of dough with butter between each layer. Turn the dough 90 degrees, and roll it out as before. Repeat the task again using the remaining butter. Make this process speedy so the butter doesn't melt.

3. Continue to roll and fold the dough as you did in Step 2, but without adding any more butter. Turn the dough 90 degrees each time you fold and roll, always in the same direction, until you have repeated the process three more times. If it's a warm day, then pop the dough into the freezer for a few minutes as you go. If the dough will be in there for longer than a few minutes, pop it into an airtight container first so it doesn't dry out.

4. Wrap the dough in two layers of plastic wrap. If you prefer not to utilise single-use plastic, then place it into an airtight container. Pop the dough into the freezer for 30 minutes to rest and cool.

5. Preheat the oven to 180 degrees Celsius (350 degrees Fahrenheit).

6. Oil a tart or flan pan.

7. Roll out the dough until it's about 3 mm (⅛ in) thick (try to estimate your quantity so you don't use more dough than necessary, as the dough should be handled as little as possible).

8. Line the pan with the dough, and allow just a little to come over the edge.

9. Blind bake the dough for 8 minutes. You can use uncooked rice to weigh down the dough and keep it in place.

10. To make the custard cream, place all of the ingredients into a bowl and whisk until smooth. Pour the liquid over the now-baked tart base. Ensure the liquid only fills two-thirds of the tart pan, allowing room for the apples.

11. To make the apple layer, mix the melted butter, cinnamon and sugar together in a bowl. Gently coat the apple slices with this mixture.

12. Lay the apple slices around your tart pan, on top of the custard cream, in a circular pattern.

13. Mix the apricot jam and lemon juice in a bowl, and brush the mixture onto the apple slices.

14. Place the pan into the oven, and bake the tart for 35 minutes or until it is solid when jiggled.

15. Serve the tart with the best cream you can find!

Apple and custard tart with rough puff pastry; right: Warm spiced apple cider

Warm spiced apple cider

Each year, we run a whole series of workshops and gatherings at the farm. The guests who arrive during autumn are almost always treated to a warm spiced apple cider. It's not hard to make, and for anyone with an apple tree in their yard (or down the road), it's the perfect way to use any apples that have been bumped, bruised or nibbled by birds. Rather than throwing these apples to the chickens, you can turn them into juice and then non-alcoholic cider.

The cider warms you from your toes up! It feels decadent, despite being the drink of common villagers since time immemorial. There is no alcohol, so kids can and will guzzle it, and it makes you feel like there's something to celebrate.

By the way, did you know that despite its name, allspice is not actually a mixture of spices? Rather, it's the dried, unripe berry from a tropical evergreen tree, *Pimenta dioica*, which is a Caribbean native. Unlike allspice, which is a single spice, mixed spice is a blend of several spices, including cinnamon, coriander seed, caraway, nutmeg, ginger and cloves.

This apple cider recipe can be adapted to suit your taste, but here's the one we use as a starting point.

Makes 8 cups (2 litres)

8 cups (2 litres) freshly pressed apple juice (we prefer it a bit 'fluffy', so we don't strain it at all. This means that it has 'bits' in it. If you prefer smooth drinking, then you'll need to strain it at the end. Another approach is to place all of your spices into a small muslin bag that's closed tightly during the simmering process and removed before you serve the cider.)

2 cinnamon sticks

2 teaspoons ground black pepper

20 cloves

1 orange, sliced

1 teaspoon allspice

1 teaspoon nutmeg

1. Mix all of the ingredients in a large stockpot.
2. Place the stockpot over low to medium heat, and simmer for at least 1½ hours.
3. Serve warm in mugs. If you fancy making an alcoholic version, add a glug of your favourite rum or whisky before serving.

Basic rhubarb compote

We harvest our rhubarb en masse, and then make this compote. It can be used immediately or kept in an airtight container in the freezer for up to 12 months. Once you've made up your compote, it's quick and easy to make a dessert or two. Try adding half a cup (125 ml) to an apple pie or mixing it with vanilla ice-cream, porridge, yoghurt, custard or chia pudding (see page 192).

Makes 4 cups (1 litre)

8–10 rhubarb stalks

Juice of 2 oranges

Dash of cinnamon, to taste (optional)

½ cup (110 g) rapadura sugar

1. Remove the leaves, ends and strings from the rhubarb stalks (use your fingers or a vegetable peeler for this last part). Wash and roughly chop the stalks.
2. Place the chopped rhubarb, orange juice and cinnamon (if using) into a saucepan, and cook over medium heat for 15 minutes.
3. Mix in the sugar, and simmer until the sugar has dissolved. Stir regularly so the sugar doesn't burn.

Fool you

Not you ... the rhubarb – rhubarb fool! This simple old English dessert intentionally mixes tart fruits with sweet whipped cream. You can dress this up or down, depending on your audience, time and pantry staples.

Serves 6

4 cups (1 litre) basic rhubarb compote (see left)

½ cup (175 g) honey

Zest and juice of 1 orange

1 vanilla bean, split and seeds scraped

Pinch of salt

¾ cup (185 ml) cream

1 tablespoon white sugar

1. Place the rhubarb compote, honey, orange zest and juice, vanilla bean and salt into a saucepan, and cook over low heat for 5–10 minutes. Stir to mix the ingredients.
2. Refrigerate the mixture until it is completely cold.
3. Whip the cream and sugar together until the mixture forms peaks.
4. Gently stir together half of the cream and half of the compote mix, and spoon it into six tall glasses.
5. Top each glass with a spoonful of cream and then a spoonful of compote mix, and serve.

DEEP CHILL

Winter is a time to tuck in, stay warm and proactively seek a state of hibernation. Some people find these harsh months a bit ho-hum, while others revel in the cosy inside days. The kettle warms gently for bottomless pots of sweet goodness; meals are slow cooked in the Rayburn stove (see page 296) and are as rich and hearty as the day is cold and dark. The food stores from the pantry become the daily offering, as the garden sits limp and lifeless except for the odd patch of silverbeet (Swiss chard) or kale.

Bare-branched trees hang grey, battered by the wind and rain, while the frosted ground stays firm and sterile for weeks on end. Whipping cold winds make your cheeks rosy, and the briskness of the air makes you feel alive.

These are the days to be in the house, a friend's kitchen or the shed. It's time to take stock of the year that's been, listing your successes and your failures, while planning for the next year.

These days are for repairing and caring, allowing yourself time for deep rest and nourishment, and taking the machinery out for a service and the tools out for an oiling. Lie low, turn inwards, go slow and take care.

SIFTING 'STUFF'

If you are a re-user, upcycler and committed second-hand buyer, it can be really hard to pass up great things when you find them – so, inevitably, you accumulate loads of stuff that doesn't have a dedicated purpose. A regular clean-up and commitment to an ordered storage process makes it easier to put your incredible 'finds' to good use rather than allowing them to languish in never-to-be-seen-again locations, unused.

While the skies are grey and the drizzle persists, don't be glum. It's the perfect excuse to audit your stuff ... all of it. Look at your kitchen cupboards, wardrobe, toolshed, pantry, kids' toy boxes, underwear drawer, linen cupboard, the third kitchen drawer down – all of those areas with dark corners that are exceptionally talented at hiding unneeded rubbish. Apply whichever philosophy you prefer: 'Does it spark joy?', 'Is this practical?', 'Have I used this in the last six months?' or 'Does it have a specific purpose?'

There are whole books on the psychology of living with less clutter, and I'm not about to write another. However, I am going to highlight the liberation and lightness that comes from shedding belongings that no longer serve you.

A culture of consumption has led the Western world to acquire more belongings than our grandparents would have imagined possible, and it's not done us any favours. It forces us to make more decisions for every action we undertake, deludes us into thinking that we need more space for storage, and fills us with expectation to endlessly update what we have, despite the existing version still working beautifully. There is also a cultural expectation to participate in the 'purchased gift' economy, which results in obligation buying rather than giving with love. Often these obligation purchases tick all the boxes, but result in unnecessary clutter that is low in quality and ill thought through – yet we feel obliged to hold on to them.

Someone once said to me: 'If you really want to know what the inside of someone's mind is like, take a look behind their closed doors.' I think of this often when I have house-sitters coming to stay, and it prompts a thorough clean-out. What does the inside of your cupboards look like?

Get 'stuff' sorted

Keep these tips in mind as you're going through your items:

- Only commit to the space you can complete at one time (cupboard, shelf, drawer, room, shed).
- Make an earnest decision that this is your once-a-year declutter, and you will not be swayed by thoughts of nostalgia, obligation, waste guilt or unrealistic expectations. Stay strong!
- Equally, don't be swayed by the idea that 'this could be very handy, I'll keep it just in case'. If it's been there for two years, and you still don't have a clear plan for its final use, then let someone else put it to use. It's not being wasted – it's being used as it was intended.

Sort your items simply into one of these categories:

- **keep to use** – define where it lives, and make this clear.
- **keep to fix/repurpose/upcycle** – only keep things with a clear and intentional end use, otherwise they go in the 'for later' pile.
- **give to others** – op shop, clothes swap, dress-up box, craft box.
- **throw it in the bin** – keep in mind that paper and cardboard can be used as a first layer under mulch in garden beds, metal can be recycled, plastic pots can often be returned to the place of purchase, books can be donated, and clothes make great rags, painting drop sheets and dog blankets. So before you bin it, think about its other myriad uses.
- **'for later'** – if it can't find a place in any of the above categories, then pop it in this pile. But you must commit to firmly finalising this pile by a set date. If this is too hard, then invite an objective friend to assist you.

Once you've decluttered, commit to a few systems to minimise the job next winter:

- **'one in, one out'** – if you buy a number of tops/shoes/bags/books from a store or op shop, then you need to donate the same number of tops/shoes/bags/books back to an op shop.
- **op shop box** – have one on the go all the time, so everyone in the house can fill it as they find things that no longer fit, bring them joy or serve their purpose.
- **glass jar box** – this is also on the go all the time, with food items that are ready to donate to your nearest co-op or bulk-buy store.
- **mending basket** – for all of those things that need a quick stitch. Pop them into this basket, and put aside an hour a week to get them all darned or hemmed at the same time.
- **dedicated spaces** – create specific places for things, such as a kids' craft cupboard, fabric store, seed store, rag bag, wrapping paper box … you get the drift.

Revel in the virtuous lightness that floods your psyche once you're done. It feels beyond good to let go of stuff in your life that can be put to better use elsewhere. It liberates you from having to deal with it in your everyday actions.

Right: We raise a toast in the bonfire light to an abundant future harvest.

WASSAIL! WASSAIL! WASSAIL!

What the heck is a wassail, you ask? In short, it's a winter tonic for your primal desires. In times gone by, villagers in cider-growing regions of western England performed a ritual each year during the depths of winter. They gathered together and – led by their ceremonial 'king' and 'queen' – they created a cacophonous racket while they marched through the trees to scare away the evil spirits and to will abundance for the following season's harvest. They drank cider aplenty from a communal 'wassail bowl', and the entire annual affair was celebratory.

At Black Barn Farm, we pick and choose which parts of the ritual we bring to life. On the whole, it has an other-worldly appeal that

allows us to forget the bitterness of winter and sneak out of our hibernating state to get jolly with our tribe on the night of the shortest day of the year. Comradeship is shared over a potluck feast in the warmth of a bonfire, while kids of all ages range free in all directions.

Dressed in ridiculous but wondrous layers of garb harking back to pagan times, we chant home-written songs that reflect our orchard life. With bellies warmed by spiced apple cider, we float through the dripping darkness while banging our sticks and carrying makeshift lanterns to light our way through the paddock to the 'mother tree'. Planted in the centre of our orchard, this tree was grafted with scion wood taken from trees on family properties and roadsides. We weave magic into leaf mandalas around the tree, before heading towards the bonfire site. A sense of nervy anticipation fills us all before the 'ghouls' carrying flame torches touch down on the ignition point, and the exploding bonfire cuts a sharp slice through the darkness to cheers of delight. We raise our voices in a chant of encouragement for future harvests, and we toast on cue to the repeated calls of 'Wassail! Wassail! Wassail!'

We love our wassail mid-winter feast. Without a doubt, it's the most nurturing annual gathering that we host. Everyone contributes just a little of their own magic, which together makes it richer than the sum of the parts. Together we create a pot of colour and chaos, and together we celebrate.

You don't need paddocks to play. A small bonfire, warmed cider and some whimsical chants with neighbours under a backyard tree are just as much fun, and they build a richness for those in your community.

POTS OF HOMEGROWN 'TEA'

A seasonal life quickly becomes filled with simple daily rituals. One of my most treasured rituals is enjoying the bottomless pot of 'tea' – or herbal blend – that is forever on the go.

Regardless of when you start your day, the most important decision is the simplest. Which cup, which teapot and which herbal blend? While our pantry hosts a range of store-bought teas, these are really the emergency go-tos. By far, the preference is for the herbs we grow and dry during the warmer months of high heat.

Over the years, I've collected teapots from all over the world – mostly from op shops or garage sales – and each of them tickles my memory bank in a very different way. Cups are similar but are more often connected to people not places, as most

have been gifts from or handmade by different friends. Choosing a teapot and cup is not a long-winded task, as I have a sense of the memories I want to spark and the joyful humans with whom I want to share my morning moment – even if it's just in my mind. Do you have a favourite cup or teapot?

TOOL-FIXING TIME

In the height of the productive season, the tools of our trade are in high demand. The days are full, so there's not much time to care for these tools. But during winter, when life is slower, we seek activities that are undercover, and the tools are mostly sitting on the shelf untouched. It's the perfect time to go through the pile of bent bottoms, twisted forks, snapped handles and loose heads, and give them all a once-over. Make or buy new handles, bang out twists, tighten nails/screws, sharpen blades and give all of the wooden handles a quick sand and oil. We just use olive oil – rancid or old oil is great, and we do it all in our machinery shed, which is dry. We know that if we give them a lick of love at least once each year during winter, then our most important food-production assets will keep going for the next season. It also saves time and money down the track.

Nourish

DEEP REST

With the darkest days wrapped around us, and daylight hours at their shortest, now is the time to turn inwards towards contemplation, reflection and self-care. Reset your pace to one that sustains, rebuild your health until you feel vital, and ensure that you take time to listen to your body, mind and soul. It's the gift that you should offer yourself without guilt or sacrifice.

Don't just rest your physical self, but take time to recalibrate your mental self. Identify the actions that erode your stamina, and take time to be in your own mind. It's more than one single day of recovery – it's a whole season of it. Here are some things to try:

◆ Take walks alone.
◆ Limit screen time – commit to full days without digital devices at all.
◆ Select a slow and gentle skill to learn, such as knitting, weaving, drawing or pottery.
◆ Actively connect with your family – read books aloud, draw or cook together, sort the seeds, play cards or write stories.
◆ Rug up and go exploring in the rain.
◆ Seek cathartic repetitive tasks, such as chopping wood or building stone walls.
◆ Take all day to make sourdough pizza bases or a loaf of bread.
◆ Create and perfect your own chai blend.
◆ Read that pile of waiting books.
◆ Take afternoon naps.
◆ Sleep in and go to bed early.
◆ Sing songs.
◆ Take baths.

◆ Plan your spring garden.
◆ Daydream uninterrupted.
◆ Scrap your to-do list, and let your days unfurl as they need to.

Luxuriate in the gift of time that you've intentionally carved out during this quiet, deep-chill season.

READ A SINGLE BOOK

The theory of multitasking leaves a lot to be desired when assessed through the lens of wellbeing rather than productivity. Taking in new information from every angle is a sure-fire way to heighten your stress response. Consequently, a simple commitment to a single communication medium is a powerful act when seeking self-nourishment.

I'm not suggesting that you do it all the time – I don't! But at least once a year, usually in the depths of winter, I select one book (or a few if I'm up for it) and down tools on other media (phones, TV, papers, magazines) for a week, so I can give my undivided attention to this one item of stimulation and thought-provoking material. It might sound simple, but I bet you can't name the last time you took a break from having multi-screen messages fighting for your brain's attention.

It's worth considering using a real book for this exercise, rather than an e-reader. There's true value in the tactility of holding the book, turning the pages, smelling the paper and being totally untouched by electronic gadgets.

WINTER WALKS

We're up most mornings for a wake-up walk, even in winter. It's brisk but invigorating, and it leaves our cheeks rosy for the day. While our winters are cold in this part of the country, they are usually clear. So it's a season for wearing layer upon layer of natural materials and breathing deeply outside.

One winter, I was racked with Ross River fever, and my 12-year-old was seeking time out from the stresses of school. The physical limitations were a mind game to manage, but it was a chance for me to really hear and respond to what we both needed.

I wiped my list clean, and we took each day as it came. Without a doubt, the most nurturing place to be was in the bush. Despite my aches and lethargy, and his fatigue and resistance, we'd don the hiking boots, fill

the water bottles and head off to a place with no expectation, no judgement and no rules. We could breath calmly, slow the internal monologue and be humbled by the magnitude of the natural world around us.

Together, we found a foot-falling rhythm, raised our heart rate for all the right reasons and let our minds be still. We had the pleasure of seeing koalas, wombats and echidnas. We marvelled at the smallest of wonders: intricate lichen patterns, vibrant fungi, twisted and intriguing shapes in the bark of trees, and old gum trees falling before our very eyes on the stillest of days. The power of biophilia was the single best way to nourish a feverish body and settle an anxious mind.

MAKE YOUR OWN CLEANING AND BATHROOM PRODUCTS

This feels like the natural time to reset your habits. If you've taken a keen interest in minimising your plastic usage (even if you haven't, now is as good a time as any), then you will have noticed that the regular culprits in your recycling bin are the multitude of bottles from your bathroom and cleaning cupboards.

If plastic reduction doesn't shake you into action, then what about considering the impact of the synthetic – often petroleum-based – chemicals on both your body and the world into which they then flow, as they wreak havoc on both. Or perhaps it's the complicated, absurdly long-winded journey they've taken to get to you, leaving a carbon footprint the size of your street in their wake.

Finally, if you're still not convinced to leave the pre-packaged cleaning muscle on the supermarket shelf, then what about considering your ability to support a local artisan at a market or teach your kids a new skill? It's much better than supporting a multinational corporate enterprise and its endless quest for the bottom line.

It's surprisingly easy to create your own DIY solutions. All you need is some time up your sleeve and a few ingredients that you probably already have in the cupboard. My theory is that if hot water, bicarbonate of soda (baking soda), orange essence, pantyhose, eucalyptus oil and vinegar can't fix it, then it's a seriously drastic problem that no fancy-pants, store-bought, chemical-filled multinational-owned liquid will be able to fix, either. So rather than succumbing to the hype surrounding branded cleaning goods, have a crack at creating your own and build new habits in your household-cleaning regime.

If making your own laundry liquid doesn't appeal to you, then consider using soap nuts (the cracked and dried berries of *Sapindus* species, which contain foaming saponins). A natural alternative to synthetic detergents, soap nuts are best packed in calico bags before throwing them into the wash, and they last a long time.

Rather than succumbing to the hype surrounding branded cleaning goods, have a crack at creating your own and build new habits.

Homemade toothpaste

It might not be minty, but it will certainly do the job! The clove oil is optional, as it can make your mouth feel a little numb – not everyone likes this feeling. The amount below will make enough for approximately 30 uses.

Makes 80 g (2¾ oz)

1 tablespoon crushed dry eggshells

2 tablespoons organic coconut oil

1 drop clove oil (optional)

8–10 drops eucalyptus oil

1 tablespoon bicarbonate of soda (baking soda)

1. To dry the eggshells, preheat the oven to 100 degrees Celsius (200 degrees Fahrenheit).
2. Spread the eggshells out on a baking tray, and place the tray into the oven for 30 minutes. Remove the tray from the oven, and set aside the eggshells to cool. Crush the eggshells using a mortar and pestle.
3. Mix all of the ingredients thoroughly, and store the toothpaste in a small pot with a lid for up to two weeks.

Do-it-yourself shampoo

It seems that DIY shampoo is the hardest to master. Most shampoos seem to miss the mark, leaving your hair limp and oily or looking like a tangled bird's nest. This one manages to find a balance, but it will make you teary if you get it into your eyes.

After shampooing your hair, follow up with another plastic-free, chemical-free solution: apple cider vinegar! If you make your own scrap apple vinegar (see page 221), this will work just as well. Because skin is naturally acidic, apple cider vinegar helps to restore your skin's natural pH, eventually resulting in a more balanced scalp.

Only make the quantity listed, as it will keep for just one month in your shower.

Makes 1 cup (250 ml)

½ cup (125 ml) coconut milk (use coconut cream if you have dry hair)

½ cup (125 ml) liquid Castile soap

20 drops essential oils, such as lavender, peppermint, rosemary or orange

1. Combine the ingredients in the shampoo container, seal tightly and then shake until the ingredients are well mixed.

Laundry liquid

It works for either hot or cold washes, and in either top or front loaders. Use about ¼ cup (60 ml) per load, or a little more for really grubby work clothes. Pre-soak stains with the liquid before adding it to the wash.

Makes 8 cups (2 litres)

8 cups (2 litres) water

½ cup (220 g) borax

½ cup (275 g) washing soda (you can use bicarbonate of soda [baking soda], but it isn't as stable or strong as washing soda)

¼ cup (60 ml) liquid Castile soap (you can use soap flakes if you'd prefer)

12 drops essential oils (one type or a mixture of them)

1 cup (250 ml) white vinegar (apple cider vinegar can be used if you make your own and are trying to avoid more plastic bottles; see page 221)

1. Pour the water, borax and washing soda into a pot, and gently boil over high heat until the powdered ingredients have dissolved.
2. Remove the pot from the heat.
3. Add the liquid Castile soap, essential oils and white vinegar to the borax mixture, and stir until the consistency is smooth. Keep stirring as the mixture cools.
4. Store the laundry liquid in well-sealed containers indefinitely.
5. Shake the liquid before use, so it's less like a gel and more like a detergent.

Window cleaner

This works best if all cobwebs and dust are vacuumed off the window first. Once the liquid has been sprayed on the window, wipe it off with newspaper.

Makes 1.2 litres (42 fl oz)

4 cups (1 litre) water

100 ml (3½ fl oz) methylated spirits

100 ml (3½ fl oz) lemon juice

1. Pour all of the ingredients into a re-usable spray bottle.
2. Shake well before use.

Multipurpose cleaner

This is good for benchtops, desks, doors and walls, and interior surfaces of the car.

Makes 4 cups (1 litre)

1 teaspoon eucalyptus oil

½ teaspoon citrus oil

2 cups (500 ml) water

2 cups (500 ml) white vinegar (apple cider vinegar can be used, too; see page 221)

1. Mix all of the ingredients together, and store the liquid in a dark spray bottle.
2. Shake well before use.

Far left: A quick pick of cumquats before simmering them in sugar syrup.

Left: Scrumped roadside apples make a good winter porridge topping and store as apple sauce for months.

Grow

WINTER CITRUS

An orange a day will keep scurvy at bay, or so the saying goes. But when you live in a climate that isn't conducive to growing citrus, it's a hard mantra to maintain. We grow a wide range of citrus (Meyer lemon, Lisbon lemon, Tahitian lime, kaffir lime, ruby grapefruit, Hamlin orange, Washington orange, navel orange, emperor mandarin, imperial mandarin and cumquats), but we've pushed the citrus-growing boundaries and made endless amendments to fulfil our hopes.

Everything is on trifoliata rootstock, which has a higher tolerance for cold weather. The trees are all planted on the eastern side of our packing shed, so they're flooded with morning sun and protected from the frost that occurs down the hill. Each year, they are wrapped in a frost blanket from the end of autumn until the middle of spring. So far, they are all still alive, but our anticipated bounty of sweet and juicy fruits still eludes us. Each year, the trees grow and produce more fruits. By the ten-year mark, we hope to have all of our vitamin C needs at our fingertips.

Cumquats are the frost hardiest of all the citrus. We keep ours in pots and simply shift them under the verandahs for the peak of winter. Their trump card is their abundance of small, tart, orange fruits. While the kids love eating them freshly picked, I prefer to cook them first. I slowly simmer them on the Rayburn stove with sugar and water, before swirling them through ice-cream for dessert.

Right: Dried citrus peel is a perfect firelighter and infusion ingredient.

Far right: Soaking and sprouting a variety of legumes, such as these mung beans, is an easy winter job.

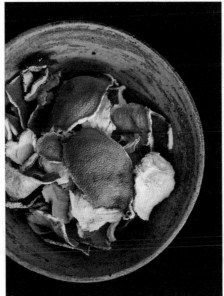

Natural firelighters

Lighting the fire in our old house is a task that we try to put off for as long as possible, because once it's lit, it has to burn until mid-spring thanks to the cold hills around us. To kick it off, we use homemade natural firelighters. Not only are they missing the toxic smells and chemical ingredients of their store-bought alternatives, but they also smell delightful as they burn – and they're free.

The process is simple. Leave your orange and mandarin peels on top of the wood box to dehydrate naturally until they're totally hard and dry. If you don't have a wood box, simply leave the peels in the sunshine (bring them in at night so they don't become damp). You can also dry them in a slow oven – 60 degrees Celsius (140 degrees Fahrenheit) – overnight, in a dehydrator overnight, or on the kitchen windowsill away from the steamy sink.

Store them in an airtight container until you're ready to use them. Voila!

SPROUTED NUTRITION

If anything takes the award for packing a nutritious punch in a pint-sized packet, then it has to be sprouted grains, seeds and legumes. Although they are tiny, they are hands-down one of the easiest ways to up your goodness quota and boost your health. I find that these are a particularly good go-to in winter, when fresh greens are not as available from my garden and more expensive to buy from the supermarket.

Sprouting grains before consuming them provides many health benefits. It neutralises the antinutrients that can cause mineral deficiencies, inflammation and bloating. It also turns dry grains into living plants, from which our bodies can gain vitamin B, carotene and vitamin C.

You can sprout loads of grains, seeds and legumes, and it's super easy to do. The main method we use is simply to soak them in a glass jar for the time listed in the chart to the right, and then pour the water out. Each day (until the sprouts appear), rinse the grains, seeds or legumes a few times until the water runs clear. It's helpful to add a touch of lemon juice or apple cider vinegar (see page 221) to the water during the soaking phase. Refrigerate the sprouts for up to five days.

Activating goodness

As well as sprouting grains, seeds and legumes, you can also activate nuts for many of the same nutritional outcomes. Activating nuts is as simple as soaking them in water (almonds for ten hours, pecans for five hours, walnuts for four hours) before dehydrating them until they are bone dry. You can then use them as required. If you are using an oven rather than a dehydrator, ensure that the temperature is no higher than 60 degrees Celsius (140 degrees Fahrenheit).

SPROUTING TIPS

If you're going to all this trouble to make sprouted seeds and grains as nutritious as possible, then start with a great foundation. Commit to buying organic seeds and grains, as many plants are sprayed with desiccants before the harvest to kill off the plant and make the harvest easier.

So you don't become overwhelmed, start with just one variety of seed. Once you're into the swing of things and you've built them into your daily rhythm, add more.

SPROUTING-TIME CHART

These are the main things we sprout, and the time they take.

GRAIN, SEED OR LEGUME	SOAKING TIME	SPROUTING TIME
alfalfa	8 hours	4 days
barley	8 hours	3 days
chickpeas	12 hours	12 hours
lentils	8 hours	12 hours
mung beans	1 day	4 days
oats	6 hours	3 days
pepitas (pumpkin seeds)	8 hours	1–2 days
quinoa	2 hours	3 days
red kidney beans	8 hours	3–5 days
sesame seeds	8 hours	2 days
sunflower seeds	2 hours	2–3 days
wheat	8 hours	3 days

CREATE A STICK FENCE

Stick fencing became our 'thing' quite by accident. Because I'm impatient and prone to being spontaneous, I bought six geese home before we were ready. We had no fences around our new vegie patch, so the geese soon demolished everything I'd planted.

We needed an inexpensive solution using something we already had, and being surrounded by bush, our fence lines were full of sticks. We had also just removed kilometres of internal fencing, so we had loads of wire rolls. Voila! Here was our solution. While it's not wombat-proof, it does keep out the chickens, geese, wallabies and dogs. As a really quick guide, here's the eight-step process for creating this type of fence.

Step 1: Collect the sticks

As strong and straight as possible. We've used eucalyptus, but there are no rules other than avoiding soft wood, which will rot too fast. We use approximately 26 sticks per 3-metre (10-foot) length.

Step 2: Cut all the sticks to size

We've stuck to 120 centimetres (47 inches), as that's the perfect height for animal exclusion.

Step 3: Install the posts

The best distance is 3 metres (10 feet) apart. We use hardwood milled posts and ensure that at least one third of each post is buried in the ground using crushed gravel with differing sediment sizes to pack them in hard. We paint the posts with wood protector first.

Step 4: Drill the holes

Drill two holes all the way through each post, one that is 20 centimetres (8 inches) down from the top, and one that is 20 centimetres (8 inches) up from the ground. Make sure you drill in the same direction as the fence line.

Step 5: Thread the wire

Measure out the length of the fence in wire, double it and add an extra 1 metre (40 inches). This is your top wire. Do the same for the bottom wire. Now thread the doubled-over wire through the holes in the top of each of the posts, and affix the wire securely at one end. Do the same for the bottom row.

Step 6: Ready the sticks

You will need the sticks to be around 8–12 centimetres (3–5 inches) apart if you want to keep children and animals out. Lay out the required number of sticks in each 'bay' so they are within easy reach.

Step 7: Place the sticks

Twist the top wire over itself four to seven times (depending on the distance you want your sticks apart), leaving a gap to insert the stick. Do the same with the bottom wire. Insert the first stick, and then twist the top and bottom wire in the *opposite* direction to the way you twisted the first time. Insert the next stick. It's crucial that you remember to switch the direction of your wire twisting after each stick, otherwise your wires will become a tangled mess.

Step 8: Pull tight

At the end of your fence, use fencing pliers to pull the top and bottom pieces of wire as tight as you can and then nail them into place, bending the nail over.

COMPOST PILES

Unless you're in a multistorey apartment, making compost is one of the most effective time-for-return activities you can do. You can even make it in a tiny backyard – and even if you don't have any of your own materials. I have vivid memories of Mum dragging hessian bags through the leafy suburban streets; they were filled to the brim with the abundance of the season to use as mulch on the garden or as the base for a compost mix. She also gathered seaweed (only taking what she needed) and grass clippings. I've been known to pounce on the local council lawnmower as they zip around parks, and they've willingly let me fill my bag with cut grass.

Compost puts to good use things that are readily available and usually need to be removed from the house or garden (such as fallen leaves, cut grass and kitchen scraps). It adds goodness to your garden by building biodiverse and nutrient-dense soil, which is ideal for growing your own food. Compost-improved soil is a gift for gardeners and the globe, because it:

+ retains soil moisture
+ builds plant immunity, which in turn suppresses plant diseases and pests, reducing the need for expensive fertilisers and manures
+ reduces the amount of organic waste going to landfill, and prevents greenhouse gas emissions and leachate that can pollute land, groundwater and waterways
+ helps to absorb and filter run-off, protecting streams from erosion and pollution.

It's a perfect, harmonious cycle! We can all get in on the act. The main trick you'll have to learn is how to get the balance right. You need a mix of 50 per cent green materials (nitrogen) and 50 per cent brown materials (carbon), with a good dose of oxygen (regular turning) and enough water to keep the mixture moist but not soaking.

A composting system can be started in old garbage bins, wooden boxes or a simple heap. You don't require fancy store-bought compost buckets. Actually, it's easier to create piles directly on the ground – just keep them tight (so that their temperature rises), cover them with a tarpaulin and water them regularly.

A heap of ingredients

Make sure that your material is cut into small pieces, so it breaks down quickly. DO add:

+ coffee grounds (brown layer)
+ dead flowers (brown layer)
+ eggshells that are well crushed (brown layer)
+ fallen leaves (brown layer)
+ old potting mix (brown layer)
+ old newspapers (brown layer)
+ sawdust, but not from treated timber (brown layer)
+ seaweed, but only collect washed-up seaweed (brown layer)
+ tea leaves and tea bags, but snip off the metal staple first (brown layer)
+ soft-stemmed plants (green layer)
+ used vegetable oil (green layer)
+ weeds, but not couch, kikuyu or nut grasses (green layer)
+ grass cuttings (green layer)
+ kitchen scraps (green layer).

DON'T add:

◆ citrus peel
◆ diseased plants
◆ animal fats
◆ glossy magazines or pamphlets
◆ large branches (anything thicker than your little finger needs to be cut into small pieces)
◆ meat and dairy products
◆ metals, plastics and glass
◆ weeds that have seeds or underground stems (such as couch).

If you are making a compost heap in winter and using what you've got access to, then the bulk of your pile will be grass, leaves and garden clippings following the end-of-harvest clean-out.

How to make a compost pile

There are just three easy steps:

1. Choose a place that won't be disturbed for at least a month. Ensure that it's not too sunny, or the pile will dry out, but not too dark and damp, or it won't get warm enough.
2. Gather your ingredients, and layer them by alternating between green and brown layers. Ensure that you don't have any green or brown layers that are too thick and that they each make up around 50 per cent of the overall mix. Water the finished pile so that it's moist but not soaking wet.
3. Turn the compost pile at least weekly using a garden fork to keep it aerated.

The compost should be ready to use on your garden beds or in your pots within about six weeks.

NATURAL PARASITE TONIC

In the lead-up to the spring egg-laying season, we get organised with the things required to keep our chickens healthy. One of these is making the black walnut parasite tonic that we add to the birds' water at a ratio of one capful to 16 cups (4 litres) of water daily during spring.

Black walnuts have long been used in herbal remedies for parasite control. They are powerfully potent, so we don't use them for human consumption – although I know folk who do. Make sure you research them thoroughly before you adopt the practice yourself.

Although black walnuts are not readily available, you can often find them in fresh food markets and online. They are the rootstock of most commercially grown walnuts. It's not uncommon to find that the odd grafted variety has died back, leaving the tree to resume life as just a black walnut, so this can be a good source.

To make the tonic, you'll need 25 sliced black walnuts and 6 cups (1.5 litres) of low-cost white spirit (vodka or gin). Push the sliced walnuts into a bottle, and cover them with the spirit. Place the lid on the bottle, and store it in a cool, dark space for six weeks before use. I often add a little more spirit to the mix later on, as I want to stretch out its use across the whole of spring.

Note that black walnut will stain anything it comes into contact with once cut (such as skin and wood), so be sure to wear gloves and use an old chopping board when cutting them up – the stain will last longer than you.

RAYBURN STOVE LOVE

When you score yourself an old house, the gift that keeps on giving is the endless draughts, heat-sapping windows, gappy floorboards and lack of insulation. While some of these are easily fixed, others are not – and freezing your bum off in winter just seems to be a part of life in an old home within a subalpine climate.

When we moved back to Stanley, Victoria, which sits at 800 metres (2600 feet) above sea level and can experience frosts as early as New Year's Day and as late as New Year's Eve, we had hoped to buy land without a house so that we didn't inherit a 140-year-old building without a temperature-sensitive design philosophy. But we searched for ten years; eventually the soil composition, slope direction, water guarantee and residual chemical levels of the land became more important, and the house was a secondary influence on the decision.

Before our first winter, we scoured second-hand online haunts and researched until the wee hours in the hope of finding a heating solution. Charlie grew up with an AGA cooker and kept leaning towards a slow-combustion wood-fired solution, but our financial reality meant that this wasn't possible. One day we spoke to a retired gent who had worked for Rayburn all his life, and he loved them so much that he spent his days bringing old ones back to their former glory. It was a long-winded conversation, speckled with repeated flourishes of adoration for the old girls, but one that ended in us committing to a Rayburn Supreme that had been rescued from a house fire but could be sandblasted to black. DONE!

We waited 12 months for the stove to be refurbished. When we finally picked her up, the half-tonne beauty spent the following two years in the shed while we found time to create a flooring foundation that was robust enough to carry her. Our teeth rattled through three winters in all before we finally had the foundation in place and the personnel on site to install her.

It was NOT instant love. I revelled in the new warmth of our home, but I just couldn't get the knack of keeping her hot without flooding the house with smoke and setting off the fire alarm. Charlie developed his love affair before I did, and in the end he mediated our relationship until it became what it is today – complete and utter devotion.

With a regular feed (and by this I mean full wheelbarrows of wood daily), she heats our radiators throughout the house, slow cooks our dinner most nights (see page 304 for our slow-cooked lamb or chicken recipe), bubbles a bottomless pot of tea and fills our kitchen with a warmth that makes me nostalgic and dries our boots all in one. Feeding her is a daily chore, but it has now formed part of our rhythm and adds exclamation marks to our days during the winter months. It's a ritual I'm glad to be done with come the longer, warmer days of spring, but one that I revel in during those short, dreary days of winter.

BAKING BREAD

Do you try your hand at anything regularly, despite being no good at it, simply because you enjoy the process? Bread-making is this for me.

The bread we eat is often hard on the outside, heavy and doughy on the inside, and quite possibly a little too tart with sourdough flavour. Despite me making it daily and having scoured instruction manuals for helpful tweaks, my final product is still sub par. However, the rhythm it adds to my routine, the feel of my hands in the flour and the smell of it cooking are gifts enough to spur the daily practice.

We still eat the lot, and the kids have nodded their approval; with plenty of butter, the bread holds its own while warm (sort of). It was disheartening and frustrating at first, but I've come to the conclusion that it's okay to embrace being mediocre at something but love the process nonetheless. That's been a liberating discovery. I'm not going to share all of my failures with you, but I am going to encourage you to try making your own bread for the sheer pleasure of the tactility and the virtue of pulling a loaf – even a flat and heavy one – fresh from the oven.

So until I improve by accident, I'm going to soldier on with my brick-like loaves and love every minute of it: both the making and the eating!

NUTTING OUT NUT MILKS

I often get asked about nut milks. I waver with these, as I resent their packaging – especially when I can swap or buy fresh goat milk in a re-usable jar from a nearby friend. But actually, I do feel much better when I avoid dairy products. Rather than buying nut milk, I find that it's relatively easy to make it myself.

I know that nut milk is contentious as it's not really 'milk', but I'm not buying into that

hot topic here. I will say that they often cop a bad rap because they generate loads of food waste, even when made at home. A simple solution is to use the left-over meal after the milking process. I've dropped a great recipe for quinoa and nut-meal vegetarian rolls on page 307.

Actually, nut milks are as rich in proteins and minerals as the milk from cows or goats, and they're pretty quick to make.

How to make almond milk

Simply follow these step-by-step instructions:

1. Get your hands on 250 g (9 oz) of nuts to make 4 cups (1 litre) of milk. If you don't like almonds, you can use cashews, brazil nuts or even hazelnuts.
2. Place the nuts into a bowl with a little salt, and thoroughly cover them with water. Leave the nuts to soak overnight.
3. Drain and rinse the nuts, and place them into a blender with 4 cups (1 litre) of water. Blend the mixture thoroughly, and then leave it to sit for 10 minutes.
4. Place the mixture into a nut-milk bag or some muslin; even an old linen tea towel would work. Let the mixture drain into a jug or bowl, making sure to squeeze the bag as dry as possible.
5. Store the nut milk in the fridge for up to three days.

Use organic nuts where possible. I add a few almonds to all milks, because it offers a sweetness you might want given there's no added sugar. Because nut milk doesn't store for very long, make smaller batches more often rather than one big batch a week. You can coordinate your soaking so that it happens at the same time you feed your sourdough starter or your kombucha scoby. If you won't have time to use your nut meal in the next 48 hours, be sure to freeze it or it'll go rancid, even in the fridge.

GET GOOD GUTS

Cool, shorter days are the nudge I need to get my **fire cider tonic** off and running. It requires a little lead time, so starting well before flu season is key.

We began making this when we found it in a funky boutique food store and realised that we had the majority of the ingredients in our patch already and could get everything else via trade or the co-op. While its popularity has taken off in recent years, it's been used as a herbal remedy to ward off illness since American herbalist Rosemary Gladstar presented her idea in the late 1970s.

I swear by it as an immunity booster and double my dose if I'm feeling like my health is wavering. The ingredients can vary depending on what you have easy access to, and it's worth making sure you only use organic ingredients. As a rule, it should always include at least the following:

- apple cider vinegar – easy to make at home (see page 221), with a million benefits. My personal favourite is that it's a digestive aid, so take a quick swig after dinner daily.
- horseradish – helps alleviate sinus congestion and headaches. Even chopping or grating horseradish has this effect, you'll see!
- rosemary – boosts the immune and circulatory systems.
- ginger – helps with digestion, infections and nausea. As a chronic morning-sickness sufferer, I can vouch for this.
- garlic – a secret superpower with antimicrobial and antibacterial properties. See pages 144–5 for a guide to growing garlic.
- onion – has similar properties to garlic, but is also great for preventing or recovering from colds or flu.
- citrus – it's a good analgesic and anti-inflammatory. I just use the peel, but it can leave a bitter aftertaste, so be careful not to use too much.
- cayenne pepper – can help move blood through the cardiovascular system. Blood circulation leads to healing.
- sage – great as a digestive aid. I have plenty of this, so I use it; not everyone likes the strong flavour, though.
- honey – soothes inflamed tissues and organs. Using local honey can also help with allergies. It's even better if you get it from your own hives.

These ingredients may seem intimidating, but the tonic is supposed to be hot and spicy to give the body a little kick. You're essentially infusing apple cider vinegar with the other flavours, straining the liquid and then adding honey to sweeten the tonic. See page 306 for the fire cider tonic recipe.

AMAZING ARTICHOKES

The perennial Jerusalem artichoke must surely be one of the easiest plants to grow. It proliferates year on year with no attention, and tolerates just about any conditions thrown at it. Then, it delivers more knobbly tubers than one could ever imagine eating, especially when they have a reputation for making most of us uncomfortably gassy.

I've long wondered if there's a way to put their abundance to use, as they really could feed an army. Could fermenting such an annual abundance be the answer to my quandary? Yes and no. Yes, because this process allows you to store large quantities of them for up to six months, and the resulting delight is versatile and has significantly fewer side effects than roasted versions. No, because preparation is a somewhat fiddly job, mostly due to the washing that's required before you can use them. However, if you are curious about these delicious yet ugly, practical yet fiddly root vegies, then give them a go!

Right: Creating fire cider tonic is fun, and the result is as potent as it is pretty (see page 306 for the recipe).

Far left: Jerusalem artichokes have sunny yellow flowers, which may be why they are also known as 'sunchokes'.

Left: Fermenting Jerusalem artichokes uses the root of the plant and is a four- to six-week process.

Fermented fartichokes

Inulin is the farting culprit, but through the process of lacto-fermentation, this long-chain carb is broken down so there's less bacteria food in the gut. Once they're fermented – which, after washing the twisted tubers, is an easy process – they can be used in a stack of ways: sliced on snack or cheese plates, served with beer and nuts, and popped into soups or salads. Here's how to ferment them:

1. Wash the tubers well. Cut them into pieces the size of pickled onions, removing any bruised or mangy bits.
2. Tip the Jerusalem artichoke pieces into a clean jar, along with mustard seeds, peppercorns, garlic, chilli, dried orange and lemon peel, dill seeds and star anise (the quantities will be based on personal preference).
3. Cover the ingredients with a 4 per cent salt brine, which is 1 tablespoon of salt in 2 cups (500 ml) of water.
4. Place a 'follower' leaf on top (grapevine, cherry or apple). This leaf sits above the brine line and holds down the fermenting artichokes. It sometimes oxidises and can go mouldy or discolour, but this doesn't matter as it is discarded when you are ready to use the fermented artichokes.
5. Place the lid on the jar. Leave the jar in a cool, dark place for four to six weeks, by which time the liquid will be cloudy and slightly bubbled.

HARVEST TIP
Although you could dig up Jerusalem artichokes any time from the end of autumn once their leaves are gone, they are actually more easily digested after they've had a few frosts, as their sugars have broken down. They will keep happily in the ground throughout winter, so the best time to harvest is mid- to late winter.

Right: We add
whatever needs to
be used as well as
lots of herbs to the
bottomless pot of
deep-winter soup.

BOTTOMLESS POT OF DEEP-WINTER SOUP

The date for this depends on the weather, but as soon as the temperature plummets and the grey skies arrive, we simultaneously kick off two of our deep-chill season tasks: lighting the Rayburn stove and starting our bottomless winter soup. I create a pot of soup (any type), which becomes the foundation for a three-month food extravaganza. It's dead easy to do.

Make your favourite soup, ensuring that there's a little more than is immediately needed, and pop the leftovers in the fridge. A day or two later, pull out the leftovers to use as the base for the next soup, including anything that needs to be cooked that day. Make a little extra of this soup, too, and place the leftovers in the fridge. If you keep the process going during winter, it evolves from being a barley and chicken soup to becoming a vegetable soup, and then a minestrone before it becomes a spicy beef soup … get the idea?

It's super quick (I literally add whatever I've got on hand), and seriously delicious (it can fall back on its base if my additions are a bit lacklustre). In addition, it can evolve to become thicker like a stew (for a hearty meal) or thinner like a broth (if you want a lighter meal).

My mum had hygiene concerns, so I've altered the process a little to soothe her worries. I only ever make enough to leave me with one or two extra portions of soup, and I decant the soup into a container so that I can wash the actual pot at least weekly. Lastly, I always pop the extra soup portions into the fridge as soon as they're cool. Just to reassure you – after many years of making it, the bottomless winter soup has never made us unwell, but you should avoid using pumpkin (squash) soup, as it tends to ferment too quickly.

Overall, this process is much quicker and more flavoursome than starting from scratch every time, and it makes for an easy meal that I don't have to think about or plan.

Slow-cooked lamb or chicken

Without a doubt, a slow-cooked lamb or chicken dish in winter evokes the ideals of country life, especially if it's pulled straight from a Rayburn stove. Actually, it's a very real part of our winter days, because of its practicality as much as our tastebuds. We often have roosters and lamb pieces in the freezer over winter, having culled our chickens and lambs in late autumn. It's an easy solution to brown off the meat, onions and garlic while we pack up after breakfast, and then tip the remaining ingredients into the pot before it cooks in the Rayburn stove until dinnertime. This allows us a full day in the paddock without having to cut it short to prepare a meal during the mid-afternoon. If you don't have a wood stove, then use a slow cooker – the meal will be just as easy to make and equally delicious.

Serves 5–8 (any leftovers can be used as the base for a soup or stew)

SLOW-COOKED LAMB

5–8 lamb pieces (shank, chump chops – whatever you prefer)

Handful of walking onions, chopped

4 garlic cloves, crushed

2 cups (500 ml) tomato passata (puréed tomatoes)

1 cup (250 ml) red wine

400 ml (14 fl oz) coconut milk

Peppercorns, to taste

Hefty thyme sprig

1 orange, halved

3 bay leaves

2 cups (500 ml) vegetable stock

Salt, to taste

SLOW-COOKED CHICKEN

1 chicken

Handful of walking onions, chopped

4 garlic cloves, crushed

3 cups (750 ml) full-cream milk

Handful of sage leaves

Handful of thyme leaves

1 lemon, halved (or 2 tablespoons preserved lemon)

1 cinnamon stick

1 cup (250 ml) white wine

1 cup (250 ml) vegetable stock

Salt, to taste

1. Preheat the oven to 120 degrees Celsius (235 degrees Fahrenheit).
2. Brown off the meat (either lamb or chicken), onions and garlic in a large cast-iron frying pan over high heat (this sears the meat, but also adds a complex umami flavour to the meal).
3. Add all of the remaining ingredients to the frying pan.
4. Place the lid on the frying pan, and place the frying pan into the oven for up to 8 hours.
5. Serve with your choice of sides, such as mashed potato, wilted greens (which are great with a squeeze of lemon juice) or soft polenta.

Fire cider tonic

Take 1–2 tablespoons of this tonic daily, either straight up or diluted with warm water or juice. If you're really game, consider replacing your usual vinegar with the tonic when you make salad dressing. It'll certainly give your salads a lift.

Makes 3 cups (750 ml)

½ cup (100 g) peeled and grated fresh ginger

½ cup (44 g) grated fresh horseradish

1 red onion, sliced

10 garlic cloves, crushed or chopped

2 jalapeño chillies, chopped (deseed if desired)

5 red chillies, sliced (deseed if desired)

2 lemons, finely sliced

1 orange, finely sliced

6 rosemary sprigs

1 tablespoon turmeric powder or 2 tablespoons grated fresh turmeric

1 teaspoon cayenne pepper

4 cups (1 litre) unfiltered apple cider vinegar (see page 221)

Honey, to taste

1. In a large sterilised jar with a wide mouth, layer all of the ingredients except the apple cider vinegar and honey.
2. Pour the apple cider vinegar over the ingredients until it reaches the top of the jar.
3. Press it all down with a piece of baking paper, so that the ingredients are all immersed in the liquid and won't touch the lid. Leave the baking paper in the jar. Place a tight-fitting lid on the jar.
4. Store the jar in a cool, dark place, turning and tipping it daily, for five or six weeks.
5. At the end of this time, strain the liquid into a clear jar (you can use the left-over solids as the base for a curry, but remove the citrus slices first). Pour the honey into it until you are happy with the sweetness.
6. Store the tonic in a sealed container in the fridge or in a cold, dark place for up to six months.

Left-over leavened crackers

Every couple of weeks, I accumulate enough unused sourdough starter to make these leavened crackers. I change up the recipe with herbs and spices – rosemary and sea salt are a favourite – or a few chia seeds, and sometimes I add turmeric, cracked pepper or even edible flowers. I make about 1 kg (2 lb 4 oz) of crackers to serve alongside pickles, dips and cheeses for our ploughman's lunches. They fill the gap between loaves of bread, and make for great snacking.

Makes 50–70 crackers

2 cups (500 ml) sourdough starter

3 cups (450 g) plain (all-purpose) flour

1 cup (250 ml) water

2 teaspoons salt

Toppings (such as sea salt, herbs and seeds)

1. In a large bowl, mix together all of the ingredients except the toppings until they form a dough. Leave the dough aside for one hour.
2. Divide the dough into four portions, and roll each into a ball. Leave the dough balls aside for eight hours at room temperature, covered with a moist tea towel.
3. Preheat the oven to 120 degrees Celsius (235 degrees Fahrenheit).
4. Roll out each ball into a flat circle on a well-floured surface. Sprinkle with your choice of toppings. Cut the dough circles like pizza, but make sure the pieces are not too wide to fit through your container opening.
5. Place the crackers onto a baking tray, and bake them in the oven for 40 minutes.
6. Allow the crackers to cool on the bench until they're crunchy. Store them in an airtight container for up to four weeks.

Quinoa and nut-meal vegetarian rolls

This is a perfect recipe for using up left-over bits in your kitchen, such as the nut meal after making nut milk and the last bits of your rough puff pastry dough.

Makes 6 meal-sized or 12–15 party-sized rolls

2 carrots, grated

Handful of fresh mixed herbs, finely chopped

Heaped tablespoon mustard

Chilli, to taste (optional)

Black pepper, to taste

2 cups (200 g) nut meal

2 cups (400 g) cooked tricolour quinoa (cooked in stock)

2 tablespoons nutritional yeast

6 sheets store-bought puff pastry or 1 batch rough puff pastry (see pages 264–5)

1. Preheat the oven to 180 degrees Celsius (350 degrees Fahrenheit).
2. Mix all of the ingredients (except the pastry) in a large bowl. You can honestly add whatever else you like, depending on your flavour preferences, garden glut or desire to bury vegies for little people. Just be sure to squeeze the mixture out so it's as dry as possible before use.
3. Roll out your pastry into the largest rectangle possible.
4. Place the mixture into a long, thin row along one side of the pastry, and then roll the pastry over it, forming a log that has an overlap of at least 5 cm (2 in) on the bottom side.
5. Cut the rolls into meal-sized or party-sized pieces, and use a fork to prick the top of the pastry on each one.
6. Place the rolls into the oven for 20–30 minutes.
7. Serve with a salad and tomato sauce (see page 228).

It's a wrap

You made it! Hopefully, you're now alert and alive and ready to go. Futuresteaders, be proud of your disruptive behaviour. Go be a change-maker!

As we embark on an era of great disruption, future-steading is about gluing together change-makers of all shapes and sizes. It's calling out to all radical homemakers, system disruptors and those with an eye for the long game so that we can move away from the old world and towards the dawning of the new age, when we seek agency over our lives and do so with joy. This is you, so raise your hand and proudly own the title of futuresteader.

People just like you and me are becoming empowered through their actions, so let's all stand together and play our part as we navigate the great disruption. Together, we are:

- choosing creative over career
- returning to our homes to raise our kids
- building locally owned social enterprises
- supporting local farmers
- growing our own food
- seeking slow over fast
- choosing voluntary simplicity over endless growth
- rediscovering the cycles of the year through connection to the natural world.

Some of our actions are small and simple, while others are groundbreaking and revolutionary. I salute every single one of them. Together, we've got this!

FUTURESTEADING PODCAST

If this book has piqued your interest and stirred some deep rumblings, then plug in your earbuds and get a weekly dose of thought provocation from the *Futuresteading* podcast, now in its third season.

I work alongside Catie Payne – a chick I've long admired for her contrary, self-aware, fresh-as-an-easterly-wind outlook on life and her frank ability to call bullshit on romanticisms. We've interviewed some wondrously normal people who are doing bloody amazing things!

Podcasts to plug in

There are many useful podcasts about homesteading, permaculture and other similar topics. Have a listen to these:

- *Futuresteading* (of course!)
- *Dumbo Feather*
- *Making Permaculture Stronger*
- *Regenerative Agriculture*
- *Unlocking Us* (Brené Brown)
- *Peak Prosperity*
- *Pip Permaculture*
- *Go Simone*
- *The Slow Home*

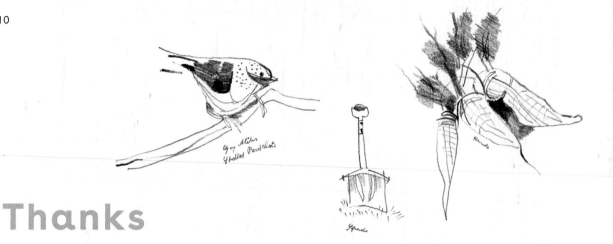

Thanks

When a friend had a dream years ago that I wrote a book, I scoffed at it – but it sowed a seed. I didn't know then that it's harder than birthing a baby and requires a solid crowd in the stands to bring it to fruition. This is a nod not only to my cheer squad, but also to the many people who have formed the path and led me on my journey of questioning, seeking of different and change-making. There have been many teachers, authors, podcast presenters, WWOOFers and general renegades in my life, and I acknowledge loudly the contribution they have made not only to me but also to all of those people they have given confidence and guidance.

Charlie – together we've landed! You are my level-headed, deep-thinking, system-challenging, self-assured soulmate, who needs little from others but puts everyone else first. It's been one hell of a ride, drums beating as one for a worthy cause. There is plenty more to come, 'as long as your eyes are blue'! The words in this book are mine, but in truth they were spurred by your ability to think, seek, learn and share. You are as brilliant as you are humble.

Harry, Bertie and Minnie – it might not feel true, but it's really all for you. You challenge, question and teach me every day. I hope that I do a little of the same for you. You are incredible humans, and together we are all doing our best.

Alice Annabel Nunan – Mum. Gran. Great-Gran. Great-Great-Gran. The original futuresteader. Stoic, stubborn, kind. Intuitive purveyor of a simple life, just doing what she knew how! Second mother figure for me and so many others, quick to swat our stealing mitts and shoo us 'chilluns' from under her feet. She issued love in spades without judgement or a critical word.

Beau Miles (Little Brother) – an instinctive futuresteader who inspires, challenges and delights in equal measure. Our book-publishing lark was nearly conjoined, but different publishing houses changed our paths. There's still time. :-)

Dad – you're a hard bastard; anti-authoritarian and creative to your core, you pushed our boundaries and applauded attempts to march to the beat of our own drum. Your complexity is derived squarely from simplicity, and your deep-reaching roots have been foundational.

Karen Webb – a wonder with a camera, you create magic by stealth. We pottered about doing just what I do, chatting our way through the seasons, while you snapped just the right moments in just the right way with just the right light. You're a true talent with a cracking laugh.

Karen Loch – thank you as much for the conversations as for the words in the margin. Your proofreading and kind guidance were the safe sounding boards needed for gentle moulding and evolution of words and themes.

Catie Payne – the best partner in crime on the mike for our podcast, my fresh-thinking confidante and my salvation when I was drowning in words. Your editing, copywriting and perspective were the shining lights that pulled me out of the trenches and made me belly laugh. You are wise beyond your years. I REALLY couldn't have done it without you.

The Murdoch Team – Jane, Megs, Justin, Mads and Dannielle – what an A team of unwavering wonders. To think we created this without ever being in the same room! Your confidence in futuresteading and your gentleness with this first-time author made it nourishing from the wordy start to the creative end. You made one heck of a team to lose my writing virginity with. xx

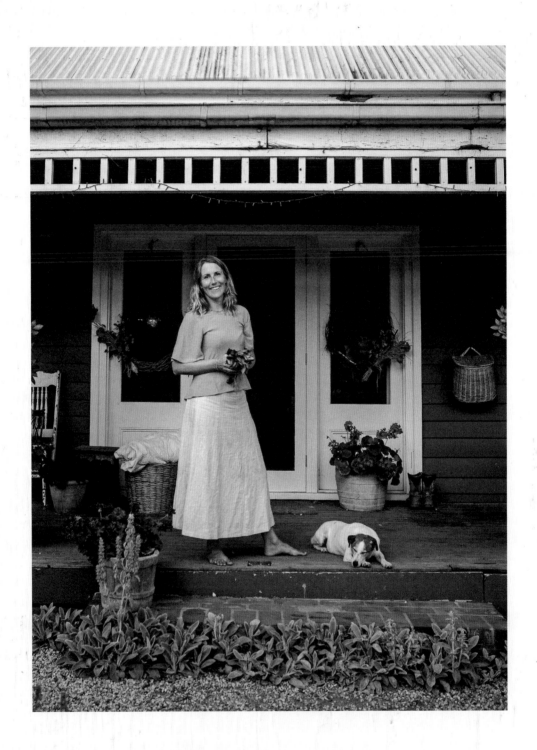

Home library

When in doubt, read more! For the sanctity of culture and knowledge, we are indebted to the thinkers who've scribed their thoughts and offered them to the tumultuous scrutiny of conjecture, conversation and celebration. They're the storytellers of their time, creating written witness to history and inspiration for imagination.

Local libraries are now our keepers of knowledge, and the book spines sit side by side on the shelf for anyone to read. Make use of this!

We've slowly built our own home library of those books that we know we'll thumb through again and again until they're dog-eared. We make a point of choosing these volumes over the screen equivalent, and our visitors, friends and WWOOFers all put them to very good use.

Books to read

If you want to upskill for resilience:

◆ *A Year of Practiculture: Recipes for living, growing, hunting & cooking with the seasons* by Rohan Anderson (Hardie Grant Books, 2015)
◆ *Grown & Gathered: Traditional living made modern* by Matt and Lentil Purbrick (Plum, 2016)
◆ *Low Tox Life: A handbook for a healthy you and a happy planet* by Alexx Stuart (Murdoch Books, 2018)
◆ *Milkwood: Real skills for down-to-earth living* by Kirsten Bradley and Nick Ritar (Murdoch Books, 2018)
◆ *RetroSuburbia: The downshifter's guide to a resilient future* by David Holmgren (Melliodora Publishing, 2018)

◆ *The Art of Fermentation: An in-depth exploration of essential concepts and processes from around the world* by Sandor Ellix Katz (Chelsea Green Publishing, 2012)
◆ *The Art of Frugal Hedonism: A guide to spending less while enjoying everything more* by Annie Raser-Rowland and Adam Grubb (Melliodora Publishing, 2017)
◆ *The Complete Book of Self-Sufficiency* by John Seymour (Corgi, 1976)
◆ *The Village: Good food, gardening and nourishing traditions to feed your village* by Matt and Lentil Purbrick (Plum, 2018)

If you need to build your knowledge of foundational systems:

◆ *Dark Emu* by Bruce Pascoe (Magabala Books, 2014)
◆ *Permaculture: Principles & pathways beyond sustainability* by David Holmgren (Holmgren Design Services, 2002)
◆ *Radical Homemakers: Reclaiming domesticity from a consumer culture* by Shannon Hayes (Left to Write Press, 2010)
◆ *Surviving the Future: Culture, carnival and capital in the aftermath of the market economy* by David Fleming (Chelsea Green Publishing, 2016)
◆ *The Biggest Estate on Earth: How Aborigines made Australia* by Bill Gammage (Allen & Unwin, 2011)
◆ *The More Beautiful World Our Hearts Know Is Possible* by Charles Eisenstein (North Atlantic Books, 2013)
◆ *The One-Straw Revolution* by Masanobu Fukuoka (New York Review of Books, 1975)

If you are eager to know more about the power of a regenerative food system:

- *Call of the Reed Warbler: A new agriculture, a new Earth* by Charles Massy (University of Queensland Press, 2017)
- *Farming Democracy: Radically transforming the food system from the ground up* edited by Paula Fernandez Arias, Tammi Jonas and Katarina Munksgaard (Australian Food Sovereignty Alliance, 2019)
- *Restoration Agriculture: Real-world permaculture for farmers* by Mark Shepard (Acres USA, 2013)
- *The Apple Grower: A guide for the organic orchardist* by Michael Phillips (Chelsea Green Publishing, 1998)
- *The Local Food Revolution: How humanity will feed itself in uncertain times* by Michael Brownlee (North Atlantic Books, 2016)
- *The Omnivore's Dilemma: A natural history of four meals* by Michael Pollan (Penguin Press, 2006)
- *The Resilient Farm and Homestead: An innovative permaculture and whole systems design approach* by Ben Falk (Chelsea Green Publishing, 2013)

If you seek inspiration to connect more deeply with your natural world:

- *Coming Back to Life: The updated guide to The Work that Reconnects* by Joanna Macy and Molly Brown (New Society Publishers, 2014)
- *Creating Sanctuary: Sacred garden spaces, plant-based medicine and daily practices to achieve happiness and well-being* by Jessi Bloom (Timber Press, 2018)

- *The Secret Network of Nature: The delicate balance of all living things* by Peter Wohlleben (The Bodley Head, 2018)

If you're keen to learn more about herbal medicine-making:

- *Healing with Whole Foods: Asian traditions and modern nutrition* by Paul Pitchford (North Atlantic Books, 2003)
- *Herbs: How to grow or gather herbal plants and use them for cookery, health and beauty* by Roger Phillips and Nicky Foy (Pan, 1992)
- *Root to Bloom: A modern guide to whole plant use* by Mat Pember and Jocelyn Cross (Hardie Grant Books, 2018)
- *The Herbalist's Way: The art & practice of healing with plant medicines* by Nancy and Michael Phillips (Chelsea Green Publishing, 2005)
- *The Nature Doctor: A manual of traditional and complementary medicine* by H.C.A. Vogel (Bookman Press, 1995)

If you want to create more ritual in your life:

- *For Small Creatures Such as We: Rituals and reflections for finding wonder* by Sasha Sagan (Murdoch Books, 2019)

MAGAZINES TO DEVOUR
- *Pip Magazine*
- *Dumbo Feather*
- *Breathe*
- *Resurgence & Ecologist*
- *Orion Magazine*
- *Biological*

Index

Published in 2021 by Murdoch Books, an imprint
of Allen & Unwin

Murdoch Books Australia
83 Alexander Street
Crows Nest NSW 2065
Phone: +61 (0)2 8425 0100
murdochbooks.com.au
info@murdochbooks.com.au

Murdoch Books UK
Ormond House
26–27 Boswell Street
London WC1N 3JZ
Phone: +44 (0) 20 8785 5995
murdochbooks.co.uk
info@murdochbooks.co.uk

For corporate orders and custom publishing, contact our business
development team at salesenquiries@murdochbooks.com.au

Publisher: Jane Morrow
Editorial Manager: Justin Wolfers
Design Manager and Cover Design: Megan Pigott
Designer: Madeleine Kane
Editor: Dannielle Viera
Photographer: Karen Webb, Capture by Karen
Illustrator: Megan Grant
Production Director: Lou Playfair

ISBN 978 1 92235 140 1 Australia
ISBN 978 1 91166 826 8 UK

A catalogue record for this
book is available from the
National Library of Australia

A catalogue record for this book is available from the National
Library of Australia

A catalogue record for this book is available from the British Library

Colour reproduction by Splitting Image Colour Studio Pty Ltd,
Clayton, Victoria
Printed by C&C Offset Printing Co. Ltd., China

The information provided within this book is for general inspiration
and informational purposes only. Individuals using or consuming
the plants listed in this book do so entirely at their own risk. Always
check a reputable source to ensure that the plants you are using are
non-toxic, organic, unsprayed and safe to be consumed. While we
try to keep the information up-to-date and correct, the author and
publisher cannot be held responsible for any adverse reactions,
and do not assume and hereby disclaim any liability to any party
for any loss, damage, or disruption caused by errors or omissions,
whether such errors or omissions result from negligence, accident,
or any other cause. Be sure to check with your local council and use
common sense when handling any potentially harmful equipment
or materials.

OVEN GUIDE: You may find cooking times vary depending on the
oven you are using. For fan-forced ovens, as a general rule, set the
oven temperature to 20°C (70°F) lower than indicated in the recipe.

TABLESPOON MEASURES: We have used 20 ml (4 teaspoon)
tablespoon measures. If you are using a 15 ml (3 teaspoon)
tablespoon add an extra teaspoon of the ingredient for each
tablespoon specified.

10 9 8 7 6 5 4 3 2 1

MIX
Paper from
responsible sources
FSC® C008047

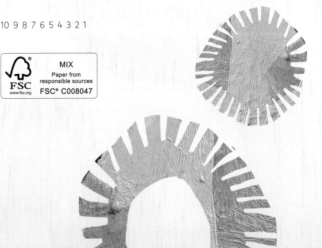